Joseph A. McCaffrey

is Assistant Professor of Philosophy
at St. Ambrose College.
He is the author of
Homosexuality: Toward a Moral Synthesis.

The
Homosexual
Dialectic

edited by

JOSEPH A. MCCAFFREY

with the special assistance of

SUZANNE M. HARTUNG

PRENTICE-HALL, INC. *Englewood Cliffs, N.J.*
A SPECTRUM BOOK

To my wife and son: JUDY and DAVID

Photographs by Diana Davies from Bethel

© 1972 by Prentice-Hall, Inc.
Englewood Cliffs, New Jersey

A SPECTRUM BOOK

ISBN: P   0–13–394577–4
          C   0–13–394585–5

Printed in the United States of America
10 9 8 7 6 5 4 3 2 1

Prentice-Hall International, Inc. (*London*)
Prentice-Hall of Australia, Pty. Ltd. (*Sydney*)
Prentice-Hall of Canada, Ltd. (*Toronto*)
Prentice-Hall of India Private Limited (*New Delhi*)
Prentice-Hall of Japan, Inc. (*Tokyo*)

Contents

Joseph A. McCaffrey

Introduction

Before 1948, the study of homosexuality, though very much a reality in the U.S.A. long before then, was almost invariably relegated to esoteric journals. These studies were frequently bent upon proving some abstract theory on the particularity of homosexuality. Where otherwise mentioned or dealt with, the subject was usually presented in such an obscure manner that its very mention or hint was enough to render understanding; and the reader's awareness of homosexuality was supposedly sufficient to insure clarity on the matter.

Although it would be unfair and absurd to dismiss the insights of theorists and artists such as Freud, Adler, Stekel, Hirschfeld, Ellis, Wilde, Gide, and Lawrence, it would be equally absurd to overlook the significance of the publication of Kinsey's *Sexual Behavior in the Human Male* in 1948. For all of its faults, and there are undoubtedly many, the Kinsey study unmercifully strangled one popular myth: that male homosexuality was an obscure phenomenon that "afflicted" only a relatively few. Of course, some astute theorists had long suspected that homosexuality was much more common than was popularly believed, but there was really no *hard* evidence to indicate this and even today those who severely criticize Kinsey have not produced any *hard* evidence to supplant him.

In effect, then, Kinsey forced many (and he himself tells of his own near disbelief at its incidence) to realize that homosexuality is not a "minute nuisance" that can be tucked away into some small corner of pluralistic America, nor a "vicious moral weakness" that can be legally purged from America's bloodstream. It was shown to be a very real and ubiquitous form of sexual expression that is shared by at least several million American men. With that book the silhouette, at least, of a dialectic took form.

Through the 1950s and the 1960s, books and articles on homosexuality have multiplied geometrically until today it is almost a full-time occupation to keep pace with the flood of literature pertaining to it. Just the quantity of literature alone points to the complexity of the matter and also to the inadequacy of any reader or anthology to deal with the question. In fact, this reader, and most others, can have only one real purpose: to indicate the depth and makeup of the dialectic as perceived by various theorists from different fields and also to portray homosexual reactions to a society where they are not only a minority but a minority that is generally despised by a majority of "straights" or heterosexuals.

Each article has been chosen with care to illustrate what is important in the dynamics of the dialectic. The fact that only two selections pertain to female homosexuality underscores the extreme disparity between the research done on male homosexuality as compared to lesbianism. Also, it is hardly surprising that some selections stand in direct opposition to one another, since dialectic is founded on and only thrives in an atmosphere of tension. And as in any anthology, there are glaring omissions for which there is only one salient excuse—space (which still has the status of an absolute).

This book, then, will help in the dialectical process that is needed when any serious challenge to traditional societal views, be they in psychology, law, morals, or sociology, is in progress. If some positive changes are wrought as a result of reading this book, its success is more than guaranteed.

Alfred C. Kinsey, Wardell B. Pomeroy, and Clyde E. Martin

Homosexual Outlet

—The Kinsey, Pomeroy, and Martin study, Sexual Behavior in the Human Male, *was published in 1948. This particular selection includes rather lengthy excerpts from Chapter 21, "Homosexual Outlet." The "Kinsey study," as it is popularly known, drew from a large number of cases, even though Kinsey himself admitted his work was based on a sample that was highly inadequate for a comprehensive view of the population. What is most important about this particular article is its demonstration of frequency and incidence and Kinsey's well-reasoned defense for his categories: heterosexuality, bisexuality, and homosexuality. The book, of course, engendered a storm of controversy because of findings like those in this excerpt.*

In the total male population, single and married, between adolescence and old age, 24 per cent of the total outlet is derived from

From *Sexual Behavior in the Human Male,* by Alfred C. Kinsey, et al. (Philadelphia: W. B. Saunders, Co., 1948). Reprinted by permission of The Institute for Sex Research, Inc., Indiana University, and the publisher, with the inclusion of the following caveat by Dr. Paul Gebhard, Director of the Institute:

"The high school educated portion of our sample (educational level 9–12) is biased by the inclusion of some groups which should have been excluded. The most important of these are prison inmates. In the nineteen forties we did not know that the sexual lives of prison inmates, even their sexual lives outside of prison, differ substantially from the sexual lives of persons never convicted for any offense. Consequently, the figures for the high school educated are often conspicuously different from those of the rest of the sample and the degree of error cannot be ascertained until the data are re-analyzed.

For this reason, and also because the distribution of our sample did not warrant such a broad generalization, the reader should ignore the column in tables (or cited in the text) entitled 'Total Population. U.S. Corrections'."

solitary sources (masturbation and nocturnal emissions), 69.4 per cent is derived from heterosexual sources (petting and coitus), and 6.3 per cent of the total number of orgasms is derived from homosexual contacts. It is not more than 0.3 per cent of the outlet which is derived from relations with animals of other species.

Homosexual contacts account, therefore, for a rather small but still significant portion of the total outlet of the human male. The significance of the homosexual is, furthermore, much greater than the frequencies of outlet may indicate, because a considerable portion of the population, perhaps the major portion of the male population, has at least some homosexual experience between adolescence and old age. In addition, about 60 per cent of the preadolescent boys engage in homosexual activities, and there is an additional group of adult males who avoid overt contacts but who are quite aware of their potentialities for reacting to other males.

The social significance of the homosexual is considerably emphasized by the fact that both Jewish and Christian churches have considered this aspect of human sexuality to be abnormal and immoral. Social custom and our Anglo-American law are sometimes very severe in penalizing one who is discovered to have had homosexual relations. In consequence, many persons who have had such experience are psychically disturbed, and not a few of them have been in open conflict with the social organization.

It is, therefore, peculiarly difficult to secure factual data concerning the nature and the extent of the homosexual in Western European or American cultures, and even more difficult to find strictly objective presentations of such data as are available. Most of the literature on the homosexual represents either a polemic against the heinous abnormality of such activity, or a biased argument in defense of an individual's right to choose his patterns of sexual behavior.

Until the extent of any type of human behavior is adequately known, it is difficult to assess its significance, either to the individuals who are involved or to society as a whole; and until the extent of the homosexual is known, it is practically impossible to understand its biologic or social origins. It is one thing if we are dealing with a type of activity that is unusual, without precedent among other animals, and restricted to peculiar types of individuals within the human population. It is another thing if the phenomenon proves to be a fundamental part, not only of human sexuality, but of mammalian patterns as a whole. The present chapter is, there-

fore, wholly confined to an analysis of the data which we now have
on the incidence and the frequencies of homosexual activity in the
white male population in this country. . . .

DEFINITION

For nearly a century the term homosexual in connection with
human behavior has been applied to sexual relations, either overt
or psychic, between individuals of the same sex. Derived from the
Greek root *homo* rather than from the Latin word for man, the
term emphasizes the *sameness* of the two individuals who are involved in a sexual relation. The word is, of course, patterned after
and intended to represent the antithesis of the word heterosexual,
which applies to a relation between individuals of different sexes.

The term homosexual has had an endless list of synonyms in the
technical vocabularies and a still greater list in the vernaculars.
The terms homogenic love, contrasexuality, homo-erotism, simili-
sexualism, uranism and others have been used in English. The
terms sexual inversion, intersexuality, transsexuality, the third sex,
psychosexual hermaphroditism, and others have been applied not
merely to designate the nature of the partner involved in the sexual
relation, but to emphasize the general opinion that individuals
engaging in homosexual activity are neither male nor female, but
persons of mixed sex. These latter terms are, however, most unfortunate, for they provide an interpretation in anticipation of any
sufficient demonstration of the fact; and consequently they prejudice investigations of the nature and origin of homosexual activity.

The term Lesbian, referring to such female homosexual relations
as were immortalized in the poetry of Sappho of the Greek Isle of
Lesbos, has gained considerable usage within recent years, particularly in some of the larger Eastern cities where the existence of
female homosexuality is more generally recognized by the public
at large. Although there can be no objection to designating relations between females by a special term, it should be recognized
that such activities are quite the equivalent of sexual relations between males. . . .

If the term homosexual is restricted as it should be, the homosexuality or heterosexuality of any activity becomes apparent by
determining the sexes of the two individuals involved in the relationship. For instance, mouth-genital contacts between males and
females are certainly heterosexual, even though some persons may

think of them as homosexual. And although one may hear of a male "who has sex relations with his wife in a homosexual way," there is no logic in such a use of the term, and analyses of the behavior and of the motivations of the behavior in such cases do not show them necessarily related to any homosexual experience.

On the other hand, the homosexuality of certain relationships between individuals of the same sex may be denied by some persons, because the situation does not fulfill other criteria that they think should be attached to the definition. Mutual masturbation between two males may be dismissed, even by certain clinicians, as not homosexual, because oral or anal relations or particular levels of psychic response are required, according to their concept of homosexuality. There are persons who insist that the active male in an anal relation is essentially heterosexual in his behavior, and that the passive male in the same relation is the only one who is homosexual. These, however, are misapplications of terms, which are often unfortunate because they obscure the interpretations of the situation which the clinician is supposed to help by his analysis.

These misinterpretations are often encouraged by the very persons who are having homosexual experience. Some males who are being regularly fellated by other males without, however, ever performing fellation themselves, may insist that they are exclusively heterosexual and that they have never been involved in a truly homosexual relation. Their consciences are cleared and they may avoid trouble with society and with the police by perpetrating the additional fiction that they are incapable of responding to a relation with a male unless they fantasy themselves in contact with a female. Even clinicians have allowed themselves to be diverted by such pretensions. The actual histories, however, show few if any cases of sexual relations between males which could be considered anything but homosexual.

Many individuals who have had considerable homosexual experience, construct a hierarchy on the basis of which they insist that anyone who has not had as much homosexual experience as they have had, or who is less exclusively aroused by homosexual stimuli, is "not really homosexual." It is amazing to observe how many psychologists and psychiatrists have accepted this sort of propaganda, and have come to believe that homosexual males and females are discretely different from persons who merely have homosexual experience, or who react sometimes to homosexual stimuli. Sometimes such an interpretation allows for only two kinds of males and two kinds of females, namely those who are heterosexual and those who are homosexual. But as subsequent data in this chapter will show, there is only about half of the male population whose sexual behavior is exclusively heterosexual, and there are only a few per cent who are exclusively homosexual. Any restriction of the term homosexuality to individuals who are exclusively so demands, logically, that the term heterosexual be applied only to those individuals who are exclusively heterosexual; and this makes no allowance for the nearly half of the population which has had sexual contacts with, or reacted psychically to, individuals of their own as well as of the opposite sex. Actually, of course, one must learn to recognize every combination of heterosexuality and homosexuality in the histories of various individuals.

It would encourage clearer thinking on these matters if persons were not characterized as heterosexual or homosexual, but as individuals who have had certain amounts of heterosexual experience and certain amounts of homosexual experience. Instead of using these terms as substantives which stand for persons, or even as adjectives to describe persons, they may better be used to describe the nature of the overt sexual relations, or of the stimuli to which an individual erotically responds.

PREVIOUS ESTIMATES OF INCIDENCE

. . . There are many persons who believe the homosexual to be a rare phenomenon, a clinical curiosity, and something which one may never meet among the sorts of persons with whom he would associate. On the other hand, there are some clinicians and some persons who have had first-hand contacts in the homosexual [world], who have estimated that something between 50 and 100 per cent of the population has such experience. . . .

Satisfactory incidence figures on the homosexual cannot be obtained by any technique short of a carefully planned population survey. The data should cover every segment of the total population. There is no other aspect of human sexual behavior where it is more fundamental that the sample be secured without any selection of cases which would bias the results. Many persons with homosexual experience very naturally hesitate to expose their histories. On the other hand, there are some who are so upset by personal conflicts or social difficulties that have developed out of their homosexual activities that they are anxious to discuss their problems with an investigator whom they have come to trust. In consequence, if one depends only upon volunteers in a survey, it is impossible to know whether homosexual histories are represented in an undue proportion, or less often than their actual incidence would demand. In order to secure data that have any relation to the reality, it is imperative that the cases be derived from as careful a distribution and stratification of the sample as the public opinion polls employ, or as we have employed in the present study. . . .

INCIDENCE DATA IN PRESENT STUDY

. . . The statistics to be given in the present section of this chapter are based on those persons who have had physical contacts with other males, and who were brought to orgasm as a result of such contacts. By any strict definition such contacts are homosexual, irrespective of the extent of the psychic stimulation involved, of the techniques employed, or of the relative importance of the homosexual and the heterosexual in the history of such an individual. These are not data on the number of persons who are "homosexual," but on the number of persons who have had at least some homosexual experience—even though sometimes not more than one experience —up to the ages shown in the tables and curves. The incidences of persons who have had various amounts of homosexual experience are presented in a later section of this chapter.

An individual who engages in a sexual relation with another male without, however, coming to climax, or an individual who is erotically aroused by a homosexual stimulus without ever having overt relations, has certainly had a homosexual experience. Such relations and reactions are, however, not included in the incidence data given here. . . . On the other hand, the data on the heterosexual-homosexual ratings which are presented later in the present chapter, do take into account these homosexual contacts in which the subject fails to reach climax. Accumulative incidence curves based upon heterosexual-homosexual ratings may, therefore, be somewhat higher than the accumulative incidence curves based upon overt contacts carried through to the point of actual orgasm.

. . . No male is included in any of the calculations shown in the present chapter unless he has had homosexual experience beyond the onset of adolescence.

In these terms (of physical contact to the point of orgasm), the data in the present study indicate that at least 37 per cent of the male population has some homosexual experience between the beginning of adolescence and old age (U.S. Corrections.[1] See Table 139, Figure 156). This is more than one male in three of the persons that one may meet as he passes along a city street. Among the males who remain unmarried until the age of 35, almost exactly 50 per cent have homosexual experience between the beginning of adolescence and that age. Some of these persons have but a single experience, and some of them have much more or even a lifetime of experience; but all of them have at least some experience to the point of orgasm.

These figures are, of course, considerably higher than any which have previously been estimated; but as already shown they must be understatements, if they are anything other than the fact.

We ourselves were totally unprepared to find such incidence data when this research was originally undertaken. Over a period of several years we were repeatedly assailed with doubts as to whether we were getting a fair cross section of the total population or whether a selection of cases was biasing the results. It has been our experience, however, that each new group into which we have gone has provided substantially the same data. Whether the histories were taken in one large city or another, whether they were taken in large cities, in small towns, or in rural areas, whether they came from one college or from another, a church school or a state university or some private institution, whether they came from one part of the country or from another, the incidence data on the homosexual have been more or less the same.

While the validity of the data on all of the sexual outlets has been tested and retested throughout the study, especial attention has been given to testing the material on the homosexual. . . .

Those who have been best acquainted with the extent of homosexual activity in the population, whether through clinical contacts with homosexual patients, through homosexual acquaintances, or through their own firsthand homosexual experience, will not find it too difficult to accept the accumulative incidence figures which are arrived at here. There are many who have been aware of the fact that persons with homosexual histories are to be found in every age group, in every social level, in every conceivable occupation, in cities and on farms, and in the most remote areas in the country. They have known the homosexual in young adolescents

---

1. [EDITOR'S NOTE: official corrections of the 1940 U.S. Census.]

AGE	TOTAL POPULATION U. S. CORRECTIONS		EDUC. LEVEL 0–8		EDUC. LEVEL 9–12		EDUC. LEVEL 13+	
	Cases	% with Exper.	Cases	% with Exper.	Cases	% with Exper.	Cases	% with Exper.
8	3969	0.0	662	0.0	490	0.0	2817	0.0
9	3969	0.1	662	0.0	490	0.2	2817	0.1
10	3969	0.5	662	0.2	490	0.6	2817	0.5
11	3968	1.7	661	1.2	490	2.0	2817	1.8
12	3968	6.1	661	5.6	490	6.3	2817	6.2
13	3968	12.6	661	11.0	490	13.7	2817	11.6
14	3965	21.3	658	17.8	490	24.1	2817	18.0
15	3957	27.7	652	24.8	488	31.1	2817	21.1
16	3934	31.6	635	27.7	483	36.0	2816	23.0
17	3874	34.5	598	27.8	462	40.9	2814	24.1
18	3738	36.7	574	29.3	426	43.7	2738	25.6
19	3507	37.5	544	29.0	389	45.0	2574	26.7
20	3203	36.7	516	28.9	348	43.4	2339	27.6
21	2830	37.0	492	29.1	305	43.6	2033	28.6
22	2428	37.1	473	29.0	283	43.5	1672	29.8
23	2113	37.3	458	29.0	258	43.4	1397	31.5
24	1822	36.5	438	29.2	232	41.8	1152	32.1
25	1636	35.4	418	28.0	216	42.1	1002	33.0
26	1493	35.6	407	28.0	202	42.6	884	32.9
27	1358	35.6	393	28.5	191	41.9	774	33.7
28	1252	35.5	379	28.2	174	42.0	699	33.9
29	1143	33.7	355	27.3	154	39.0	634	33.6
30	1049	32.4	339	26.5	137	38.7	573	33.7
31	973	31.3	319	25.4	125	36.8	529	34.2
32	915	30.5	307	26.1	116	34.5	492	32.9
33	856	31.0	295	25.4	113	36.3	448	33.9
34	804	29.9	287	23.7	105	35.2	412	34.7
35	747	27.5	273	22.3	92	33.7	382	34.0
36	703	27.2	260	22.7	87	32.2	356	33.7
37	641	26.1	242	21.9	76	30.3	323	33.4
38	611	25.4	234	20.9	70	30.0	307	33.2
39	556	25.3	212	20.8	64	29.7	280	33.6
40	509	25.0	194	21.6	58	29.3	257	32.7
41	474	23.3	183	20.2	53	26.4	238	31.9
42	445	23.3	174	19.5	50	28.0	221	31.2
43	399	22.9	159	20.1			192	32.8
44	369	23.5	146	21.9			177	31.1
45	340	22.9	135	21.5			161	32.9

Table 139. Accumulative incidence data on total homosexual outlet

Covering the life span, including pre-marital, extra-marital, and post-marital experience. In three educational levels, and in the total population corrected for the U. S. Census of 1940.

and in persons of every other age. They have known it in single persons and in the histories of males who were married. In large city communities they know that an experienced observer may identify hundreds of persons in a day whose homosexual interests are certain. They have known the homosexuality of many persons whose histories were utterly unknown to most of their friends and

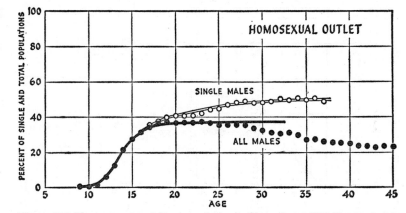

Figure 156. Homosexual outlet: accumulative incidence in total U. S. population and in single population alone

Black line shows percent of total population which has ever had homosexual experience by each of the indicated ages. Hollow line shows percent of the population of single males which has ever had experience. All data corrected for U. S. Census distribution. The incidence for the total population is lower than the incidence for the single population because the males who marry have less homosexual experience and bring down the averages when they are included in the calculations with the single males.

acquaintances. They have repeatedly had the experience of discovering homosexual histories among persons whom they had known for years before they realized that they had had anything except heterosexual experience. . . .

The number of males who have any homosexual experience after the onset of adolescence (the accumulative incidence) is highest in the group that enters high school but never goes beyond in its educational career. In that group 55 per cent of the males who are still single by 30 years of age have had the experience of being brought to climax through a physical contact with another male. Among the boys who never go beyond grade school the corresponding figure is 45 per cent, and for the males who belong to the college level, 40 per cent. The accumulative incidence figures for the whole of the life span (Figure 157) are a bit higher for all of these groups, inasmuch as there are some males who do not have their first homosexual experience until after they are 30 years of age.

Among single males in the population, the highest active incidence figures occur in the older age groups. Between adolescence and 15 years of age about 1 male in 4 (27%) has some homosexual

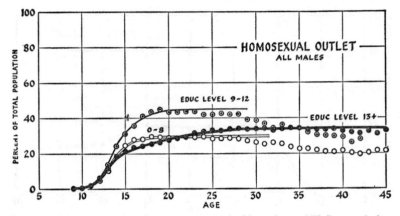

Figure 157. Homosexual outlet: accumulative incidence in total U. S. population for three educational levels

Showing percent of each population that has ever had homosexual experience by each of the indicated ages. All data based on total population, irrespective of marital status.

experience. The figures rise to nearly 1 male in 3 in the later teens and appear to drop a bit in the early twenties. Among those who are not married by the latter part of their twenties, the incidence is about 1 male in 3, and the figures increase slightly among older unmarried males (39%). There are some minor differences in the trends in the different social levels.

The drop in the active incidence figures between 21 and 25 appears so consistently through all of the calculations, that there is reason for believing that it represents an actual fact in the behavior of the population. During their late teens, many males experience considerable personal conflict over their homosexual activities, because they have become more conscious of social reactions to such contacts. Particularly in that period, many individuals attempt to stop their homosexual relations, and try to make the heterosexual adjustments which society demands. Some of these individuals are, of course, successful, but in a certain number of cases they finally reach the point, somewhere in their middle twenties, where they conclude that it is too costly to attempt to avoid the homosexual, and consciously, deliberately and sometimes publicly decide to renew such activities. Another factor which certainly contributes to the decrease in active incidence in the early twenties is the fact that heterosexually oriented males are then marrying in great numbers,

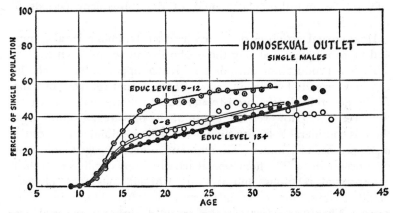

Figure 158. Homosexual outlet: accumulative incidence among single males, in three educational levels

and this leaves an increasingly select group at older ages in the single population.

The active incidence figures are highest among single males of the high school level. In the late teens nearly every other male of this level (41%) is having some homosexual contact, and between the ages of 26 and 30 it is had by 46 per cent of the group. Among the males of the grade school level about 1 in 4 (22 to 27%) has any homosexual experience in any age period of the pre-marital years. Among the males who belong to the college level only about 1 in 5 has homosexual experience between adolescence and 15 (22%), 1 in 6 (16%) has such relations in the later teens, and less than 1 in 10 (10%) has homosexual relations between the ages of 21 and 25. Among males who never go beyond grade school, about the same number of individuals is involved while they are actually in grade school, during their late teens when they are out of school, and in all the subsequent years until they marry. Among the males who stop their schooling at high school levels a larger number is involved after they have left school. For the males who belong to the college level, the largest number is involved while they are in high school, but the number steadily decreases in later years.

Homosexual activities occur in a much higher percentage of the males who became adolescent at an early age; and in a definitely smaller percentage of those who became adolescent at later ages. . . . It [those who became adolescent at an early age] is the group which possesses on the whole the greatest sex drive, both in early adolescence and throughout most of the subsequent periods of their lives.

Homosexual activities occur less frequently among rural groups and more frequently among those who live in towns or cities. . . . This is a product not only of the greater opportunity which the city may provide for certain types of homosexual contacts, but also of the generally lower rate of total outlet among males raised on the farm. . . . [However] in certain of the most remote rural areas there is considerable homosexual activity among lumbermen, cattlemen, prospectors, miners, hunters, and others engaged in out-of-door occupations. The homosexual activity rarely conflicts with their heterosexual relations, and is quite without the argot, physical manifestations, and other affectations so often found in urban groups. There is a minimum of personal disturbance or social conflict over such activity. It is the type of homosexual experience which the explorer and pioneer may have had in their histories.

On the whole, homosexual contacts occur most frequently among the males who are not particularly active in their church connections. They occur less frequently among devout Catholics, Orthodox Jewish groups, and Protestants who are active in the church. The differences are not always great, but lie constantly in the same direction. . . .

FREQUENCIES

Since the incidence of the homosexual is high, and since it accounts for only 8 to 16 per cent of the total orgasms of the unmarried males and for a rather insignificant portion of the outlet of the married males, it is obvious that the mean frequencies must be low in the population as a whole. Even when the calculations are confined to those males who are having actual experience, the average frequencies are never high.

These low rates are in striking discord with the fact that homosexual contacts could in actuality be had more abundantly than heterosexual contacts, if there were no social restraints or personal conflicts involved. The sexual possibilities of the average male in his teens or twenties are probably more often assayed by males than by females, and younger males who are attractive physically or who have attractive personalities may be approached for homosexual relations more often than they themselves would ever approach females for heterosexual relations. A homosexually experienced male could undoubtedly find a larger number of sexual partners among males than a heterosexually experienced male could find among females. It is, of course, only the experienced male who understands that homosexual contacts are so freely available. The considerable taboo which society places upon these activities and upon their open discussion leaves most people in ignorance of the channels through which homosexual contacts are made; and even among males who desire homosexual relations, there are only a relatively few who have any knowledge of how to find them in abundance. Consequently many homosexual individuals may go for months and even for years at a stretch without a single contact which is carried through to orgasm.

The heterosexual male finds a regular outlet if he locates a single female who is acceptable as a wife in marriage. The homosexual male is more often concerned with finding a succession of partners, no one of whom will provide more than a few contacts, or perhaps not more than a single contact. Some promiscuous males with homosexual histories become so interested in the thrill of conquest, and in the variety of partners and in the variety of genital experiences that may be had, that they deliberately turn down opportunities for repetitions of contacts with any one person. This necessity for finding new partners may result in their going for some days or weeks without sexual relations.

Even the most experienced homosexual males may be inhibited from making all the contacts that are available because of preferences for particular sorts of partners. A male who has highly developed esthetic tastes, one who is emotionally very sensitive, one who over-reacts to situations which do not entirely please him, one who develops a preference for a partner of a particular age or a particular social level, of a particular height or weight, with hair of a particular color, with particular genital qualities, or with other particular physical aspects—a male who refuses to have sexual relations except under particular circumstances, at particular hours of the day, and in particular sorts of environments—may turn down hundreds of opportunities for contacts before he finds the one individual with whom he accepts a relation.

Many of the males who have homosexual histories are acutely aware that they are transgressing social custom and engaging in activity which has a certain amount of peril attached to it if it becomes known to the society in which they live. Consequently, many such males become oversensitive to the precise situations under which they accept relationships. All of these handicaps make for discord between homosexual partners, and this lessens the number of opportunities for successful relations.

Long-time relationships between two males are notably few. Long-time relationships in the heterosexual would probably be less frequent than they are, if there were no social custom or legal restraints to enforce continued relationships in marriage. But without such outside pressures to preserve homosexual relations, and with personal and social conflicts continually disturbing them, relationships between two males rarely survive the first disagreements.

There are some males whose homosexuality is undoubtedly the product of inherent or acquired timidity or other personality traits which make it difficult for them to approach other persons for any sort of social contact. Such males find it easier to make contacts with individuals of their own sex. Their homosexuality may be the direct outcome of their social inadequacies. Even with their own sex, however, these timid individuals may find it very difficult to approach strangers. They may resort to taverns, clubs, and other places where they know that homosexual contacts may be easily obtained, but are likely to go alone, and may go regularly for weeks and months without speaking to anyone in the assemblage. The low rates of outlet of some of these individuals are as extreme as any in the whole male population.

There are some males who are primarily or even exclusively homosexual in their psychic responses, but who may completely abstain from overt relations for moral reasons or for fear of social difficulties. Left without any socio-sexual contacts, some of these persons have essentially no outlet, and some of them are, therefore, very badly upset.

For these several reasons, average frequencies among males with homosexual histories are usually low, and there are very few high frequencies. In any particular age group, in any segment of the population, it is never more than about 5.5 per cent of the males who are having homosexual relations that average more than once every other day (3.5 per week). Calculating only for the males who actually have homosexual experience, there are never more than 5.2 per cent that have frequencies averaging more than 6.0 per week during their most active years. Considering that it is 25 per cent of the entire population which has total sexual outlets which average more than 3.5 per week, and considering that 24 per cent of the married males have outlets that average more than 6.0 per week in their most active period, it is apparent that outlets from the homosexual are definitely low.

Among single males who are having homosexual experience the average frequencies rise from 0.8 per week in early adolescence to about 1.3 per week at age 25 and 1.7 per week by age 35. Since the frequencies of total sexual outlet steadily decrease with advancing age, it is to be noted that the homosexual supplies an increasing proportion of the orgasms for the single males who are having such contacts: 17.5 per cent of the orgasms in early adolescence, 30.3 per cent in the early twenties, 40.4 per cent by age 40. This increased dependence of this older male upon his homosexual outlet parallels the increased dependence which the heterosexual male places upon coitus as a source of outlet. The situation is, however, accentuated in the case of the homosexual because the younger male may be restrained by considerable doubts as to the advisability of continuing in a socially taboo activity.

The frequencies of homosexual contacts differ considerably at different social levels. The least frequent activity is to be found in the college level. Comparing active populations of college and high school levels, there is 50 to 100 per cent more frequent activity among the males of the high school group. The grade school level stands intermediate between the other two groups. The differences between the social levels are most marked in the early age periods.

The considerable amount of homosexual experience among males of the high school level is a matter for note. . . .

THE HETEROSEXUAL-HOMOSEXUAL BALANCE

Concerning patterns of sexual behavior, a great deal of the thinking done by scientists and laymen alike stems from the assumption that there are persons who are "heterosexual" and persons who are "homosexual," that these two types represent antitheses in the sexual world, and that there is only an insignificant class of "bisexuals" who occupy an intermediate position between the other groups. It is implied that every individual is innately—inherently —either heterosexual or homosexual. It is further implied that from the time of birth one is fated to be one thing or the other, and that there is little chance for one to change his pattern in the course of a lifetime. . . .

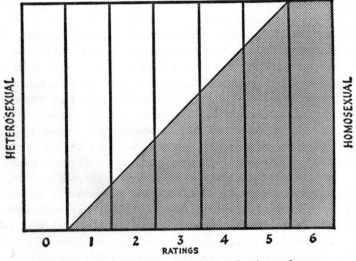

Figure 161. Heterosexual-homosexual rating scale

Based on both psychologic reactions and overt experience, individuals rate as follows:

0. Exclusively heterosexual with no homosexual
1. Predominantly heterosexual, only incidentally homosexual
2. Predominantly heterosexual, but more than incidentally homosexual
3. Equally heterosexual and homosexual
4. Predominantly homosexual, but more than incidentally heterosexual
5. Predominantly homosexual, but incidentally heterosexual
6. Exclusively homosexual

The histories which have been available in the present study make it apparent that the heterosexuality or homosexuality of many individuals is not an all-or-none proposition. It is true that there are persons in the population whose histories are exclusively heterosexual, both in regard to their overt experience and in regard to their psychic reactions. And there are individuals in the population whose histories are exclusively homosexual, both in experience and in psychic reactions. But the record also shows that there is a considerable portion of the population whose members have combined, within their individual histories, both homosexual and heterosexual experience and/or psychic responses. There are some whose heterosexual experiences predominate, there are some whose homosexual experiences predominate, there are some who have had quite equal amounts of both types of experience.

Some of the males who are involved in one type of relation at one period in their lives, may have only the other type of relation at some later period. There may be considerable fluctuation of patterns from time to time. Some males may be involved in both heterosexual and homosexual activities within the same period of time. For instance, there are some who engage in both heterosexual and homosexual activities in the same year, or in the same month or week, or even in the same day. There are not a few individuals who engage in group activities in which they may make simultaneous contact with partners of both sexes.

Males do not represent two discrete populations, heterosexual and homosexual. The world is not to be divided into sheep and goats. Not all things are black nor all things white. It is a fundamental of taxonomy that nature rarely deals with discrete categories. Only the human mind invents categories and tries to force facts into separated pigeon-holes. The living world is a continuum in each and every one of its aspects. The sooner we learn this concerning human sexual behavior the sooner we shall reach a sound understanding of the realities of sex.

While emphasizing the continuity of the gradations between exclusively heterosexual and exclusively homosexual histories, it has seemed desirable to develop some sort of classification which could be based on the relative amounts of heterosexual and of homosexual experience or response in each history. Such a heterosexual-homosexual rating scale is shown in Figure 161. An individual may be assigned a position on this scale, for each age period in his life, in accordance with the following definitions of the various points on the scale:

0. Individuals are rated as 0's if they make no physical contacts which result in erotic arousal or orgasm, and make no psychic responses to individuals of their own sex. Their socio-sexual contacts and responses are exclusively with individuals of the opposite sex.

1. Individuals are rated as 1's if they have only incidental homosexual contacts which have involved physical or psychic response, or incidental psychic responses without physical contact. The great preponderance of their socio-sexual experience and reactions is directed

toward individuals of the opposite sex. Such homosexual experiences as these individuals have may occur only a single time or two, or at least infrequently in comparison to the amount of their heterosexual experience. Their homosexual experiences never involve as specific psychic reactions as they make to heterosexual stimuli. Sometimes the homosexual activities in which they engage may be inspired by curiosity, or may be more or less forced upon them by other individuals, perhaps when they are asleep or when they are drunk, or under some other peculiar circumstance.

2. Individuals are rated as 2's if they have more than incidental homosexual experience, and/or if they respond rather definitely to homosexual stimuli. Their heterosexual experiences and/or reactions still surpass their homosexual experiences and/or reactions. These individuals may have only a small amount of homosexual experience or they may have a considerable amount of it, but in every case it is surpassed by the amount of heterosexual experience that they have within the same period of time. They usually recognize their quite specific arousal by homosexual stimuli, but their responses to the opposite sex are still stronger. A few of these individuals may even have all of their overt experience in the homosexual, but their psychic reactions to persons of the opposite sex indicate that they are still predominantly heterosexual. This latter situation is most often found among younger males who have not yet ventured to have actual intercourse with girls, while their orientation is definitely heterosexual. On the other hand, there are some males who should be rated as 2's because of their strong reactions to individuals of their own sex, even though they have never had overt relations with them.

3. Individuals who are rated 3's stand midway on the heterosexual-homosexual scale. They are about equally homosexual and heterosexual in their overt experience and/or their psychic reactions. In general, they accept and equally enjoy both types of contacts, and have no strong preferences for one or the other. Some persons are rated 3's, even though they may have a larger amount of experience of one sort, because they respond psychically to partners of both sexes, and it is only a matter of circumstance that brings them into more frequent contact with one of the sexes. Such a situation is not unusual among single males, for male contacts are often more available to them than female contacts. Married males, on the other hand, find it simpler to secure a sexual outlet through intercourse with their wives, even though some of them may be as interested in males as they are in females.

4. Individuals are rated as 4's if they have more overt activity and/or psychic reactions in the homosexual, while still maintaining a

fair amount of heterosexual activity and/or responding rather definitely to heterosexual stimuli.

5. Individuals are rated 5's if they are almost entirely homosexual in their overt activities and/or reactions. They do have incidental experience with the opposite sex and sometimes react psychically to individuals of the opposite sex.

6. Individuals are rated as 6's if they are exclusively homosexual, both in regard to their overt experience and in regard to their psychic reactions.

It will be observed that this is a seven-point scale, with 0 and 6 as the extreme points, and with 3 as the midpoint in the classification. On opposite sides of the midpoint the following relations hold:

> 0 is the opposite of 6
> 1 is the opposite of 5
> 2 is the opposite of 4

It will be observed that the rating which an individual receives has a dual basis. It takes into account his overt sexual experience and/or his psychosexual reactions. In the majority of instances the two aspects of the history parallel, but sometimes they are not in accord. In the latter case, the rating of an individual must be based upon an evaluation of the relative importance of the overt and the psychic in his history.

In each classification there are persons who have had no experience or a minimum of overt sexual experience, but in the same classification there may also be persons who have had hundreds of sexual contacts. In every case, however, all of the individuals in each classification show the same balance between the heterosexual and homosexual elements in their histories. The position of an individual on this scale is always based upon the relation of the heterosexual to the homosexual in his history, rather than upon the actual amount of overt experience or psychic reaction.

Finally, it should be emphasized again that the reality is a continuum, with individuals in the population occupying not only the seven categories which are recognized here, but every gradation between each of the categories, as well. Nevertheless, it does no great injustice to the fact to group the population as indicated above.

From all of this, it should be evident that one is not warranted

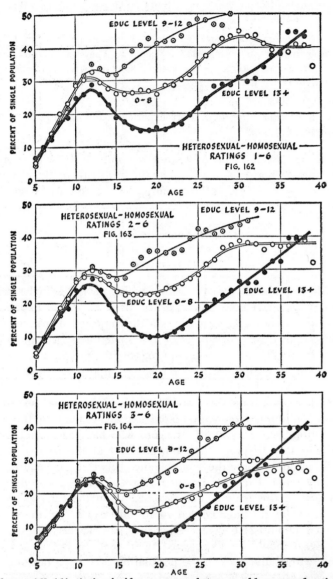

Figures 162–164. Active incidence curves: heterosexual-homosexual ratings, by age and educational level, among single males

Top figure, 162, shows percent of single males who have at least incidental (or more) homosexual reactions or experience (ratings 1–6) in each year. Middle figure, 163, shows percent of single males who have more than incidental homosexual reactions or experience (ratings 2–6). Bottom figure, 164, shows percent of single males who have as much as or more homosexual than heterosexual reactions or experience (ratings 3–6), in each year.

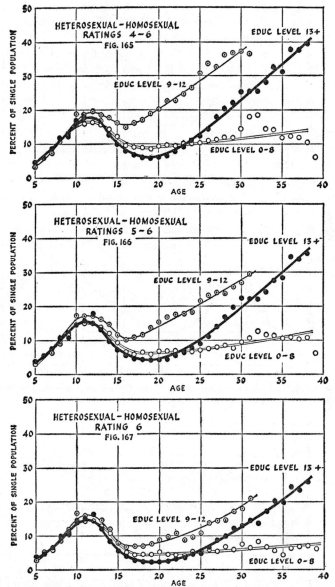

Figures 165–167. Active incidence curves: heterosexual-homosexual ratings, by
age and educational level, among single males

Top figure, 165, shows percent of single males who have more homosexual than
heterosexual reactions or experience (ratings 4–6) in each year. Middle figure, 166,
shows percent of single males who have more or less exclusively homosexual reactions
or experience (ratings 5–6). Bottom figure, 167, shows percent of single males who are
exclusively homosexual (rating 6) in each year.

in recognizing merely two types of individuals, heterosexual and homosexual, and that the characterization of the homosexual as a third sex fails to describe any actuality. . . .

Everywhere in our society there is a tendency to consider an individual "homosexual" if he is known to have had a single experience with another individual of his own sex. Under the law an individual may receive the same penalty for a single homosexual experience that he would for a continuous record of experiences. In penal and mental institutions a male is likely to be rated "homosexual" if he is discovered to have had a single contact with another male. In society at large, a male who has worked out a highly successful marital adjustment is likely to be rated "homosexual" if the community learns about a single contact that he has had with another male. All such misjudgments are the product of the tendency to categorize sexual activities under only two heads, and of a failure to recognize the endless gradations that actually exist.

From all of this, it becomes obvious that any question as to the number of persons in the world who are homosexual and the number who are heterosexual is unanswerable. It is only possible to record the number of those who belong to each of the positions on such a heterosexual-homosexual scale as is given above. Summarizing our data on the incidence of overt homosexual experience in the white male population and the distribution of various degrees of heterosexual-homosexual balance in that population, the following generalizations may be made:

> 37 per cent of the total male population has at least some overt homosexual experience to the point of orgasm between adolescence and old age (Figure 156). This accounts for nearly 2 males out of every 5 that one may meet.

> 50 per cent of the males who remain single until age 35 have had overt homosexual experience to the point of orgasm, since the onset of adolescence (Figure 156).

> 58 per cent of the males who belong to the group that goes into high school but not beyond, 50 per cent of the grade school level, and 47 per cent of the college level have had homosexual experience to the point of orgasm if they remain single to the age of 35 (Figure 158).

63 per cent of all males **never have overt** homosexual experience to the point of orgasm after the onset of adolescence (Figure 156).

50 per cent of all males (approximately) **have neither overt nor psychic** experience in the homosexual after the onset of adolescence (Figures 162–167).

13 per cent of the males (approximately) **react erotically** to other males **without having overt** homosexual contacts after the onset of adolescence.

30 per cent of all males **have at least incidental homosexual experience** or reactions (*i.e.*, rate 1 to 6) over at least a three-year period between the ages of 16 and 55. This accounts for one male out of every three in the population who is past the early years of adolescence (Figure 168).

25 per cent of the male population **has more than incidental homosexual experience** or reactions (*i.e.*, rates 2–6) for at least three years between the ages of 16 and 55. In terms of averages, one male out of approximately every four has had **or** will have such distinct and continued homosexual experience.

18 per cent of the males have at least **as much of the homosexual as the heterosexual** in their histories (*i.e.*, rate 3–6) for at least three years between the ages of 16 and 55. This is more than one in six of the white male population.

13 per cent of the population **has more of the homosexual than the heterosexual** (*i.e.*, rates 4–6) for at least three years between the ages of 16 and 55. This is one in eight of the white male population.

10 per cent of the males are **more or less exclusively homosexual** (*i.e.*, rate 5 or 6) for at least three years between the ages of 16 and 55. This is one male in ten in the white male population.

8 per cent of the males are **exclusively homosexual** (*i.e.*, rate a 6) for at least three years between the ages of 16 and 55. This is one male in every 13.

4 per cent of the white males are **exclusively homosexual throughout their lives,** after the onset of adolescence (Figure 168).

BISEXUALITY

Since only 50 per cent of the population is exclusively hetero-sexual throughout its adult life, and since only 4 per cent of the population is exclusively homosexual throughout its life, it appears that nearly half (46%) of the population engages in both hetero-

AGE	CASES	HETEROSEXUAL-HOMOSEXUAL RATING: ACTIVE INCIDENCE TOTAL POPULATION—U. S. CORRECTIONS							
		X	0	1	2	3	4	5	6
		%	%	%	%	%	%	%	%
5	4297	90.6	4.2	0.2	0.3	1.2	0.3	0.2	3.0
10	4296	61.1	10.8	1.7	3.6	5.6	1.3	0.5	15.4
15	4284	23.6	48.4	3.6	6.0	4.7	3.7	2.6	7.4
20	3467	3.3	69.3	4.4	7.4	4.4	2.9	3.4	4.9
25	1835	1.0	79.2	3.9	5.1	3.2	2.4	2.3	2.9
30	1192	0.5	83.1	4.0	3.4	2.1	3.0	1.3	2.6
35	844	0.4	86.7	2.4	3.4	1.9	1.7	0.9	2.6
40	576	1.3	86.8	3.0	3.6	2.0	0.7	0.3	2.3
45	382	2.7	88.8	2.3	2.0	1.3	0.9	0.2	1.8

Table 147. Heterosexual-homosexual ratings for all white males

These are active incidence figures for the entire white male population, including single, married, and post-marital histories, the final figure corrected for the distribution of the population in the U. S. Census of 1940. For further explanations see the legend for Table 141.

sexual and homosexual activities, or reacts to persons of both sexes, in the course of their adult lives. The term bisexual has been ap-plied to at least some portion of this group. Unfortunately, the term as it has been used has never been strictly delimited, and con-sequently it is impossible to know whether it refers to all individ-uals who rate anything from 1 to 5, or whether it is being limited to some smaller number of categories, perhaps centering around group 3. If the latter is intended, it should be emphasized that the 1's, 2's, 4's, and 5's have not yet been accounted for, and they con-stitute a considerable portion of the population.

In any event, such a scheme provides only a three-point scale (heterosexual, bisexual, and homosexual), and such a limited scale does not adequately describe the continuum which is the reality in nature. A seven-point scale comes nearer to showing the many gradations that actually exist. . . .

SCIENTIFIC AND SOCIAL IMPLICATIONS

In view of the data which we now have on the incidence and frequency of the homosexual, and in particular on its co-existence

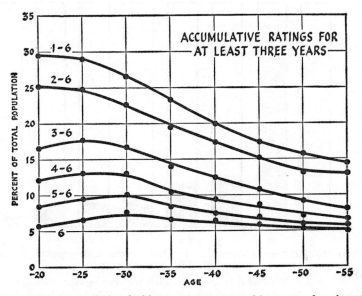

Figure 168. Accumulative incidence of heterosexual-homosexual ratings **in** total male population (single and married), by age periods

Based on U. S. Corrected data. Based only on ratings held by each individual for **a** period of at least three years. All accumulative incidence curves should rise; these drop in older age periods because (1) younger males today may be more often involved in homosexual activity, or (2) older males forget their earlier experience, or (3) older males deliberately cover up their homosexual experience. Certainly the data for the earlier age periods are the most reliable.

with the heterosexual in the lives of a considerable portion of the male population, it is difficult to maintain the view that psycho-sexual reactions between individuals of the same sex are rare and therefore abnormal or unnatural, or that they constitute within themselves evidence of neuroses or even psychoses.

If homosexual activity persists on as large a scale as it does, in the face of the very considerable public sentiment against it and in spite of the severity of the penalities that our Anglo-American culture has placed upon it through the centuries, there seems some reason for believing that such activity would appear in the histories of a much larger portion of the population if there were no social restraints. The very general occurrence of the homosexual in

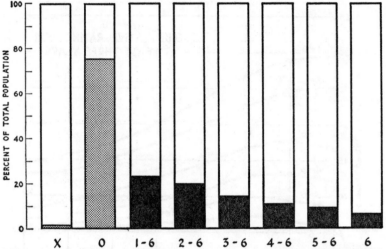

Figure 169. Heterosexual-homosexual ratings in total male population (single and married) in any single year

Based on U. S. Corrected data (last line of Table 150). Passing experiences eliminated from data by showing only ratings which have involved a period of at least three years after the males turned 16. Percent shown as "X" have no socio-sexual contacts or reactions.

ancient Greece, and its wide occurrence today in some cultures in which such activity is not as taboo as it is in our own, suggests that the capacity of an individual to respond erotically to any sort of stimulus, whether it is provided by another person of the same or of the opposite sex, is basic in the species. That patterns of heterosexuality and patterns of homosexuality represent learned behavior which depends, to a considerable degree, upon the mores of the particular culture in which the individual is raised, is a possibility that must be thoroughly considered before there can be any acceptance of the idea that homosexuality is inherited, and that the pattern for each individual is so innately fixed that no modification of it may be expected within his lifetime.

The opinion that homosexual activity in itself provides evidence of a psychopathic personality is materially challenged by these in-cidence and frequency data. Of the 40 or 50 per cent of the male population which has homosexual experience, certainly a high proportion would not be considered psychopathic personalities on the basis of anything else in their histories. It is argued that an

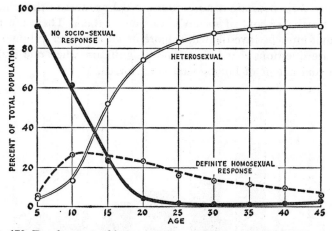

Figure 170. Development of heterosexuality and homosexuality by age periods

Active incidence curves, corrected for U. S. population. Males with no socio-sexual response (rating X) rapidly disappear between the ages of 5 and 20. Males whose responses are chiefly heterosexual (rating 0 or 1) rapidly increase in number until they ultimately account for 90 per cent of the whole population. Males who are more than incidentally homosexual in response or overt activity (ratings 2–6) are most abundant in pre-adolescence and through the teens, gradually becoming less abundant with advancing age.

individual who is so obtuse to social reactions as to continue his homosexual activity and make it any material portion of his life, therein evidences some social incapacity; but psychiatrists and clinicians in general might very well re-examine their justification for demanding that all persons conform to particular patterns of behavior. As a matter of fact, there is an increasing proportion of the most skilled psychiatrists who make no attempt to re-direct behavior, but who devote their attention to helping an individual accept himself, and to conduct himself in such a manner that he does not come into open conflict with society.

There are, of course, some persons with homosexual histories who are neurotic and in constant difficulty with themselves and not infrequently with society. That is also true of some persons with heterosexual histories. Some homosexual individuals are so upset that they have difficulty in the accomplishment of their business or professional obligations and reach the point where they find it difficult to make the simplest sort of social contact without friction. It is, however, a considerable question whether these persons have homosexual histories because they are neurotic, or whether their neurotic disturbances are the product of their homosexual activities and of society's reaction to them. These are matters that must be investigated in more detail in a later volume; but they are questions that become more significant when one realizes the actual extent of homosexual behavior. . . .

Jack H. Hedblom

The Female Homosexual:
Social and Attitudinal Dimensions

—*Studies on lesbianism (Sapphic love or female homosexuality) are far too rare in the literature on homosexuality. They are often merely intuitional and based on highly personal observations. This previously unpublished article by Hedblom, on the other hand, places the study of lesbianism on a scientific level, and it must rank as one of the finer studies available at this time on the subject.*

RESEARCH IN TABOO AREAS

There are problems involved in researching clandestine behavior that are not encountered in more traditional research. These difficulties include locating the activity itself, and are compounded by the unwillingness of the subjects to be studied. A research method particularly suited to this type of study is participant observation. Although the data derived from this method does not have "sense" built into it, the data does generate hypotheses. A problem in using this method is organizing the data to serve this generative purpose. The technique has often been criticized because the case history material generates more random observations than hypotheses. Polsky has suggested that

> Successful field research depends upon the investigator's ability to look at people, listen to them, think and feel with them. It does not depend fundamentally on some impersonal apparatus, such as

"The Female Homosexual: Social and Attitudinal Dimensions." © 1972 by Jack H. Hedblom. Used by permission of the author. This research was funded in part by The Biomedical Research Foundation, State University of New York at Buffalo. The author wishes to acknowledge the support of Dr. John Sirjamake.

a camera or a tape recorder or a questionnaire that is imposed between the investigator and the investigated. . . . A problem for many sociologists today, the result of curricula containing as much scientism as science, is that these capacities far from being trained in him are trained out of him.[1]

Merton has also argued that the timing of hypothesis formulation is irrelevant since the validity of the hypothesis always rests upon replication of studies.[2] Whyte in evaluating his experience and researching the data for *Street Corner Society* addressed this problem.

> Logic then plays an important part. But I am convinced that the actual evolution of research ideas does not take place in accord with the formal statements we read on research methods. The ideas grow up, in part, out of our immersion in data and out of the whole process of living. Since so much of this process of analysis perceives on the unconscious level, I am sure that we could never present a full account of it. . . .[3]

As Simon and Gagnon stated:

> The lesbian represents an excellent example of a need to integrate our understanding about deviant and conventional processes. Where, one might ask, is the research literature that reports upon the attributes and activities of the lesbian when she is not acting out her deviant commitment? The answer is that there is virtually none. As a result [sic] any research must rely upon an exceedingly thin scientific literature.[4]

It appears that there is a need to establish greater continuities between what Garfinkel [5] has called ethnomethodological concerns and traditional survey techniques. The study reported has attempted to base the validity of its survey instrument on the period of participant observation.

1. Ned Polsky, *Hustler, Beats and Others* (New York: Aldine Publishing Co., 1967), pp. 127–28.
2. Robert Merton, *Social Theory and Social Structure,* rev. ed. (Glencoe: The Free Press, 1957), pp. 93–95.
3. William Foote Whyte, *Street Corner Society* (Chicago: University of Chicago Press, 1954), p. 280.
4. William Simon and John Gagnon, "Femininity in Lesbian Community," *Social Problems,* XV, 2 (1967), 213.
5. Harold Garfinkel, *Studies in Ethnomethodology* (Englewood Cliffs, N.J.: Prentice-Hall, Inc., 1967), pp. 3–4.

The Focus: Homosexuality

Despite an extensive literature treating lesbian themes in drama, art, and history, little attention has been paid to lesbianism itself. There are very few scientific studies on the extent of lesbianism, the life styles of lesbians, and the nature of their community. This study employs both observation and survey techniques and was done in Philadelphia between 1964 and 1970. Its principal focus is on the careers and life styles of lesbians. In order to maximize sample size and to avoid possible bias by having the questionnaire administered by a straight male, a field investigator was hired who was herself homosexual.

Becoming a homosexual often involves a matter of degree, not an either/or decision. Persons having occasional homosexual experiences were not included in this study. We also excluded persons who had made a homosexual adjustment in a total institution where no heterosexual outlets exist. Such persons identified themselves as heterosexual and most often made an exclusively heterosexual adjustment upon change in the living conditions. We therefore defined the lesbian as a female who focuses her sexual attentions, fantasies, and activities upon members of her own sex. Persons who are so defined must identify themselves as homosexual, and as Goffman stated:

> . . . participate in a special community of special understanding wherein members of one's own sex are defined as the most desirable sex object and sociability is energetically organized around the pursuit and entertainment of these objects.[6]

The nature of the homosexual commitment creates a very specialized social-psychological milieu in which one must establish a social career. This milieu may be considered a subcultural phenomenon characterized by patterns of beliefs, goals, and statuses that are different from the host society although not necessarily antithetical to it. It is important to note that only a small portion of the life style is taken up by the acting out of homosexual activities. The social career of the female homosexual can only be understood by considering the total range of her social and sexual activity.

6. Erving Goffman, *Stigma: Notes on the Management of Spoiled Identity* (Englewood Cliffs, N.J.: Prentice-Hall, Inc., 1963), pp. 143–44.

Lesbianism: A Covert Phenomenon

Given an uninformed public that is somewhat embarrassed at the mention of sex in any form, it is not surprising that Western European culture is loath to admit the existence of female homosexuality at all. The lesbian has a low detectability when compared with the male homosexual. She is accordingly treated differentially by law enforcement officers and suffers less discrimination at the hands of the community than does her male counterpart.[7] Adverse public opinion becomes manifest only when the lesbian identifies herself by performance, association, or unique dress.

The homosexual commitment encompasses the entire life style; the simple fact of being a homosexual places an individual in a very special relationship to society. Life style is intrinsically interwoven in a specialized community that is based entirely on that difference. Adequate measures of the extent of homosexuality depend upon the willingness of the rather specialized covert homosexual community to be studied or to include temporarily in its membership persons who are scientifically interested in manifestations of the phenomenon itself.

THE FEMALE HOMOSEXUAL: A UNIQUE COMMITMENT

There are basic biological and social differences between the male homosexual and the female homosexual. The female reflects the impact of her socialization as a female. She is concerned with the establishment of a home. She relates sex to love and is more likely to abstain from sex until she meets "the right person." She tends to be more passive in her search for a mate, even in the established marketplace of the homosexual community. Women are a more homogeneous group than men by virtue of their rigid socialization and are on the whole conditioned to be less aggressive and assertive. Stearn noted that women, including the lesbian, are trained to marital fidelity.

> The lesbian prided herself on the chastity of the lesbian group as compared to the male homosexual. . . . It was not unusual for lesbians to remain true to one woman. "Like other women," a lesbian

7. It is for this reason that official arrest statistics are not indicative of the scope or extent of female homosexuality.

told me, "we think in terms of a monogamous ideal, even when we don't practice it." [8]

Lesbians are exposed to the same subtle influences and experiences as heterosexual females, many of which occur before actual sexual experience.[9] The effectiveness of the lesbian's socialization is evident in that her career is an almost exact duplication of the female heterosexual's.

ESTIMATE OF SIZE OF
THE HOMOSEXUAL COMMUNITY

It is difficult to estimate the size of the female homosexual community. It is more elusive than the male subculture and less obvious in its deviation, and for this reason, its size is often underestimated. The lesbian is more difficult to detect by virtue of her training in sexual repression, which is far more systematic for the female than for the male. Hooker suggests that lesbians maintain a front of heterosexuality that becomes an integral part of their life style. This pretense makes the lesbian's already low detectability even lower.[10] Hooker refers to female homosexuality as an iceberg phenomenon, indicating that most of the community lies beneath the surface of society. Further, she states that the majority of homosexuals belong to the submerged group and seldom attend homosexual meetings, join homosexual organizations, or frequent homosexual bars. The female homosexual community consists of a series of loosely knit or overlapping networks of friends bonded together by their difference and their need to be themselves among others who do not stigmatize their identity.

Existing statistics do not indicate the extent of female homosexuality nor is it revealed by arrest statistics, since very few women are arrested for homosexuality. The inability to establish population parameters seriously limits the use of sampling techniques for a representative sample. The best estimate is that homosexuality is found at least as frequently among women as among men.

8. Jess Stearn, *The Grapevine* (New York: Doubleday & Co., 1964), p. 13.

9. Simon and Gagnon, *op. cit.*, pp. 212–21.

10. Evelyn Hooker, "The Homosexual Community," a paper delivered at the Fourteenth Annual Congress of Applied Psychology, Copenhagen, 1961. General editor, Gehard Heilson, Copenhagen, 1962, pp. 40–59.

EXPLANATORY MODELS

Theories of the causality of homosexuality are varied and often conflicting. However, three approaches are basic to the subject. The medical model dominates the literature on the ideology of homosexuality. It assumes that homosexuality is the result of an underlying psychological or physical pathology. Homosexuality is, therefore, a symptom of this pathology, and it is treated as a condition that can be "cured." The psychiatric implications of this model are clear. Obviously, the homosexual adjustment is resistant to change, but it can be ameliorated and result in a "normal heterosexual adjustment." As Robertiello states:

> Homosexuality is the symptom of an illness. Certain traumatic experiences in childhood cause anxieties of the homosexual that do not allow him to express his sexual feelings toward a member of the opposite sex and at the same time compel him to express them towards a member of his own sex. It is not a matter of choice but of compulsion. Most homosexuals are unhappy, suffering people. Some of them may rationalize that theirs is the best life—at least for them, but all of them have an inner dissatisfaction with their method of adaptation. This dissatisfaction is not only reflective of society's disapproval, it is also based on an awareness of the basic lack of fulfillment and the compulsive pattern connected with their activity.[11]

The psychoanalytical approach is evidenced in the following:

> I sort of gravitated toward my father and Jack toward my mother, while Louise was cuddled by all of us. She was the baby and even Jack could accept her, and that's the way it all started. Now I understand the whole business, when I find my case history written up by an orthodox Freudian analyst. My name was Electra and I used to sit upon my daddy Agamemnon's lap and I fell in love with him, while little Jackie Oedipus was falling in love with mama Jocasta. It is all so clear, except that Jackie Oedipus grew up to like women because I was in love with daddy, so it doesn't explain everything, at least not to me.[12]

11. Richard Robertiello, *Voyage from Lesbos* (New York: The Citadel Press, 1959), pp. 15–16. Editorially we note that the homosexual tends to detest his adjustment as well as himself.

12. Donald Webster Cory, "The Lesbian in America," *America's Troubles— A Casebook on Social Conflict* (Englewood Cliffs, N.J.: Prentice-Hall, Inc., 1969), p. 264.

This model precludes the possibility of there being a psychologically healthy homosexual. Bergler, in *Homosexuality—Disease or Way of Life*,[13] stated:

> . . . It has been recently discovered that homosexuality is a curable disease.

> . . . There are no healthy homosexuals. The entire personality structure of the homosexual is pervaded by the unconscious wish to suffer; this wish is gratified by self-created trouble-making. This "injustice-collecting" (technically called psychic masochism) is conveniently deposited in the external difficulties confronting the homosexual. If they were to be removed—and in some circles in large cities they have been virtually removed—the homosexual would still be an emotionally sick person.

We criticize this point of view since it denies that homosexuality can be a viable adjustment. The contact between patient and therapist has, most often, been initiated by the homosexual himself. It is therefore the maladjusted rather than the comfortably adjusted homosexual who seeks treatment. Court agencies espouse the medical orientation and use treatment to justify probation or parole. Since the nature of these contacts is essentially therapeutic, the assumption of an underlying pathology is understandable. However, the population upon which the medical model is based is restricted to homosexuals who are experiencing difficulty in adjusting to their homosexuality and to their social role. There is, therefore, a bias in the model that reflects only the sick homosexual and ignores the possibility of a well-adjusted homosexual who is content with her difference, finds meaningful relationships in her world, and enjoys a productive life.

In 1957 Hooker examined this perspective in *The Adjustment of the Male Homosexual*. In her study, thirty well-adjusted homosexuals were matched for age, I.Q., and education with thirty apparently well-adjusted heterosexuals. Judges were asked to distinguish between the groups. They were unable to do so.[14]

The Wolfenden committee, an English investigatory body, was highly critical of the medical conception of homosexuality. It asserted that the traditional view of disease requires that there be

13. New York: Collier Books, 1956, p. 7.
14. Maurice Leznoff and William A. Wesley, "The Homosexual Community," *Social Problems*, III (April, 1956), 457–63.

abnormal symptoms, that the symptoms be caused by pathological conditions, and that the causes of these symptoms be both necessary and sufficient conditions for their existence. It pointed out that persons may manifest peculiar behavior that is deviant within our frame of reference and still be "normal." It held also that considerations of behavior as normal or abnormal represented culturally biased value judgments and as such were less than scientific. Homosexual activity, according to the committee, did not manifest sufficient symptomatology to imply an underlying pathology. Homosexual persons, according to the committee, were virtually indistinguishable from nonhomosexual.[15] The committee alleged that medical organizations and agencies in general had a vested interest in defining homosexuality as a disease.

The Wolfenden committee further rejected the medical analogy.

> The alleged psychopathological causes for homosexuality have also been found to occur in others besides the homosexual. . . . In the absence of the physical pathology, psychopathological theories have been constructed to explain the symptoms of various forms of normal behavior and mental illness. . . . They are theoretical constructions . . . and not facts.[16]

The claim that homosexuality is an illness carries a further implication that the sufferer cannot help his condition and, therefore, carries a diminished responsibility for his actions. Even if homosexuality could properly be described as a disease, we should not accept this correlation. There are no prima facie grounds for supposing that homosexuality is any less controllable than heterosexuality.[17] The committee suggested further that:

> It is obvious that only a minority of homosexuals or, for that matter, those who indulge in homosexual acts fall into the hands of the police and it is even likely also that a minority of such persons find their way to a doctor's consulting room. But it is impossible to determine what proportion of persons concerned these minorities represent. Still less on this evidence, what proportion of the total population falls within the description homosexual. These figures (derived figures), therefore, cannot be relied on as an indication of

15. Sir John Wolfenden, et al., Report of the Departmental Committee on Homosexual Offenses and Prostitution (London: Her Majesty's Stationery Office, 1957).

16. Ibid., p. 119.

17. Ibid., p. 120.

the extent of homosexuality or homosexual behavior among the community as a whole.[18]

The Family Interaction Model

Those researchers concerned with the influence of institutions on behavior have focused on parental roles to explain the development of the homosexual. Recent research has isolated the following model. The father is described as detached or hostile or both. He has resigned his role as father and as household head. In the face of this resignation, the mother tends to be loving and overprotective. She is seductive toward sons and presents a strong identification model for daughters, who contrast her with a weak, ineffectual, yet exploitative male parent.

Schrieber and Wilber, who isolated the pattern described above, noted that it required two parents to create the homosexual child. If the father encouraged the son to be masculine, the latter did not become homosexual. Similarly, the mother's encouragement in heterosexuality acted as a deterrent. They noted that unhappy marriages promoted homosexuality because they tended to cause displacement of love object, resulting in the mother using the son as husband substitute.

In the case of female homosexuality, the mother's relationship with the daughter is a kind of chaotic struggle in which the child loses continually; the mother uses rejection, degradation, and guilt in order to control her child. The child rebels against the mother but at the same time wants her love. At the onset of puberty, warned about the dangers of heterosexual dating, the daughter considers the female the more desirable sex object and, at the same time, a mother substitute.[19]

This analytical model may be criticized from several points of view. Initially, the model ignores the possibility of primary influences other than the family. Peers and basic institutions such as the school and the church are ignored. It is assumed that the patterns established when the family is the single or primary source of socialization are immutable in later years. This orientation likewise ignores the possibility of the reenforcement of homosexual urges or fantasies by supportive structures, such as the awareness of other homosexuals and interaction with them. The model likewise ig-

18. *Ibid.*, p. 125.
19. Schrieber and Wilber, "Homosexual Men and Women," *Science Digest* (April, 1964), 55–64.

nores the likelihood of homosexual siblings or the order of birth of the child who becomes homosexual. Our own studies have found that the incidence of homosexual siblings and cousins in families that have produced one homosexual is greater than is reported in the literature. This is not surprising, given the continuity of socialization between siblings and cousins. Siblings and cousins share at least one common parent and are socialized by a milieu that we can tentatively suggest produces some continuity of personality.

Wahl noted family influence in the case of homosexuality.[20] He suggests that the most common family structure that produces homosexuality is one having a weak or absent same-sexed parent, coupled with a dominating, overprotective, seductive, opposite-sexed parent.

> The child exposed to this condition may conclude (in the case of the male) that women are stronger and more reliable than men; and children being prone to identify with a power source may identify, therefore, not only with the mother but also with her sexual object choice. Another common variation is the family history of a sadistic and a punitive opposite-sexed parent, coupled with a submissive, ineffectual or absent same-sexed parent.[21]

Wahl notes also that other factors, extrafamilial factors, are important in inducing homosexuality. He numbers among these the presence of a supportive structure or a group that provides rationalization of homosexual activity. Morse likewise observed that parental influences play an important role in the development of the homosexual personality.[22] He suggested that a family that wants a child of one sex and gets a child of another sex tends to create psychological problems for the child by forcing or favoring activities most appropriate for the opposite sex. He cites, as an example, the father who wanted a son and got a daughter but who treated the daughter as if she were a son.

> Mom would be in the kitchen making dinner or doing the dishes, she says, and Dad and I would be out in the backyard tossing a ball back and forth. In the fall it was football, in the spring and

20. Charles W. Wahl, ed., *Sexual Problems—Diagnosis and Treatment in Medical Practice* (New York: The Free Press, 1967).

21. *Ibid.*, p. 97.

22. Benjamin Morse, *The Lesbian* (Derby Conn.: Monarch Books, 1961), pp. 90–91.

summer baseball. Mom would do the housework and I would play catch with Dad.[23]

The root of homosexuality is, therefore, not neurosis but rather the social-psychological milieu based on the relationship between parents and child. The child's basic role in the family and the effectiveness of the roles played by the parents strongly affect the early psychosexual commitment of the child.

The most persuasive argument for the family model of homosexuality identifies the father as a crucial parent and homosexuality as arising either from the father's inability to accept the appropriate sexual role of the child or his passivity, ineffectiveness, or domination by the female parent. McGee viewed the child's relationship to the father as central, and observed that it was not so much the absolute quality of the relationship that is important as how the child perceived the relationship.

> . . . One can now begin to see the different ways in which a child may become homosexual because of a pattern of relationship in which the entire family is involved. . . . Some of the most recent work being done on the subject, for example, that of the sociologist Dr. Eva Bene, points to the surprising conclusion that the really crucial relationship in the case of both male and female homosexuals is not with the mother but with the father.[24]

The family model does not explain the occurrence of homosexual experiences themselves. It does not explain how one homosexual meets another nor how they resolve their status problems. It does not explain the pervasiveness of the homosexual commitment nor how behavior and identity continue without supportive structures. It does not provide a mode whereby we can understand the female homosexual's identification and social career.

The lesbian's commitment to a unique community or subculture is a defense against stigmatization of her identity. The subculture establishes a status system based on qualities already possessed by individual members. Participation in it is a kind of problem-solving behavior. The antithetical values of the subculture are learned, adapted, and exhibited in a manner similar to those in the host

23. *Ibid.,* p. 36.
24. Bryon McGee, *One in Twenty—A Study of Homosexuality in Men and Women* (London: Secker and Warburg, 1966), p. 28.

culture. The individual continues as an active participant in the host society as well as in the homosexual subculture.

Homosexuality creates innumerable difficulties for a female in playing her social roles. A homosexual commitment affects her associations, entertainment activities, and occupational roles, as well as delimiting the possibility of certain types of social mobility. The subculture protects the homosexual from mixed feelings about herself and provides her with associations that are essentially accepting. Since her social career is focused primarily upon her sexual identification, her commitment places her in a special relationship to the larger society and to the conventional patterns of interaction which comprise it.

The lesbian community is a continuing collectivity of associations. Persons involved in it have a common identity resulting from a stigmatized social designation. The community facilitates sexual union, provides a source of identity, and offers an opportunity for the lesbian to relax the front she traditionally presents to the heterosexual community. It reduces the possibility of embarrassing oneself by making advances to a straight person and provides an ideology and justification for homosexual behavior itself.

MODEL COMBINATIONS

Individually, neither of these models provides a sufficiently broad framework to understand the phenomenon of lesbianism. Of the two approaches, the medical model presents the greatest difficulty. It is based on value judgments that define heterosexual morality as absolute rather than culturally relative and excludes inversion as a viable sexual adjustment. The family interaction model emphasizes parental roles and children's perception of them to the exclusion of other social variables. The model does not explain the persistence of the homosexual adjustment in the face of its pejorative definition and ignores the supportive structure of social interaction. While the role of the family cannot be ignored, neither can the role of other social institutions, including the supportive structure of the homosexual community in perpetuating the life style of the lesbian.

Given the inherent weakness of each model, a combination of models must be used to locate the etiology of inverted psychosexual identity in the role-structure of the family and the social support for the ongoing homosexual activity in the specialized community of the lesbian. The life of the female invert will be explored within this theoretical frame of reference. We examine the role-structure of the lesbian's home as she perceives it. We likewise examine her dating patterns, marriage arrangements, occupations, and patterns of sexual behavior. The process of becoming homosexual is considered in terms of the age at which first fantasy, contact, emotional involvement, and finally entry into the homosexual community occurs. The following tables best describe the sample.

SAMPLE CHARACTERISTICS

In summary, the heterosexual marital status of the sample includes fifty-seven persons who had never married, one married person, three separated persons, and four divorced. Thirty-one of the sample are homosexually married; thirty-four are not. The educational descriptions indicate a larger percentage of respondents have graduated from high school, have college experience, have graduated from college or attended graduate school, than we expected to find in a heterosexual population. Forty-six percent of the respondents have attended college or are in the process of attending college. Forty-eight percent of the sample hold occupations that are skilled or semiskilled, with 32 percent in professional occupations or technical categories. Fifteen percent of the sample are in the professional category. This distribution shows a large percentage of respondents in the middle class or upper-middle class. This is not interpreted to mean that most female homosexuals originate predominantly in these social classes. The analysis of fathers' occupations indicates that parents of respondents were both lower class and middle class as well as some upper class.

The data indicate a high achievement pattern among homosexual females. Lesbians carry the responsibility for maintaining themselves rather than being supported by a male partner. Their occupational roles and goals are, therefore, culturally defined as masculine.

THE COMMUNITY

We have previously discussed the nature of the homosexual community. Respondents indicated involvement in activities unique to this homosexual world and interaction with a network of friends, themselves homosexual. The most accessible public meeting place

Sample Characteristics*

A. Age

		Homosexually Married	Unmarried	Total
6.	41–45	3	2	5
5.	36–40	4	3	7
4.	31–35	4	3	7
3.	26–30	9	18	27
2.	21–25	11	7	18
1.	16–20	0	1	1

46 of 65 total, or 70% of sample, are 30 years old or less.
20 of 31 married or 68% of married sample are 30 years old or less.
26 of 34 unmarried or 76% of unmarried sample are 30 years old or less.

B. Years of Schooling

	Married	Unmarried	Total
Graduate work	3	3	6
College			
Graduate	3	3	6
3 years	1	4	5
2 years	3	2	5
1 year	3	4	7
High school			
Graduate	15	15	30
3 years	2	2	4
2 years		1	1
1 year	1		1
Grade			
8			
7			
6			
5			

C. Occupation

	Married	Unmarried	Total
Professional	4	5	9
Technical	5	6	11
Skilled	6	8	14
Semiskilled	5	12	17
Unskilled	5	2	7
Blue collar	5		5
No answer	1	1	2

*When figures do not total 65, respondents have not answered the question.

D. RELIGIOUS AFFILIATION

	Homosexually Married	Unmarried	Total
Protestant	9	12	21
Catholic	16	16	32
Jewish	1	2	3
Other	5	3	8
(1 no answer)			

E. RACE (self-defined)

White	31	33	64
Negro		1	1
Mongol			
Other			

F. MARITAL STATUS (heterosexual)

Single	24	33	57
Married	1		1
Separated	3		3
Divorced	3	1	4

G. CHILDREN

Male	2
Female	4
None	61

GROUPINGS BY AGE

H. RELIGION

Group	Total	Protestant	Catholic	Jewish	Other
1. 16–20	1				1
2. 21–25	18	6	9	1	2
3. 26–30	27	9	14	1	3
4. 31–35	7	3	3		1
5. 36–40	7	1	3	1	1
6. 41+	5	2	3		
Total		21	32	3	8

I. RACE (64 White, 1 Negro who is in 26–30 category)

J. MARITAL STATUS

Group	Total	Single	Married	Separated	Divorced
1. 16–20	1	1			
2. 21–25	18	16		1	1
3. 26–30	27	24	1	1	1
4. 31–35	7	6			1
5. 36–40	7	6		1	
6. 41+	6	4			1
Total		57	1	3	4

K. FATHER PERCEIVED AS HEAD OF HOUSE   MOTHER PERCEIVED AS HEAD OF HOUSE

Group	Total	No Answer	Yes	No	No Answer	Yes	No
1. 16–20	1			1		1	
2. 21–25	18	2	10	6	1	7	10
3. 26–30	27	3	15	9	2	10	15
4. 31–35	7		4	3		2	5
5. 36–40	7	1	5	1	1	1	5
6. 41+	5		5			1	4
Total		6	39	20	4	22	39

L. PARENTAL OCCUPATION

	Father	Mother	Total
Professional	10	6	16
Technical	7	3	10
Skilled	20	3	23
Semiskilled	9	40	49
Unskilled	4	1	5
Blue collar		2	2
Totals	50	55	105

M. PARENTAL YEARS OF SCHOOL

	Father	Mother	Total
Graduate work	2	2	4
College			
Graduate	10	3	13
3 years			
2 years	2	6	8
1 year		1	1
High school			
Graduate	22	21	43
3 years		2	2
2 years	4	1	5
1 year	2	7	9
Grade			
8	2	5	7
7	3	5	8
6	4	3	7
5	2	1	3
Totals	53	57	110

for the lesbian is the homosexual bar. In the career of the typical lesbian, the bar plays several roles, i.e., that of sexual marketplace, clearinghouse for information, meeting place, place for finding peer associations, and above all, a neutral meeting ground. Bar attendance is a predictable part of the lesbian's life. It provides, in addition, psychological reinforcement for homosexual identity as well as opportunity to interact freely without the necessity of putting up a front. Typically, lesbians visit bars two or three times a month. Twenty-nine percent of respondents attend bars at least six times per month. Twenty-three percent of respondents indicate that they had met 100 percent of their friends in homosexual bars. As the female homosexual becomes more involved with the subculture of homosexuality, the importance of the homosexual bar as a sexual marketplace tends to diminish.

Respondents indicate that they have had sexual relations with girls met in bars as well as with girls met through friends. The greater percentage of these relationships has occurred through friends or contacts outside the bar (32 percent). Thirty percent of respondents, on the other hand, indicate that they have met only 20 percent of the persons with whom they had shared a sexual relationship through friends. The pattern of responses stresses the mutual importance of the homosexual community and the homosexual bar. The availability of one facility is not diminished by that of the other. Given the clandestine nature of homosexual bars and their limited number, it is not surprising that most of them are peopled by a cross-section of the homosexual world.

Sixty-four of the sample of sixty-five indicate that they prefer a stable relationship to any other. This affects the nature of "dating" as it occurs in the homosexual world since in the gay world one is not "dating someone"—one is "going with someone." Dating patterns are characterized by a kind of perpetual "going steady." The stable relationship acts as a defense against charges of promiscuity. Most respondents are involved in a marriage arrangement. Seventy-one percent of respondents have had such an arrangement, and 75 percent have had two or fewer such relationships. Twenty-nine percent of respondents, however, have had three or more such relationships. These marriage-like relationships have no legal or social support outside the homosexual community. Although they tend to be impermanent, they are easier to establish than heterosexual marriages, which involve formal announcement and public rituals in their formalization. The homosexual marriage arrangement finds its analogy in the heterosexual world in "living to-gether," or trial marriage. There have been no comparisons of homosexual marriages with "trial marriages" in the literature.

The existence of a community composed of homosexuals is re-vealed by the fact that 84 percent of respondents reported that the majority of their friends were homosexual. This percentage is im-pressive when one considers that homosexuals are involved in school or are employed in the straight world most of the time. Seventy-six percent of respondents indicate that they keep up a heterosexual front when interacting with the heterosexual community. This "leading two lives" severely limits social interaction with persons met occupationally or otherwise in the heterosexual community. Younger respondents are less likely to pretend heterosexuality, which indicates a growing militancy against discrimination and definition as abnormal or sick. Respondents resent having to main-tain a heterosexual front and believe that the choice of love object has nothing to do with the quality of love itself and that homo-sexual love is "normal."

Homosexual females defend themselves by defining their "nor-malcy" in terms of numbers. Whenever they estimate the size of the homosexual community, they observe that there are many more female inverts than the public is aware of. They imply that if a large number of persons are involved in homosexual activities, they must be "normal."

A majority of respondents (84 percent) indicate that they are comfortable with nonhomosexuals. This suggests the effectiveness of the heterosexual front, which makes possible a considerable ex-change between homosexual and heterosexual communities. The posture of heterosexuality allows the female invert to act as a sin-gle girl in the straight community. Since she was socialized in the straight community, such behavior is natural to her regardless of her sexual commitment. That she comfortably interacts with the heterosexual community indicates that she has adjusted to her role in the homosexual community and is comfortable with it. The group reinforcement of homosexual identity is indicated by 79 percent of respondents who assert that homosexuality is as normal as heterosexuality.

Entrance into the homosexual community does not immediately follow awareness of individual homosexual commitment or first physical homosexual contact. Initial homosexual contacts are nei-ther exploitative nor characterized by the respondent's seduction into a homosexual commitment. Instead, they are a willing, cooperative exploration of homosexual tendencies. Fourteen percent of the respondents indicated that first physical contact occurred before the age of ten. Seventy-nine percent of the respondents had a physical experience before the age of twenty and before entry into the homosexual community. Only 20 percent of the respondents report that their first physical experience occurred after twenty but before twenty-five. Respondents, however, indicate that they first chose homosexuals as their principal social group between the ages of twenty and thirty, with 45 percent making this choice before twenty-five years of age and 35 percent between the ages of twenty-six and thirty. Only four made this decision after the age of thirty. Physical experience thus precedes entrance into the homosexual community by a considerable period of time. Most respondents assert that their grammar school and high school experiences were not affected by awareness of homosexuality or the physical experience itself, thus indicating peer support for heterosexual dating patterns and attitudes.

Typically, the lesbian, regardless of her growing involvement with the homosexual community or awareness of her homosexuality, continues heterosexual dating for a considerable time. She has little or no support for her homosexuality from the homosexual community unless she is involved in it. Her peers and family exert pressures on her to conform to a more ordinary life and define this period in her life as a "fun period." They relax these pressures on her as she grows older and assumes the role of an adult female. With eventual emancipation from the parental home, the lesbian has opportunities to explore life styles and sexual patterns. It is ordinarily at this point that serious involvement with the homosexual community begins.

Membership in the homosexual community is obviously the result of feelings and events, not necessarily sexual in nature, that lead to self-awareness and self-acceptance as a homosexual; she then seeks out homosexuals as her principal social group. By this act, she minimizes the stigma of her identity as something different from the normal population and finds support for her emotional being as well as social career. One function of the homosexual community is to provide rationalizations that lessen the stigma of homosexuality. Seventy-three percent of respondents indicate that they believe homosexuals to be particularly creative (more creative than heterosexuals), and 80 percent perceive homosexuals to be particularly sensitive to others (more sensitive also than heterosexuals).

Indicative of the supportive quality of the homosexual subculture, 85 percent of the respondents indicate that they are generally happy. Sixty-five percent of the sample indicate that they would leave the choice of homosexuality vs. heterosexuality to their children. The fact that such perceptions have wide support in the homosexual community indicates that the community itself presents an ideology which provides a means whereby a positive identity can be established for its members.

The negative perception of the homosexual life style is therefore based on the discrimination and the stigmatized identity of the homosexual commitment as viewed by the heterosexual world. It is not intrinsic to the nature of homosexuality itself. However, the transient quality of the homosexual liaison, the covert nature of the "gay" life, the need for concealment, and the distorted self-image of the homosexual support the conclusion that the heterosexual is a more fulfilling existence than the homosexual life style.

SOCIAL AND ATTITUDINAL DIMENSIONS

Involvement with the homosexual community for the lesbian typically begins between the ages of twenty and thirty. Fifty-eight percent of respondents chose homosexuals as their principal social group between the ages of twenty-one and twenty-five, and 35 percent between the ages of twenty-six and thirty. The social career of a typical lesbian begins with emancipation from family and from adolescent peer associations. Entrance to the community is a gradual process, preceded by homosexual fantasies, and characterized by physical homosexual contacts occurring over a long time.

Sixty-seven percent of the respondents report that their grade and high school experiences were not overly affected by awareness of homosexual tendencies or commitment. Most respondents continued heterosexual dating after their awareness of homosexual proclivities, probably believing them transitory or part of a phase, after which they would be "normal" again. The milieu of the teenager offers little support for nonconforming sexual behavior. Pressures for conventional life style are exerted by peers and family.

Despite clear-cut boundaries between heterosexual and homosexual worlds, interchanges between them do occur. Eighty-nine percent of the respondents report that they have dated men during their homosexual careers. A good proportion (37 percent) of the respondents have also had sexual experience with men. Dating heterosexual men has sexual connotations and is not carried on principally for cover or escort purposes. Respondents date straight men more often than gay men. Eighty-five percent of the respondents indicate that they do not date gay men exclusively. The need for a male escort has been overemphasized in the literature.[25]

Homosexual dating patterns differ from those of the heterosexual world. Due to the covert nature of homosexuality, homosexual dating involves house parties, group outings, and other collective activities that conceal their homosexual nature. Dating means something different in the homosexual community from what it does in the heterosexual. Moreover, there is an emphasis on youth, with the girls being called "kids." However, there is also an emphasis upon couples. One does not "date around" in the homosexual community; one looks for a partner. Some 60 percent of the respondents report that they do not date girls whom they meet in homosexual bars. Instead they rely on a network of friends and associates in the homosexual community for "dates" or other forms of interaction.

Eighty-six percent of respondents indicate that they interact with the heterosexual world with a degree of ease. A larger percentage of married couples were more comfortable with straight persons than were unmarried persons. This interaction with the heterosexual community indicates the efficacy of the front of heterosexuality that homosexuals present to the heterosexual word and is also a measure of comfort with themselves. Forty-nine (or 75 percent) of the respondents report that they keep up a front for the benefit of straight friends or acquaintances.

It has been commonly assumed that there is more understanding between the male homosexual world and the female homosexual world than exists between either perspective and the heterosexual world. The data does not support this. If anything, the data indicates that as great a gulf of misunderstanding exists between the male and female homosexual worlds as exists between the homosexual and heterosexual worlds. Female homosexuals regard the male homosexual community pejoratively. Eighty-five percent of the respondents indicate that they consider female homosexual marriage arrangements more stable than their male counterparts.

25. Respondents typically date once a week, with married persons dating less frequently than unmarried persons. Seventy-nine percent of respondents, after being instructed to disregard their present involvements, indicate that they date at least once per week and three or four times a month.

Ninety-eight percent of the sample view the male homosexual community as being more promiscuous than the female and as having more extremes in its milieu. The male homosexual is also perceived as having more "one-night stands" than his female counterpart.[26] He is viewed as being more oriented toward immediate gratification than toward establishment of a relatively permanent association. This perception indicates differences in attitudes toward sex between the male and female homosexual. Conversely, the female homosexual typically considers her world as happy for her, differing from the heterosexual community only to the extent that homosexuality is stigmatized as unnatural.

Seventy-five percent of the respondents believed that the female homosexual's drive for authority and achievement patterns is greater than those of the heterosexual female. Respondents indicate that they consider themselves as stable and as mentally healthy as they would be in the straight world. Ninety-one percent of the respondents say they have never sought professional help to overcome their homosexuality. Twenty-six percent indicate they have sought specialized help with adjustment problems that did not pertain to their homosexuality.

SEXUAL AWARENESS AND ACTIVITY

Nearly one-half of respondents (42 percent) experienced homosexual fantasies between the ages of eleven and fifteen, 28 percent between the ages of six and ten, and 30 percent after the age of fifteen. Some period of time lapsed between their first fantasies and first physical homosexual contacts. A further period of time followed before respondents fully identified with the homosexual community.

A cherished notion in the heterosexual community is that homosexuality begins as the result of the seduction of children by older homosexuals. To ascertain the relationship between respondents and the person with whom they had shared their first physical experience, we found that 47 percent of the respondents played an initially passive, but willing role. Fifty-three percent indicated that they had played an initially dominant role and were the seducers. Based on this data, we state that persons are not seduced into ho-

---

26. One-night stand in this instance is meant to designate a contact between two strangers whose purpose is gratification of sexual need rather than constituting an attempt at establishing a relationship of any other kind.

mosexuality. Initial contacts are the result of mutual willingness to explore homosexuality. Psychosexual identity has already been formed before the first physical contact, and homosexual females experiment with the dimensions of their sexual universe just as heterosexuals experiment with theirs.

As the respondent matures and increases her involvement with the homosexual community, there is a decreasing pressure to date from peers and family. This is accompanied by an emphasis upon her emergent role as an adult female. It is at this point in her social career that the female homosexual begins a serious involvement with the subculture of female homosexuality.

The basic role in the homosexual world that the individual assigns herself pertains directly to the type of role she will act out socially. The physical aspects of the role are more flexible than the social aspects. Only 18 percent of the sample indicate that they play the physical role of the female exclusively (femme). The remainder of the sample indicate that they play both the dominant (butch) and submissive roles interchangeably. On the basis of this data, female homosexual roles—i.e., (male) dominance vs. (female) submission—are more social in their basic dimensions than they are physical. Social roles are a method whereby the homosexual subculture organizes dating and pursuit patterns as well as areas of responsibility in social interaction. Social roles apparently have little to do with the sexual roles played out by respondents.

Respondents indicate that 20 percent of their dates with other lesbians result in a sexual liaison (55.9 percent of respondents). Respondents who indicate that 100 percent of their dates result in sexual contact are probably exaggerating. Twenty-seven percent of the respondents indicate that oral sex was a part of their first physical contact. Oral sex was not expected to have occurred as the first sexual contact. Manual stimulation was the expected mode of exploration because it is a simple extension of self-arousal. Forty percent of the respondents achieved orgasm on first contact, 5 percent on second contact, and 51 percent on subsequent contacts. The immediacy of sexual gratification may be explained from two perspectives. It is related to the fantasies and anticipation preceding the physical act and the willingness of the respondents to engage in physical homosexual acts, and to their previous experience with physical manipulation and masturbation common to childhood. It is possible also that absence of a fear of penetration encourages the enjoyment of sexual relations. Women are tender, gentle, and aware of female anatomy and its sensitivities. These factors encourage an early and facile sexual response.

Thirty-seven respondents have had sexual relations with a man. Typically these occurred between twenty-one and twenty-five years of age, with some proportion between twenty-six and thirty years of age. Thirty-three respondents who have had sexual relations with a man indicate that penetration by the male occurred. Therefore, heterosexual relationships involving lesbians are not comprised simply of those oral acts to which they are accustomed. Relations between them are not a mock version of the homosexual relationship, but are complete heterosexual acts. Respondents typically adopt a passive role in these relationships, which was predictable, given the fact that women are traditionally socialized to do so. The female homosexual does not prefer sex with a woman because she has had no experience with a man; it is as likely that she has had such an experience as not.

Forty-eight percent of the respondents who have had sex with a man indicate that oral-genital contact occurred. Typically the act was mutual. Forty-eight percent of the respondents achieved orgasm with a man and 50 percent had not, but this did not disturb their identity as female homosexuals. The choice of sex object is based not upon her inability to have satisfying sexual relations with a man but upon more complicated criteria rooted in her psychosexual identity. More than a third of the respondents having sexual relations with a man had this experience within the twelve-month period preceding their completion of the questionnaire. Some have had sexual liaisons within the previous six months. Nevertheless, these individuals thoroughly identify with the homosexual community and accept their psychosexual identity as lesbians. Unmarried respondents engage in mutual oral sex more often than do the married groups. Oral sex is apparently related to whether the respondents achieve orgasm with the man.

SUMMATION

The social career of the female homosexual occurs within a subcultural context that parallels closely the career of the heterosexual woman. Her principal interaction with the straight community involves her employment. The majority of her friends are lesbians. She perceives her stigmatized identity and maintains a front of heterosexuality for the straight community and, in part, her family.

The lesbian views herself as being less promiscuous than male homosexuals and as more likely to enter into long-term, stable relationships. She associates sex with an emotional bond between persons and is less likely to "cruise" for sex partners. Her dating patterns indicate that she is "going with" someone or "married" in the homosexual sense of the word.

Although the lesbian attends homosexual bars, of equal importance in her social career is the network of friends and associates in the homosexual community. The group supports her definition of homosexuality as normal and a viable sexual adjustment. She perceives homosexuals as being more sensitive and more creative than nonhomosexuals. Due to her independence from males, her occupational aspirations are masculine; and her achievement patterns, both scholastic and occupational, are higher than heterosexual females.

The lesbian does not become involved with the homosexual community until she has completed high school and begun emancipation from family and adolescent, heterosexual peers. Fantasies about women and an initial physical sexual experience precede community entry by a considerable period of time.

Respondents are comfortable around the straight community but choose the homosexual community for friendships after the age of twenty. They define themselves as being in the "gay life" and are generally happy with it. Despite clear-cut boundaries between the homosexual and heterosexual worlds, the lesbian enjoys interchanges across the boundaries in sexual and nonsexual senses. A large number of lesbians have sexual relations with men, with a surprising number of these contacts resulting in orgasm.

The lesbian's sexual career begins before her homosexual social career. Her first contact occurs typically before the age of twenty, with a good percentage having physical contact before the age of fifteen. Respondents typically focused on females as their principal sex object prior to this time. The nature of the first physical contact is varied. The majority of respondents indicate that only manual stimulation occurs. Almost one-third of the population indicate that oral sex was a part of their first contact. This was unrelated to whether orgasm was achieved. These activities are similar to those of young heterosexuals who often substitute manual stimulation for "going all the way."

The life of the lesbian can be understood only within the framework of limitations imposed upon her by her subculture and the host culture, which both stigmatizes and discriminates against her. Her life style is as much a function of that discrimination as it is of her difference from the nonhomosexual community. The patterns of her initial sexual awareness and involvement with a milieu that accepts her commitments parallels the experience of the heterosexual woman's involvement with the heterosexual world of couples.

Due to the nature of the sampling procedures of the study, we have generated only nominal data. For this reason we cannot generalize from this data to the larger population of female homosexuals. Despite this limitation, certain findings recommend themselves for further study.

If family structure is related to producing the homosexual commitment, as this study suggests, investigations should include more than examinations of how respondents perceive the dominance of each parent. Research into the role-structure of the family might produce interactional configurations that are conclusive to producing the homosexual. The question of homosexual siblings and cousins requires further exploration in that female homosexuals are more likely to have inverted siblings and cousins than heterosexuals.

Since sexual fantasies about women preceded actual physical experience, which in turn preceded entry into the homosexual subculture, further study should focus upon the ages at which each stage of the lesbian career occurs. It would be fruitful to ascertain how many females fantasized sexually about women, went on to have a satisfying homosexual physical experience, but did not enter the homosexual subculture, developing, rather, a heterosexual life style. A question might be raised as to how such individuals differ from those who continued in their homosexuality and became so self-identified. Comparing these two groupings, how would their family structures differ? Do elements in family relationships exist for those who become heterosexual that do not exist for those who become overtly homosexual?

This study has suggested that the nature of the first physical contact is mutually explorative. Further study would indicate if this is so and whether or not the role of seduced or seducer is related to the sexual role eventually played by either party. Such concerns might extend to the nature of the relationship leading to the first marriage arrangement. Examination of this dimension of the social career should analyze roles played, age differentials, if any exist, the length of time the arrangement lasted, how the break-up occurred, and whether or not the respondents continued in the basic role-pattern of dominance or submission (butch vs. femme) manifest in this first marriage relationship.

The achievement patterns, both occupational and educational, of female homosexuals appear to be higher than a comparable group of heterosexual females. Occupations or areas of study might be isolated that are particularly attractive to the lesbian—i.e. teaching, nursing, or other occupations whose professional orientation guarantees a degree of independence. Although the achievement patterns and occupational aspirations of lesbians may be related to their unwillingness to attach themselves to a male provider, these motivations may also be related to other more fundamental dimensions of the personality dynamic.

Lesbians perceive differences between their life style and that of the male homosexual. Such differences should be explored in terms of sexual activities as well as social and attitudinal dimensions. It is possible that great differences exist between the social careers of the male and female homosexuals and that they are not etiologically related.

The nature of the homosexual marriage should be investigated as to where meetings resulting in such liaisons occur and what age differentials typify initial marriage relationships. Further analysis should include how long such relationships exist and how subsequent marriage relationships differ from the initial relationship. A role breakdown might include such areas as occupation, education, income differentials, ownership patterns, and the like.

With regard to her experience with men, further analysis should pinpoint when such relationships typically occur in the career, how they occur, and whether or not they are an aspect of heterosexually oriented data. A relationship may exist between the length of involvement with a heterosexual career and the probability of heterosexual experience or dating occurring. Exploring the sexual career of the lesbian further, attention should be paid to her experience with other women—age at first homosexual experience, age at second experience, and duration of the relationship resulting in the first physical experience, as well as the length of time between the first homosexual partner and the second. The number of men and women the typical lesbian is intimate with in her career needs to be explored, as well as how often sexual relations occur between married couples per week, how often per week the single girl is successful in arranging a sexual liaison, and the typical length of time between such marriage arrangements.

How the U.S. lesbian social career and the content of the sub-culture differ from a European sample (in that the homosexual identity is less stigmatized in certain countries) needs to be investigated. Differences should exist between samples drawn from these countries and a random sample of homosexuals derived from the American population. It is expected that as negative definitions of identity of the homosexual decrease, the importance of the unique homosexual community as the source of social interaction will also decrease, as will the need to maintain a heterosexual front. The covert quality of the homosexual community may disappear, and interchanges across the boundaries separating the heterosexual and homosexual worlds may increase. Although this may be accompanied by an apparent rise in the incidence of homosexuality, such integration of the heterosexual and homosexual worlds will augment the possibilities of sexual adjustments for lesbians presently isolated. The probability of a percentage of lesbians eventually making a heterosexual adjustment would be increased by this interchange.

It is mandatory that the parameters of the research universe be established, as well as the ecological distribution of homosexuals. Since sampling depends largely upon educated guesses about the research population, further research on that population will depend upon an accurate means of estimating its size. This is perhaps the next task awaiting the researcher.

BIBLIOGRAPHY

ACHILLES, NANCY. *The Homosexual Bar.* Unpublished M.A. Thesis, University of Chicago, 1964.

ARMON, VIRGINIA. "Some Personality Variables in Overt Female Homosexuality," *Journal of Projective Techniques,* XXIV (1960), 292–309.

BEACH, FRANK A., ed. *Sex and Behavior.* New York: John Wiley & Sons, Inc., 1965.

DE BEAUVOIR, SIMONE. *The Second Sex.* H. M. Parshley, ed. New York: Alfred A. Knopf, 1968.

BECKER, HOWARD S. and GEER, BLANCHE. "Participant Observation and Interviewing, A Comparison," *Human Organizations,* XVI, 3 (Fall, 1957).

BENE, EVA. "On the Genesis of Female Homosexuality," *Journal of Psychiatry*, III (1965), 815–21.

BERG, CHARLES. *Fear, Punishment, Anxiety and the Wolfenden Report.* London: George Allen & Unwin, Ltd., 1957.

BERG, CHARLES and KRICH, A. M. *Homosexuality.* London: George Allen & Unwin, Ltd., 1958.

BERGLER, EDMUND, M.D. *Homosexuality, Disease or Way of Life?* New York: Collier Books, 1962.

————. "Homosexuality and the Kinsey Report," *Homosexuality—A Subjective and Objective Investigation.* London: Ruskin House, 1958.

————. "Lesbianism, Facts and Fiction," *Marriage Hygiene*, I, 4 (May, 1948).

————. "The Respective Importance of Reality and Phantasy in the Genesis of Female Homosexuality," *Journal of Criminal Psychopathology*, V (1943), 27–48.

BLALOCK, HUBERT M. *Social Statistics.* New York: McGraw-Hill, 1960.

BONAPARTE, MARIE. *Feminine Sexuality.* New York: International Universities Press, 1953.

CAPRIO, FRANK S., M.D. *Female Homosexuality, A Psychodynamic Study of Lesbianism.* New York: Grove Press, 1962.

CARO, JO. "The Kinsey Interview Experience—As Seen by a Psychiatric Social Worker," *The Homosexual and His Society—A View From Within.* New York: The Citadel Press, 1964, pp. 191–201.

COHEN, ALBERT K. *Delinquent Boys.* Glencoe, Ill.: The Free Press, 1955.

CORY, DONALD WEBSTER. *The Homosexual in America.* New York: Paperback Library, Inc., 1951.

————. "The Lesbian in America," *America's Troubles—A Casebook on Social Conflict.* Englewood Cliffs, N.J.: Prentice-Hall, Inc., 1969.

————. "Lesbianism—As Seen by a Sexual Non-Conformist," *The Homosexual and His Society—A View from Within.* New York: The Citadel Press, 1963.

———— and LEROY, JOHN P. *The Homosexual and His Society—A View From Within.* New York: The Citadel Press, 1963.

DANIEL, SUZAN. "The Homosexual Woman in Present Day Society," *International Journal of Sexology*, VII, 5 (May, 1954), 223–24.

DENITZ, SIMON and RECKLESS, W. C. *Critical Issues in the Study of Crime.* Boston: Little, Brown & Co., 1968.

ELLIS, ALBERT. *Homosexuality, Its Causes and Cure.* New York: Lyle Stewart, Inc., 1965.

————. "Introduction—From the First to the Second Kinsey Report,"

The Homosexual and His Society—A View From Within. New York: The Citadel Press, 1963.

———. *The Rack.* London, Melbourne, Toronto: William Heinemann Ltd., 1958.

"Female Homosexuality," *Science News Letter* (Jan. 14, 1961), 30–31.

"Female Homosexuals," *The Science Digest* (Oct., 1966).

FORD, CLELLAN S. and BEACH, FRANK H. *Patterns of Sexual Behavior.* New York: Harper & Row, Publishers, 1951.

FREDERICO, DIANA. *Diana—A Strange Autobiography.* New York: The Citadel Press, 1939.

FREEMAN, HOWARD E. and KIRTZ, NORMA R., eds. *America's Troubles—A Casebook on Social Conflict.* Englewood Cliffs, N.J.: Prentice-Hall, 1969.

GAGNON, JOHN H. and HOOKER, EVELYN. "Sexual Behavior: Deviation: Social Aspects," *Encyclopedia of Social Sciences,* XIV, 215–33.

GAGNON, JOHN H. and SIMON, WILLIAM, eds. *Sexual Deviance, The Lesbian: A Preliminary Overview.* New York: Harper & Row, Publishers, 1969.

GARFINKEL, HAROLD. *Studies in Ethnomethodology.* Englewood Cliffs, N.J.: Prentice-Hall, Inc., 1967.

GIALLOMBARDO, ROSE. "Social Roles in a Prison for Women," *Social Problems,* XIII (Winter, 1966), 268–88.

GIANNELL, A. STEVEN. "Giannell's Criminosynthesis Theory Applied to Female Homosexuality," *Journal of Psychology,* LXIV (1966), 213–22.

GIESE, HANS. "Differences in the Homosexual Relations of Man and Woman," *The International Journal of Sexology,* VII, 4 (May, 1954).

GOFFMAN, IRVING. *Behavior in Public Places.* New York: Free Press Paperback, 1963.

———. *Stigma: Notes on the Management of Spoiled Identity.* Englewood Cliffs, N.J.: Prentice-Hall, Inc., 1963.

HAMMER, MAX. "Homosexuality in a Women's Reformatory," *Corrective Psychiatry and Journal of Social Therapy,* XI, 168–69.

HELMER, WILLIAM J. "New York's Middle-Class Homosexuals," *America's Troubles—A Casebook on Social Conflict.* Englewood Cliffs, N.J.: Prentice-Hall, Inc., 1969.

HOFFMAN, MARTIN. *The Gay World.* New York: Basic Books, 1968.

HOOKER, EVELYN. *The Homosexual Community.* A paper delivered at the Fourteenth Annual Congress of Applied Psychology. Gerhards Heilson, ed. Copenhagen: 1962.

———. "A Preliminary Analysis of Group Behavior of Homosexuals," *The Journal of Psychology,* XLII (1965), 217–25.

KEISER, SILVAN and SCHAFFER, DORA. "Environmental Factors in Homosexuality in Adolescent Girls," *Psychoanalytic Review*, XXXVI (1965), 283–95.

KINSEY, ALFRED C. *et al*. *Sexual Behavior in the Human Female*. Philadelphia: W. B. Saunders Co., 1953.

——. *Sexual Behavior in the Human Male*. Philadelphia: W. B. Saunders Co., 1948.

KIRKHAM, GEORGE L. *The Female Offender*. San Jose, Calif.: The Spartan Book Store, San Jose College, 1966.

KLUCKHOHN, FLORENCE R. "The Participant–Observer Technique in Small Communities," *The American Journal of Sociology*, XLV (Nov., 1940), 331–43.

Lesbian, "My Kind of Loving," *Twentieth Century* (Spring, 1963), 147–48.

LEZNOFF, MAURICE and WESLEY, WILLIAM A. "The Homosexual Community," *Social Problems*, III (April, 1956), 457–63.

LIEBOW, ELLIOT. *Talley's Corner*. Boston: Little, Brown & Company, 1967.

LINDER, ROBERT. "Homosexuality and the Contemporary Scene," *A View From Within*. New York: The Citadel Press, 1963.

LOMBARDO, GIA. *Society of Women*. New York: John Wiley & Sons, 1966.

MACKENZIE, D. F. "Homosexuality and the Justice Department," *New Zealand Medical Journal*, LXVI (1967), 745–48.

MAGEE, BRYAN. "The Facts About Lesbianism," *The New Statesman* (March 26, 1965), 491–93.

——. *One in Twenty—A Study of Homosexuality in Men and Women*. London: Secker and Warburg, 1966.

MARLOW, KENNETH. "Some Notes on Being Homosexual," *In Their Own Behalf*. New York: Appleton-Century-Crofts, 1968.

MARMOR, JUDD. *Sexual Inversion, The Multiple Routes of Homosexuality*. New York: Basic Books, 1965.

McCAGHY, CHARLES H., *et al*. *In Their Own Behalf—Voices From the Margin*. New York: Appleton-Century-Crofts, 1968.

MEAKER, MARYANN (ANN ALDRICH, pseudonym). *We Walk Alone*. New York: Facet Press, 1955.

MERCER, J. D. *They Walk in Shadow*. New York: Comet Press, 1959.

MERTON, ROBERT. *Social Theory and Social Structure*, rev. ed. Glencoe: The Free Press, 1957.

MORSE, BENJAMIN. *The Lesbian*. Derby, Conn.: Monarch Books, 1961.

——. *The Sexual Revolution*. Derby, Conn.: Monarch Books, 1962.

PARDES, HERBERT, *et al*. "A Rare Case of Overt and Mutual Homosexuality in Female Identical Twins," *Psychiatric Quarterly*, XLI (1967), 108–33.

POLSKY, NED. *Hustlers, Beats and Others.* New York: Aldine Publishing Co., 1967.

RECHY, JOHN. *City of Night.* New York: Grove Press, 1963.

REES, J. T. and USILL, H. V. *They Stand Apart.* New York: The Macmillan Co., 1955.

"Research with Adolescents Sheds New Light on Early Lesbianism," *Science News of the Week,* XCVI (July 19, 1969), 45.

ROBERTIELLO, RICHARD. "These Tragic Women," *Newsweek* (June 15, 1959), 62–63.

————. *Voyage From Lesbos.* New York: The Citadel Press, 1959.

ROWE, DILYS. "A Quick Look at the Lesbians," *Twentieth Century* (1962–63), 67–72.

RUITENBEEK, HENDRICK M. *The Problems of Homosexuality in Modern Society.* New York: E. P. Dutton & Co., 1963.

RUSHING, WILLIAM A. *Deviant Behavior and Social Process.* Chicago: Rand McNally & Co., 1969.

SAGARIN, EDWARD and MACNAMARA, DONALD. *Problems of Sex Behavior.* New York: Thomas Y. Crowell Co., 1968.

SCHAFER, STEPHEN. *The Victim and His Criminal—A Study in Functional Responsibility.* New York: Random House, 1968.

SCHAFFER, ALBERT, *et al. Understanding Social Problems.* Columbus: Charles E. Merrill Publishing Co., 1970.

SCHREIBER, R. F. and WILBER, C. B. "Homosexual Men and Women," *Science Digest* (April, 1964), 55–64.

SCHUR, EDWIN M. *Crimes Without Victims.* Englewood Cliffs, N.J.: Prentice-Hall, Inc., 1965.

SELLTIZ, CLAIRE, *et al. Research Methods in Social Relations.* New York: Holt, Rinehart and Winston, 1961.

SHERWIN, ROBERT VEIT. "Female Sex Crimes—As Seen by an Attorney," *A View From Within.* New York: The Citadel Press, 1963.

SHILS, EDWARD A. and RAY, DONALD P., eds. *Trends in Social Science.* New York: Philosophical Library, 1961.

SHORT, JAMES F. JR., ed. *Gang Delinquency and Delinquent Subcultures.* New York: Harper & Row, Publishers, 1968.

SIMON, JULIAN L. *Basic Research Methods in Social Science—The Art of Empirical Investigation.* New York: Random House, 1969.

SIMON, WILLIAM and GAGNON, JOHN. "Femininity in the Lesbian Community," *Social Problems,* XV, 2 (1967), 212–21.

SJOBERG, GIDION and NETT, ROGER. *A Methodology for Social Research.* New York: Harper & Row, Publishers, 1968.

STEARN, JESS. *The Grapevine.* New York: Doubleday & Co., 1964.

————. *The Sixth Man*. New York: McFadden Books, 1962.

STONE, WALTER N., *et al.* "The Treatment of a Homosexual Woman in a Mixed Group," *International Journal of Group Psychotherapy*, XVI (1966), 425–33.

SUTHERLAND, EDWIN H. *The Professional Thief*. Chicago: The University of Chicago Press, 1937.

SYKES, GRESHAM. *Crime and Society*, second ed. New York: Random House, 1967.

TURK, AUSTIN T. *Criminality and Legal Order*. Chicago: Rand McNally & Company, 1969.

WAHL, CHARLES WILLIAM, ed. *Sexual Problems—Diagnosis and Treatment in Medical Practice*. New York: The Free Press, 1967.

WARD, DAVID A. and KASSEBAUM, GENE G. "Homosexuality: A Mode of Adaptation in a Prison for Women," *Social Problems*, XII (1964–65), 159–77.

WESTWOOD, GORDON. *Society and the Homosexual*. New York: E. P. Dutton & Co., 1963.

WHYTE, WILLIAM FOOTE. *Street Corner Society*. Chicago: University of Chicago Press, 1954.

WILBUR, CORNELIA B. "Homosexual Men and Women," *Science Digest* (April, 1964), 55–64.

WILDEBLOOD, PETER. *Against the Law*. London: Penguin Books, Inc., 1955.

WITTENBERG, RUDOLPH. "Lesbianism as a Transitory Solution of the Ego," *Psychoanalytic Review*, XLIII (1956), 348–57.

WOLFENDEN, SIR JOHN, *et al. Report of the Departmental Committee on Homosexual Offenses and Prostitution*. London: Her Majesty's Stationery Office, 1957.

WOLFGANG, MARVIN E. and FERRACUTI, FRANCO. *The Subculture of Violence*. London: Tavistock Publications, 1967.

Laud Humphreys

New Styles in
Homosexual Manliness

—Laud Humphreys has been a close observer of the "gay world," which has undergone some rather severe changes in the life styles of its members, especially in the idea of "manliness." The Lessard selection could be profitably read in conjunction with this article.

Near the heart of a metropolis on the eastern seaboard, there is a historic park where homosexuals have been cruising for at least a hundred years. As an aging man told me:

> Back around 1930, when I was a very young man, I had sex with a really old fellow who was nearly 80. He told me that when he was a youngster—around the end of the Civil War—he would make spending money by hustling in that very park. Wealthy men would come down from the Hill in their carriages to pick up boys who waited in the shadows of the tree-lined walks at night.

In our motorized age, I have observed car drivers circling this park and adjoining residential blocks for the same sexual purposes. On a Friday night, unless the weather is bitter cold, a solid line of cars moves slowly along the one-way streets of this area, bumper to bumper, from 9:00 P.M. until 5:00 in the morning. The drivers pause in their rounds only long enough to exchange a few words with a young man on the sidewalk or to admit a willing passenger. There is no need to name this park. A knowledgeable person can find such pickup activity, both homosexual and heterosexual, in every major city of the Western world.

Cruising for "one-night-stands" is a major feature of the market economy in sex. In *The Wealth of Nations* Adam Smith postulated the ideal form of human relationship as being specific, depersonalized, short-term and contractual. This capitalist ideal is realized in the sex exchange of the homosexual underworld perhaps more fully than in any other social group, and the cruising scene of the gay world may continue for another hundred years or more. There are indications, however, that in the affluent, highly industrialized centers of our civilization the popularity of this sort of activity is declining. No one, of course, could make an up-to-date count of all the participants in even a single segment of the sexual market, and no base is available from which to estimate variations in such activity over time. One can only depend on careful observers of the scene, chief among whom are the participants themselves. I can report, then, what respondents tell me, checking their observations against my own of the past six years.

DECLINE OF CRUISING

Even with this limited source of data, it is still possible to discern a trend away from the traditional cruising for pickups as the major activity of the homosexual market. Men still make sexual contracts with other men along the curbstones of our cities and in the shadowy places of public parks, but at least three social factors are acting to alter and curtail those operations and to increase the popularity of other forms of sexual exchange.

The most obvious factor affecting the cruising scene along this nation's roadways is perhaps the least important: the matter of crime in the streets. As a criminologist, I am yet to be convinced that the streets are actually less safe than they were 10, 30 or 100 years ago. American streets have been the scenes of assaults and robberies for generations. Slums expand into certain areas, making some streets more dangerous than they were; but slums also contract, leaving once dangerous streets more safe. I doubt, however, that it is any more dangerous to pick up a hitchhiker in 1970 than it was in 1940.

Moreover, anyone seeking deviant sex is engaged in a risky activity, and usually knows it. Indeed, risk in the pursuit of sex simply increases the appeal of the homosexual markets for millions of American men. The chances they take add an element of adventure to the gaming encounters and, for many participants, serve as an aphrodisiac. In fact, of course, most of the moral risk—and much of the physical danger—encountered by homosexuals comes from vice squad operations. The mugger is no more to be feared than the violent policeman. When I interviewed him, the man I quoted above was still recuperating from a severe beating at the hands of a patrolman. Two years ago, an active member of the homophile movement was shot to death by a vice squad detective in a Berkeley, California, park. But such attacks by police and youthful toughs are nothing new in homosexual market places.

Nevertheless, crime in the streets is of importance in curtailing homosexual cruising, if only because it is perceived and publicized as being on the increase. It thus becomes more an excuse than a deterrent. Since the man who cruises for sex has always been vulnerable to such victimization, that alone does not serve as a major factor in his decision to switch to another form of sexual exchange. But, if he is driven by other social forces to a new market place, he may use the widely perceived threat of violence as an excuse for changing.

Another factor in contemporary society that does effectively turn men away from this sort of sexual liaison is the growing scarcity of time. To cruise for sex requires leisure. The successful cruiser must have plenty of time to devote to his favorite sport. As with fishing, one dare not be hurried. It takes a great deal of time to size up a trick, to convince him that you are a legitimate score, for both parties to signal their intentions and to effect a contract. More time is required to find a safe locale for the sexual act—an out-of-the-way place to park, an apartment or hotel room, a *pied-à-terre* maintained for this purpose. For cruising, expressways and fast cars are scarcely more advantageous than cobblestone streets and carriages; in this as in so many things, technological advance represents no gain because it has not been accompanied by increased leisure. The plague of anomie, caused by a people with too much time on its hands, has yet to descend on us.

The Swedish economist Staffan B. Linder discusses the actual fate of *The Harried Leisure Class*:

> We had always expected one of the beneficent results of economic affluence to be a tranquil and harmonious manner of life, a life in Arcadia. What has happened is the exact opposite. The pace is quickening, and our lives in fact are becoming steadily more hectic.

The clock on the cover of a paperback edition of Thorstein Veblen's *The Theory of the Leisure Class* has no hands. But Veblen was careful to point out that he used the term "leisure" not to "connote indolence or quiescence. What it connotes is non-productive consumption of time." As Veblen indicated, it is consumption, not production, that is inefficient and time wasting. Indeed, so much time is consumed in our society, Linder says, that there is an increasing scarcity of it. The upper stratum of society that Veblen defined as the Leisure Class at the end of the nineteenth century must now be defined as the Jet Set: "Superficial people in the rich countries [who] are often in a greater hurry than anyone else. They are enormously busy, even if it is sometimes difficult to see with what."

There was a time when a man of means could dally with a maid in a Victorian attic room or spend a leisurely afternoon with his mistress. He could afford to cruise for a pickup or manage a tryst in some sylvan glade. As Linder states, "To court and love someone in a satisfactory manner is a game with many and time-consuming phases." The pleasures of the bed are declining, he continues, in three ways: "Affairs, which by their very nature occupy a great deal of time, become less attractive; the time spent on each occasion of lovemaking is being reduced; the total number of sexual encounters is declining."

Among the evidence that tends to support Linder's hypotheses is that gathered in a recent study of the sexual behavior of Frenchmen. Jacques Baroche notes that the fabled Gallic lover is leaving his mistress and turning to the fleeting sex act. One man interviewed in the research states that "only one thing counts in love—it is the brief encounter."

IMPERSONALIZATION

Cruising operations may have led to the ideal type of relationship for a laissez faire capitalist of a century ago, but the market economy has since produced social factors necessitating transformation of its own sexual adjunct. It is no longer sufficient for human relationships to be depersonalized, short-term and contractual, such as that which might be expected to result from a pickup on the streets. In the sexual sphere, at least, relationships must now be utterly impersonal, highly expedient, fleeting in nature. The capitalist criteria have become more demanding.

In my study of the impersonal sex that occurs in public rest rooms, *Tearoom Trade,* I wrote:

> What the covert deviant needs is a sexual machine—collapsible to hip-pocket size, silent in operation—plus the excitement of a risk-taking encounter. In tearoom sex he has the closest thing to such a device. This encounter functions, for the sex market, as does the automat for the culinary, providing a low-cost, impersonal, democratic means of commodity distribution.

The sexual encounter in the tearoom constitutes the epitome of libidinal enterprise for the contemporary, consuming society. An old man on the toilet stool, serving as habitual insertee in fellatio with a succession of commuters, could better meet the standards of Madison Avenue only if he were an antiseptic machine with a coin slot in his forehead and stereo speakers for ears.

Approaching the phenomena of impersonal sex from a psychoanalytic standpoint rather than a socioeconomic one, Rollo May says in *Love and Will*: "The Victorian person sought to have love without falling into sex; the modern person seeks to have sex without falling into love." My objection to May's analysis (other than his apparent ignorance of Steven Marcus' *Other Victorians*) is its implication that modern man knows what he seeks. We pursue what we have been conditioned to seek, what is expedient for members of the consuming society. We are subject to the subliminal suggestion that love and sex are essentially indistinguishable and any distinctions irrelevant. As with Coca-Cola, things go better with sex.

The increasing scarcity of time has differing effects upon the various segments of American society. As Linder suggests, some men simply find it more expedient to take their sex at home. Millions of others, however, limited or lacking in the conjugal exchange of goods and services, are turning to market places of impersonal sex, such as the tearooms. For instance, my data indicate that Roman Catholic religious affiliation is a causal factor in tearoom participation, because that church's prohibition of the use of artificial contraceptives limits the sexual outlet in marriage. Of the married men in my sample of tearoom participants, 50 percent are Roman Catholic or married to a Roman Catholic, as compared to 26 percent of married men in the control sample. For some single men, primarily those with higher educational levels, masturbation provides a sufficiently expedient sexual outlet. Others must turn to impersonal sexual exchanges to meet these needs.

The overall effect is the increasing impersonalization of the sexual markets. Prostitutes are now offering five-minute "blow jobs" in the parking garages of major cities, while the free service of tearooms increases in popularity. As more "straight" men, those lacking in homosexual identity and self-image, turn to impersonal sexual outlets provided by the gay world, others who seek homosexual relationships find the tearooms more rewarding than cruising the streets. America's sexual answer to the increasing scarcity of time, tearoom activity, seems to counter Linder's prediction that "the total number of sexual encounters is declining." Perhaps Sweden is lacking in such facilities.

VIRILIZATION

If the scarcity of time in our society were the only factor influencing homosexual market operations, why aren't all men with homosexual interests crowding into the nation's public toilets to satisfy their growing demand for what can be found there? There is, however, another social factor acting upon the gay world to produce a countertendency. The cruising scene, so familiar to those interested in the homosexual subculture, is yielding to attacks from two sides: it is not sufficiently impersonal and expedient for some, and too much so for others. Sexual exchanges in the gay underworld are experiencing a polarization, torn between a growing impersonalization on the one hand and increasing virilization on the other.

By virilization, I refer to the increasingly masculine image of the gay scene. Few gay bars are now distinguished by the presence of limp wrists and falsetto voices. Increasingly, these centers for the homosexual subculture are indistinguishable from other hangouts for youths of college age. Girls are now common among the patrons in gay bars. Beards, leather vests, letter jackets and boots have their place alongside the more traditional blue jeans and T-shirts. If any style predominates, it is that of the turned-on, hip generation.

As Tom Burke pointed out in *Esquire* a year ago, just when the public seemed ready to accept the sort of homosexual portrayed in *The Boys in the Band* that life style began to fade away: "That the public's information vis-à-vis the new deviate is now hopelessly out-dated is not the public's fault. It cannot examine him on its own because, from a polite distance, he is indistinguishable from the heterosexual hippie." Although this "new homosexuality" is in-creasingly evident on both coasts, as well as on campuses across the country, it is just beginning to appear in the gay bars and coffee-houses of Denver, Omaha and St. Louis. The hip, masculine image for homosexuals is not yet as universal, the transformation not so dramatic, as Burke would have us believe. "The majority of con-temporary homosexuals under forty," he claims, "are confirmed potheads and at least occasional acid-trippers." Such a statement makes good copy, but there is no evidence for it. My sample of tearoom participants included fewer drug users than the control samples indicate are in the nondeviant population. But my re-search subjects were, by definition, only those who seek the im-personal sex of tearooms. My current research in the homosexual ecology of a sample of cities throughout the nation indicates a far higher proportion of pot smokers, perhaps 20 percent, among the population who engage in homosexual activity than I encountered during my field research six years ago. Clearly, the youth counter-culture with its attendant styles of dress and drug use has spawned a young, virile set to coexist with the effete martini sippers of the traditional gay world.

The new emphasis in the homosexual subculture, then, is upon virility: not the hypermasculinity of Muscle Beach and the motor-cycle set, for these are part of the old gay world's parody on hetero-sexuality, but the youthful masculinity of bare chests and beads, long hair, mustaches and hip-hugging pants. The new generation in gay society is more apt to sleep with a girl than to mock her speech or mannerisms. Many of these young men (along with the older ones who imitate their style) frown upon an exclusive orienta-tion to homosexual or heterosexual activity. The ideal is to be a "swinger," sensitive to ambisexual pleasures, capable of turning on sexually with both men and women.

In a crowded gay bar in Boston I recently watched this new facet of the subculture in action. Neither the young men nor the girls scattered throughout the room were at all distinguishable from any other college-age group in the taverns of that city. There were fewer women, to be sure, but the dress, appearance and conversa-tions were typical of any campus quadrangle. A handsome youth in a denim jacket and pants introduced an attractive young girl to a group standing at the bar as his fiancée. One man remarked, with a grin, that he was jealous. The young man, whom I shall call Jack, placed an arm around the shoulders of his fiancée, and, pulling her head toward his, explained: "Tom here is an old lover of mine." "Aren't we all!" another member of the party added, upon which all within earshot laughed.

After the bar closed, I was invited, along with the young couple, to join a number of patrons for "some group action" in a nearby apartment. A rather common, two-room pad with little furniture but many pillows and posters, the apartment was illuminated by only a single lightbulb suspended from the kitchen ceiling. Once our eyes had adjusted to the darkness of the other room, we could see about a dozen men, stretched in a number of stages of undress and sexual activity over the mattress and floor at the far end of the room. Excusing himself, Jack joined the orgy. In a few minutes, I could discern that he was necking with one man while being fellated by another.

Having explained my research purposes on the way to the apartment, I sought to explore the girl's reactions to her lover's apparent infidelity. I asked whether it bothered her. "Does it arouse me sexusually, do you mean?" she replied. "No. Like, does Jack's behavior upset you?" With a laugh, she answered, "No, not at all. Like, I love Jack for what he is. You know, like, he swings both ways. If that's his thing, I groove on it. He could have left me home, you know—that's what some guys do. They leave their chicks home and, like, feed them a lot of shit so they can slip out and get their kicks. One of the things I dig most about Jack is that he shares everything with me. Having secrets just leads to hangups." "But don't you feel even a bit jealous?" I probed. "Like, woudn't you rather be making love to him than standing here rapping with me?" "Why should I?" she said. "Like, Jack and I'll go home and ball after this is over. He's a beautiful person. Being able to share himself with so many different people makes him more beautiful!"

Later, Jack and his fiancée left those of us who were bound for an all-night restaurant. Arm in arm, they headed for the subway and a pad in Cambridge. Their story, I think, is an accurate reflection of the morality of the youth counterculture, both in its easy acceptance of a variety of sexual expressions and its nondefensive trust that the deeper, personal relationships are the more important ones.

SUBCULTURAL DIVERSITY

Like the scarcity of time, such norms of the counterculture have differing effects upon the sexual markets and life styles of the gay world, depending upon the permeability of various segments of the homosexual society. In order to outline and gauge these changes, it is necessary to construct a taxonomy of the homosexual community. Once we are able to consider its diverse segments in relation to each other, we can compare their reactions to some of the forces of contemporary society.

In my study of tearoom sex, I delineated four basic types of participants in these impersonal encounters: trade, ambisexuals, the gay and closet queens. These men are differentiated most clearly by the relative autonomy afforded them by their marital and occupational statuses. When one engages in sexual behavior against which the society has erected strong negative sanctions, his resources for control of information carry a determining relationship to his life style, as well as to his self-image and the adaptations he makes to his own discreditable behavior. An example of this principle of classification would be that married men who are bound hand and foot to their jobs have more to fear—and less to enjoy—from their clandestine encounters because they have relatively fewer means of countering exposure than men of greater autonomy.

I have chosen the word "trade" from the argot of the homosexual community because it best describes that largest class of my respondents, the married men with little occupational autonomy. In its most inclusive sense in the gay vocabulary, this term refers to all men, married or single, who think they are heterosexual but who will take the insertor role in homosexual acts. Except for hustlers, who will be discussed later, most of these men are married. As participants in homosexual activity, they are nonsubcultural, lacking both the sources of information and the rationalization for their behavior that the gay circles provide. Generally, the trade are of lower-middle or upper-lower socioeconomic status. They are machinists, truck drivers, teachers, sales and clerical workers, invariably masculine in appearance, mannerisms and self-image. Single men, I have found, are generally less stable in sexual identification. Once they begin to participate in homosexual relations, therefore, their straight self-image is threatened, and they tend to drift into the less heterosexual world of the closet queens or gay bar crowd. Apart from an exclusive concern with tearoom operations, however, I think it preferable to allow for the inclusion of some single men in the trade classification.

Moving into the upper strata of society, it is difficult to find participants in homosexual activity who think of themselves as strictly heterosexual. Americans with the higher educational level of the upper-middle and upper classes tend to find literary justification for their ventures into deviant sexual activity. The greater occupational autonomy of these men enables them to join in friendship networks with others who share their sexual interests. If these men are married, they tend to define themselves as "ambisexual," identifying with a distinguished company of men (Alexander the Great, Julius Caesar, Shakespeare, Walt Whitman and a number of movie stars) who are said to have enjoyed the pleasures of both sexual worlds. In this classification are to be found business executives, salesmen with little direct supervision, doctors, lawyers and interior decorators.

College students join with artists, the self-employed and a few professional men to constitute the more autonomous, unmarried segment of the gay society. These men share enough resources for information control that they are unafraid to be active in the more visible portions of the homosexual subculture. In the tearoom study, I refer to them as "the gay," because they are the most clearly definable, in the sociological sense, as being homosexual. They are apt to have been labeled as such by their friends, associates and even families. Their self-identification is strongly homosexual. Because their subcultural life centers in the gay bars, coffeehouses and baths of the community, I will refer to them here as the "gay bar crowd."

The fourth type identified in my previous research are the "closet queens." In the homosexual argot this term has meanings with varying degrees of specificity. Occasionally, trade who fear their own homosexual tendencies are called closet queens. Again, the term may be used in referring to those in the subculture who feel that they are too good or proper to patronize the gay bars. In its most general sense, however, it is employed to designate those men who know they are gay but fear involvement in the more overt, bar-centered activities of the homosexual world. Because they avoid overt participation in the subculture, the married ambisexuals often receive the closet queen label from the gay bar crowd. I should like to maintain the distinctions I have outlined between ambisexuals and closet queens, however, because of the contrasting marital and socioeconomic statuses of the two groups. As I employ the term in my tearoom typology, the closet queens are unmarried teachers, clerks, salesmen and factory workers. Living in fear that their deviance might be discovered, they tend to patterns of self-hatred, social isolation and lone-wolf sexual forays.

There is a fifth type of man who is seldom found in tearooms, where money does not change hands, but who plays an important role in the homosexual markets. I mean the hustlers, homosexual prostitutes who operate from the streets, theaters and certain bars, coffeehouses and restaurants of the urban centers. The majority of these "midnight cowboys" share a heterosexual self-image. Indeed, since relatively few of them make a living from sexual activity, there is strong evidence that, for most hustlers, the exchange of money functions more to neutralize the societal norms, to justify the deviant sexual behavior, than to meet economic needs.

My observations suggest that there are at least three subdivisions among male prostitutes. One large, relatively amorphous group might properly be called "pseudo-hustlers." For them the amount of money received holds little importance, a pack of cigarettes or a handful of change sufficing to justify their involvement in the forbidden behavior, which is what they really wanted. Another large number of young men would be called "semiprofessionals." This type includes members of delinquent peer groups who hustle for money and thrills. Unlike the pseudo-hustlers, these young men receive support and training from other members of the hustling subculture. They are apt to frequent a particular set of bars and coffeehouses where a strict code of hustling standards is adhered to. Although a minority of these boys rely upon their earnings for support, the majority gain from their hustling only enough to supplement allowances, using their take to finance autos and heterosexual dates.

New to the sexual markets are the "call boys." Advertising in the underground papers of such cities as Los Angeles, San Francisco and New York as "models," these young men charge an average fee of $100 for a night or $25 an hour. I have seen a catalogue distributed by one agency for such hustlers that provides frontal nude, full-page photographs of the "models," complete with telephone numbers. In general, the call boys share a gay or ambisexual identity and take pride in their professional status. The appearance of these handsome, masculine youngsters on the gay scene is an important manifestation of the virilization of the homosexual market.

These five basic types constitute the personnel of the gay world. The hustlers and trade, few of whom think of themselves as homosexual, are the straight world's contribution to the gay scene. Without their participation, the sex exchanges would atrophy, becoming stale and ingrown. The ambisexual enjoys the benefits of his status, with a well-shod foot firmly planted in each sexual world. He need not be as covert as either the closet queen or trade and, when out of town on a business trip, may become very overt indeed. The open, visible members of the homosexual community are the hustlers and those I have called, for the purposes of this taxonomy, the gay bar crowd. With this classification in mind, it is possible to see how the contemporary social forces are diffused and filtered through interaction with each class of persons in the gay community.

POLARIZATION OF MARKET ACTIVITY

As the growing scarcity of time drives an increasing number of American males from every walk of life into one-night-stand sexuality, the impersonalized sex exchange thrives. Rest stops along the expressways, older tearooms in transportation terminals, subways, parks and public buildings—all enjoy popularity as trysting places for "instant sex." The more expedient an encounter's structure and the greater the variety of participants, as is the case with tearoom sex, the less attractive are the time-demanding liaisons of the cruising grounds.

The trade and closet queens, in particular, find their needs met in the impersonal sex market of our consuming society. Here they can find sex without commitment, an activity sufficiently swift to fit into the lunch hour or a brief stop on the way home from work. The ambisexuals—many of them harried business executives—prefer the tearooms, not only for the speed and anonymity they offer, but also for the kicks they add to the daily routine.

Covert members of the gay society provide impetus to the impersonalization of the homosexual market. My study of tearoom participants revealed that trade, closet queens and ambisexuals share highly conservative social and political views, surrounding themselves with an aura of respectability that I call the breastplate of righteousness. In life style, they epitomize the consuming man of the affluent society. In tearooms, they fill the role of sexual consumers, exchanging goods and services in every spare moment they can wring from the demands of computerized offices and automated homes. At the same time, however, their conservatism makes them nearly impervious to the pressures of the youth counterculture.

On the overt side of the gay world, the virile influence of hip culture is having profound effects. Already poorly represented in the tearoom scene, the gay bar crowd is preconditioned to embrace some of the stronger norms of the flower people. At least in word, if not always in deed, these overt leaders of the gay community espouse the deeper, more personal type of relationship. Theirs is a search for lovers, for men with whom they may build abiding relationships. Moreover, like hippies, these men flaunt some of the more sacrosanct mores of the straight society. With the hustlers, they share a sense of being an oppressed minority. On the whole, they are happy to discard the effeminate mannerisms and vocabulary of low camp in return for the influx of the new blood, the turned-on generation.

Arrival of the new bold masculinity on the gay bar scene has made the bars more suitable for hustlers of drinking age. As recently as 1967, I have seen hustlers ejected from a midwestern bar that now plays host to many of them. In those days, they were too easily identified by their rough, masculine appearance that contrasted with the neat effeminacy of the other customers. On both coasts, and increasingly in other parts of the country, bars and coffeehouses are now replacing the streets as sexual markets for hustlers and their scores.

One might surmise that the meeting of hustlers and the gay bar crowd in the same branch of the sexual market would signify a countertendency to what I see as a personalization of sex on the more virile side of the sexual exchange. But this, I think, is to misunderstand prostitution, both heterosexual and homosexual. Hustling involves many deeply personal relationships, often accompanied by a sense of commitment. Admittedly with much futility, prostitutes generally seek love and hope for the lover who will keep them. Persons who lack knowledge of the tearooms and other scenes of thoroughly impersonal sex fall victim to the stereotype of the frigid prostitute who values the customer only for his money. In reality, prostitution is at the corner grocery end of the market economy spectrum. Tearoom sex ranks near the public utility extreme of the continuum.

The addition of the hip set with its virile, drug-using, ambisexual life style has transformed the gay bar into a swinging, far less inhibited setting for sexual contact. The old bar is familiar from gay novels: a florid, clannish milieu for high-pitched flirtation. Patrons of the new bars are justifiably suspicious of possible narcotics agents; but black, white, lesbian, straight women, heterosexual couples, old and young mix with an abandon unknown a decade ago.

Gay bathhouses, once little more than shabby shelters for group sex, although still active as sexual exchanges, are now becoming true centers for recreation. The underground press, along with homophile publications such as the *Los Angeles Advocate,* provide a medium for such facilities to compete in advertising their expanding services. Such advertisements, limited as they may be to underground newspapers, are distinctive marks of the new virilized sex exchanges. By advertising, bars, baths and even hustlers proclaim their openness. It is as if this overt portion of the homosexual community were announcing: "Look, we're really men! Mod men, to be sure, children of the Age of Aquarius; but we are real men, with all the proper equipment, looking for love." In the 1970s it will be very difficult for a society to put that down as deviant.

RADICALIZATION

The new generation's counterculture has also had its impact on the homophile movement, a loose federation of civil rights organizations that reached adolescence about the same time as the flower children. Beginning with the Mattachine Foundation, established around 1950 in Los Angeles, the homophile movement has produced a history remarkably parallel to that of the black freedom movement. Frightened by the spirit of McCarthyism, its first decade was devoted primarily to sponsoring educational forums and publications, along with mutual encouragement for members of an oppressed minority.

During the sixties, with the leadership of attorneys and other professional men, it began to enlist the support of the American Civil Liberties Union in using the courts to assure and defend the civil rights of homosexuals. About the time ministers marched in Selma, clergymen (inspired, perhaps, by the stand of the Church of England in support of homosexual law reform in that nation) began to join the movement as "concerned outsiders." The National Council on Religion and the Homosexual was formed, and, with clergy as sponsors and spokesmen, members of the movement entered into dialogues with straights.

With the proliferation of organizations for the homosexual, a variety of social services were initiated for the gay community: bulletins announcing social events; referral services to counselors, lawyers and doctors; venereal disease clinics; legal guides for those who might suffer arrest; lonely hearts clubs. As they gained strength, the organizations began to foster changes in legislation and to organize gay bar owners for defense against pressures from both the police and organized crime.

In the mid-sixties, the first homosexual pickets began to appear, and the North American Conference of Homophile Organizations (NACHO) held its first national meeting. San Francisco's Society for Individual Rights (SIR), now the largest homophile group, was created and soon began to use picketing and techniques of applying political pressure. "Equal" signs in lavender and white appeared on lapels. But the new militancy began, significantly enough, with demonstrations by Columbia University's Student Homophile League in 1968. At that year's NACHO meetings, the movement's official slogan was adopted: "Gay is Good!"

Radicalization of the movement seems to have peaked in 1969. In that year, homosexuals rioted in New York, shouting "Gay Power!", and the Gay Liberation Front was organized. Student homophile organizations were recognized on half a dozen campuses. By the end of 1970, such groups were recognized on about 30 campuses.

THE BACKLASH—NORMALIZATION

Meanwhile, older leaders who had felt the sting of public sanctions recoiled in fear. Not only did the shouts of "Gay Power!" threaten to unleash a backlash of negative sentiment from a puritanical society, but the militants began to disrupt meetings, such as that of NACHO in San Francisco in the fall of 1970. As one homophile leader states: "The youngsters are demanding too much, too fast, and threatening to destroy all that has been gained over 20 painful years." Countless closet queens, who had joined when the movement was safer and more respectable, began to pressure the old militants to return to the early principles and activities of the movement.

An example of such reaction took place in St. Louis early in

1970. The campus-activist founders of the newly formed but thriving Mandrake Society were voted out of office and replaced by a conservative slate. Pages of the Mandrake newsletter, formerly occupied with items of national news interest, warnings about police activity and exhortations for homosexuals to band together in self-defense, have since been filled with notices of forthcoming social events. A Gay Liberation Front has been formed in that city during the past few months.

In his report to the membership on the year 1969, SIR's president criticized the "developing determined and very vocal viewpoint that the homosexual movement must be 'radicalized'" by aligning with the New Left on such issues as draft resistance, Vietnam, the Grape Boycott, student strikes and abortion. He replied to this demand: "SIR is a one-issue organization limiting itself to a concern for the welfare and rights of the homosexual as a homosexual. The SIR position has to be more like the American Civil Liberties Union than to be like a political club." While SIR's members recovered from the St. Valentine's Sweetheart Dance, the Gay Liberation Front at San Francisco State College threatened to take over all men's rooms on campus unless the administration grant them a charter.

As the process of normalization, with its emphasis on respectable causes, like social events and educational programs, asserts itself in established organizations of the gay world, more closet queens may be expected to join the movement. At the same time, Gay Liberation groups, cheered on by others of the New Left, should be expected to form on all the larger campuses of the nation. This marks a distinct rift in the homophile movement. At present, one finds an alignment of loyalties, chiefly along the dimensions of age and occupational status. Younger homophiles who enjoy relatively high autonomy follow a red banner with "Gay Power!" emblazoned upon it. (The motto of the recent Gay Liberation Conference was "Blatant Is Beautiful!") Older men—and those whose occupations require a style of covert behavior—sit beneath a lavender standard, neatly lettered "Gay Is Good!"

Sensitive to the need for unity, some leaders of the older homophile organizations plead for the changes needed to keep the young "Gayrevs" within the established groups. One such appeal is found in the April, 1969, issue of *Vector*:

It's time that we took some long, hard looks. If we want a retreat for middle-aged bitchery. A television room for tired cock-suckers.

An eating club and community theatre—then let us admit it and work toward that.

If we are, as we say we are, interested in social change—then let's get on the ball. Let's throw some youth into our midst. But I warn you . . . they don't want to live in 1956 (and neither do I).

UNITY IN ADVERSITY

In August of 1970, SIR began picketing Macy's in San Francisco to protest the arrest of 40 men in that store's restrooms. Young men in sandals demonstrated alongside the middle-aged in business suits, together suffering the insults and threats of passersby. Recently, they have called for a nation-wide boycott of the Macy's chain by homosexuals. Resulting internal struggle brought the resignation of Tom Maurer, SIR's conservative president. Present indications are that this large organization is successfully maintaining communications with both sides of the activist rift.

Meanwhile, New York's Gay Activists Alliance, dedicated to non-violent protest, has provided youthful leadership for homophiles of varying ideological persuasions in the campaign to reform that state's sodomy, fair employment and solicitation statutes. In both Albany and San Diego, organizations with reformist emphases have taken the name of Gay Liberation Front.

Although severe enough to confound social scientists who attempt to describe or analyze *the* homophile movement, the rift between homophile groups has yet to diminish their effectiveness. Much anger was generated when invading radicals disrupted the 1970 meetings of NACHO, but that organization has yet to enjoy what anyone would call a successful conference anyway. Meanwhile, the hotline maintained by the Homophile Union of Boston serves as a center of communication for the nine, varied homophile groups that have developed in that city during the past eighteen months.

Three factors promote cooperation between the conservative, reform and radical branches of the homophile movement. First, instances of police brutality in such widely scattered cities as New York, Los Angeles, San Francisco and New Orleans have brought thousands of homosexuals together in protest marches during the past year. Nothing heals an ailing movement like martyrs, and the police seem pleased to provide them. Because a vice squad crusade is apt to strike baths and bars, parks and tearooms, all sectors of the homosexual market are subject to victimization in the form of arrests, extortion, assaults and prosecution. There is a vice squad behind every active homophile group in America. With a common enemy in plain clothes, differences in ideology and life style become irrelevant.

Second, the *Los Angeles Advocate* has emerged as the homosexual grapevine in print. With up-to-date, thorough news coverage rivaling that of the *Christian Science Monitor* and a moderate-activist editorial policy, this biweekly is, as it claims, the "Newspaper of America's Homophile Community." With communication provided by the *Advocate* and inspiration gained from the successes of the Women's Liberation Movement, the larger homophile organizations appear to be moving into a position best described as moderately activist.

Finally, a truly charismatic leader has appeared on the homophile scene. The Rev. Troy Perry, founder of the Metropolitan Community Church, a congregation for homosexuals in Los Angeles, was arrested during a fast in front of that city's Federal Building in June of 1970. The fast coincided with "Gay Liberation Day" marches of 2,000 persons in New York and 1,200 in Los Angeles. An articulate, moving speaker, Perry began to tour the nation for his cause. I have seen him honored by a standing ovation from an audience of a hundred main-line Protestant and Catholic clergy in Boston. Because he commands general respect from both gay libs and liberals in the movement, it is impossible not to draw a parallel between this minister and Martin Luther King. When I suggested that he was "the Martin Luther King of the homophile movement," he countered that "Martin Luther *Queen* might be more appropriate." As an evangelical religious movement spreads from the West Coast, replacing drugs as a source of enthusiasm for many in the youth counterculture, Perry's position of leadership should increase in importance.

Just as the world of female homosexuals should benefit from the trend towards liberation of women, so the male homosexual world of the 1970s should thrive. Divisions of the movement may provide the advantages of diversification. The new blood provided by the Gay Liberation Front, alarming as it may be to some traditionalists, is much healthier than the bad blood that has existed between a number of NACHO leaders.

Concurrently, the same social forces that are dividing and transforming the homophile movement have polarized and strengthened the homosexual markets. By now, the consuming American should know that diversification in places and styles of exchange is a healthy indicator in the market economy. Both virilization and impersonalization will attract more participants to the market places of the gay world. At the same time, traditionalists will continue to cruise the streets and patronize the remaining sedate and elegant bars. When threatened by the forces of social control, however, even the closet queens should profit from the movement's newly-found militance.

Irving Bieber, et al.

Conclusions

—Irving Bieber, et al., are responsible for a major study, Homosexuality: A Psychoanalytic Study of Male Homosexuals, *that deals with 106 patients with homosexual proclivities. The study is an empirical attempt at determining the cause of homosexuality, its classification, and its curability. The section chosen for reprint here is the Summary of the book, and in it the reader can find the essential conclusions of the authors. This study has a critically important place in literature concerning homosexuality.*

This study provides convincing support for a fundamental contribution by Rado on the subject of male homosexuality: A homosexual adaptation is a result of "hidden but incapacitating fears of the opposite sex."

A considerable amount of data supporting Rado's assumption has been presented as evidence that fear of heterosexuality underlies homosexuality, e.g., the frequent fear of disease or injury to the genitals, significantly associated with fear and aversion to female genitalia; the frequency and depth of anxiety accompanying actual or contemplated heterosexual behavior.

We have described the specific types of disturbed parent-child relationships which have promoted fear of heterosexuality (discussed in psychodynamic detail later on) and we have emphasized throughout these chapters the role of parents in the homosexual outcome. The data have also demonstrated that many of the homosexuals in our sample showed evidences of heterosexual interest and desire manifested in dreams, fantasies, and attempts at heterosexual activity.

From *Homosexuality: A Psychoanalytic Study of Male Homosexuals,* by Irving Bieber, et al. (New York: Basic Books, 1962). © 1962 by Society of Medical Psychoanalysts, Basic Books, Inc., Publishers, New York. Reprinted by permission.

The capacity to adapt homosexually is, in a sense, a tribute to man's biosocial resources in the face of thwarted heterosexual goal-achievement. Sexual gratification is not renounced; instead, fears and inhibitions associated with heterosexuality are circumvented and sexual responsivity with pleasure and excitement to a member of the same sex develops as a pathologic alternative.

Any adaptation which is basically an accommodation to unrealistic fear is necessarily pathologic; in the adult homosexual, continued fear of heterosexuality is inappropriate to his current reality. We differ with other investigators who have taken the position that homosexuality is a kind of variant of "normal" sexual behavior.

Kinsey *et al.* did not regard homosexuality as pathologic but rather as the expression of an inherent capacity for indiscriminate sexual response. In support of this assumption the authors referred to the high frequency of homosexual experiences in the preadolescence of American males. Thus, an assumption of normalcy is based on the argument of frequency though, in fact, frequency as a phenomenon is not necessarily related to absence of pathology. For example, most people in New York will contract a cold during a given period of time. This expectancy will show a normal probability distribution but respiratory infections are patently pathologic conditions.

Kinsey *et al.* also stated that the personality disturbances associated with homosexuality derive from the expectation of adverse social reactions. Although most H-patients [homosexual patients] in our study were apprehensive about being exposed as homosexuals, these were secondary responses to a primary disorder. Further, anxiety about social acceptance would not account for the many significant differences between homosexuals and heterosexuals which were found among the large number of items tapped; in particular, hostility to the H-father, to brothers rather than to sisters, the close relationship with the mother, and so forth. Moreover, some patients had no apparent problems about social acceptance. Without minimizing its importance, the emphasis upon fears of censure and rejection as promotive of the personality disorders associated with homosexuality seems to be a quite superficial analysis of this complex disorder.

Ford and Beach, in accord with Kinsey *et al.*, also imply that homosexuality is not pathologic but that "the basic mammalian capacity for sexual inversion tends to be obscured in societies like our own which forbid such behavior and classify it as unnatural."

The authors compare the sporadic and indiscriminate "homosexual" behavior frequently observed among infrahuman species (though heterosexual behavior is not extinguished in hardly any instances and is reinstated with no apparent change), with human homosexual behavior where cognitive and highly complex patterns are involved and where, at least in our society, fear of heterosexuality is salient. Based on the frequency of homosexual phenomena, the authors state, "The cross-cultural and cross-species comparisons presented . . . combine to suggest that a biological tendency for inversion of sexual behavior is inherent in most if not all mammals including the human species." Following their logic, one might assume that any frequently occurring sexual aberration may be explained by postulating an inherent tendency. A pathologic formation, i.e., homosexuality, viewed as an inherent tendency points to a confusion between the concept of adaptational potential and that of inborn tendency.

Ford and Beach do not distinguish between *capacity* and *tendency*. *Capacity* is a neutral term connoting *potentiality* whereas *tendency* implies the probability of action in a specific direction. In our view, the human has a capacity for homosexuality but a tendency toward heterosexuality. The capacity for responsivity to heterosexual excitation is inborn. Courtship behavior and copulatory technique is learned. Homosexuality, on the other hand, is acquired and discovered as a circumventive adaptation for coping with fear of heterosexuality. As we evaluate the maturational processes, a homosexual phase is not an integral part of sexual development. At any age, homosexuality is a symptom of fear and inhibition of heterosexual expression. We do not hold with the now popular thesis that in all adult males there are repressed homosexual wishes. In fact, most adult heterosexual males no longer have the potential for a homosexual adaptation. In the comparison sample one-fourth of the cases revealed no evidence of homosexual propensities—conscious or unconscious. If we assume that homosexuality is a pathological condition, and our data strongly support this assumption, we would no more expect latent homosexuality to be inevitable among well-integrated heterosexuals than we would expect latent peptic ulcer to be inevitable among all members of a healthy population.

Another approach to the question of homosexuality as behavior within a normal range is found in Hooker's work. In this investigation projective techniques were utilized to determine whether homosexuality and homosexual adjustment could be distinguished from that of heterosexuals. It was found that the differences sought between the two populations could not be reliably distinguished. The conclusion was that "homosexuality may be a deviation in sexual pattern which is within the normal range psychologically." Since the tests and adjustment ratings were performed by competent workers and the implication of the findings and conclusions are at marked variance with those of our own and other studies, we suspect that the tests themselves or the current methods of interpretation and evaluation are inadequate to the task of discriminating between homosexuals and heterosexuals.

Still another type of argument is that homosexuality in certain individuals is related to genetic factors. In Kallman's twin studies, homosexuality among monozygotic twins was investigated. Each sibling of forty pairs was found to be homosexual. Kallman placed enormous emphasis on genetic factors; yet, he contradicted his own position by stating that the sexual impulse is easily dislocated by experiential factors. Even assuming a genetic determination, it cannot be strongly operative if sexuality responds so sensitively to nongenetic influences. We propose that the study should have included psychoanalytic treatment for at least some of the pairs studied. Had a shift to heterosexuality occurred in the course of treatment, as it had in one-fourth of the homosexuals in our sample, the reversibility would have cast doubt on the significance of genetic determinants in homosexuality. Though reversibility in itself is not a sufficient argument against the genetic position, there is so much evidence on the side of the nurture hypothesis and so little on the side of the nature hypothesis, that the reliance upon genetic or constitutional determinants to account for the homosexual adaptation is ill founded.

A point of view which has gained some acceptance in psychoanalytic circles is that homosexuality is a defense against schizophrenia; that is to say, if the H-patients had not become homosexual they would have become schizophrenic. Our findings do not support this hypothesis. One-fourth of the homosexual cases were diagnosed as schizophrenic; thus, homosexuality obviously had not defended these homosexuals against schizophrenia. Further, there were no schizophrenic sequelae among those H-patients who became exclusively heterosexual.

The idea that paranoia is a defense against homosexuality goes back to Freud's early analysis of the Schreber case. According to anecdotal data offered by E. A. Weinstein[1] homosexual content was absent in the delusional systems during the acute paranoid states of native Virgin Islanders. We propose that schizophrenia and homosexuality represent two distinct types of personality maladaptation which may or may not coexist.

An analysis of the data obtained on the schizophrenic homosexual and comparison cases was made. The analysis was not presented in this volume since it was not central to our study. We did find, however, that with certain item clusters, those patients who were diagnosed as schizophrenic in the H-sample were more like the schizophrenic heterosexuals than like the other nonschizophrenic homosexuals. On other item clusters, however, the schizophrenic homosexuals resembled other H-patients more than they did heterosexual schizophrenics. For example, on item clusters tapping father-son relationships, the schizophrenic patients in both samples were significantly more fearful, more distrustful, and had fewer friendly, accepting, and respectful relationships with significantly more frequently hostile and unsympathetic fathers than was noted among the nonschizophrenic H- and C-patients. [C-patients stands for comparison group.] But on the Six Developmental Items and on the item tapping aversion to female genitalia, the responses converged according to sexual adaptation, e.g., schizophrenic and nonschizophrenic homosexuals resembled each other more than they did schizophrenic and nonschizophrenic comparison patients whose responses also converged on these items.

The differences in psychopathology between the homosexuals and schizophrenics suggest that the time in life when predisposing influences became effective may have occurred earlier among schizophrenics. The nonschizophrenic homosexuals may not have been exposed to as severe pathogenic influences until the appearance of behavior construed by parents as heterosexual; this usually occurs in the early phase of the Oedipus Complex.

Freud's formulations on so-called "narcissistic" love object choice are supported by our findings in the Adolescent Study. Reciprocal identifications and love for an exchanged self-image were noted among the adolescents.

Freud postulated that castration anxiety, which he deemed to be a major factor in homosexuality, was strongly reinforced in the male child upon his shocked discovery of the absence of a penis in

1. United States Public Health Psychiatrist to the Virgin Islands, 1958–1960.

the female. Our study does not provide data directly bearing upon this hypothesis although our findings permit us to make certain inferences. Fear of and aversion to the female genitalia were reported for approximately three-fourths of the homosexual patients in contrast to only one-third of the heterosexuals. If the assumed anxiety reaction in the young male goes beyond a transitory childhood experience so as to become a determining force in masculine psychosexual development, we could expect a much higher frequency of fear and aversion to female genitalia among heterosexuals. Such was not the case among the heterosexual patient sample. We conclude that the male child's reaction to the observed absence of a penis in the female may be an important determinant of anxiety but only when reinforced by other determinants of anxiety related to sexuality. The significant association between fear and aversion with other items of the questionnaire indicates to us that the aversion is a defense against fear of heterosexuality.

Our findings are replete with evidence of a close mother-son relationship and confirm the observations of Freud and other investigators that "mother fixation" is related to homosexuality. The data also provide convincing evidence of the importance of the Oedipus Complex in the etiology of homosexuality. Our material highlights the parental distortions of this phase of child development, as noted in the overcloseness and seductiveness of the H-mother and the hostility of the H-father.

The data on identification of the homosexual partner with family members support two other of Rado's assumptions: (1) heterosexual impulses may be acted out in the homosexual act or homosexual relationship; (2) the homosexual adaptation frequently includes attempts to solve problems involving the father.

The identification of the homosexual partner with the mother and sisters, which occurred in some patients of our sample, suggests that heterosexual strivings were being acted out in these homosexual relationships. On the other hand, the identification of the homosexual partner with a father or brothers who were hated and feared suggests that these patients were making reparative attempts to solve relationship problems originating with the father and/or brothers.

Rado had also stated that two other determinants of homosexual behavior are "temporary expedience" and "a desire for surplus variation." We are in disagreement with these views. We do not base our differences on material derived from our study since our sample

Klein:
restitution

was composed of patients who were not "sporadic" homosexuals, and they had well-established homosexual patterns—but rather upon psychiatric reports on military personnel during World War II. Lewis and Engel have abstracted the major psychiatric papers published during the war years; none referred to expedient homosexual behavior despite the deprivation of women for millions of men. Further, a member of the Research Committee who had had the opportunity to observe all homosexuals apprehended for homosexual activity in a particular Theater of Operations did not clinically observe patients with the motivations Rado has proposed. Homosexual behavior was relatively uncommon in the armed forces of Great Britain and the United States. It occurred in individuals with premilitary homosexuality, or occasionally in individuals under the influence of alcohol as might occur in civilian life.

The assumption of "surplus variation" could apply to any aberrant sexual activity. Clinical experience has shown that aberrant behavior is always pathologically motivated. The "doing-it-for-kicks" assumption does not adequately explain aberrant sexuality. We are committed to Rado's own proposition that homosexuality is an adaptation to fear of heterosexuality, and we extend this proposition to account for all homosexual behavior.

Theories which postulate that homosexuality is a coincidental phenomenon in a more comprehensive psychopathologic process are given minimal support by our data. The construct proposed by Ovesey differentiates *actual* (acted-out) homosexuality from *pseudo*homosexuality ("latent" or unconscious). Dependency and inhibited assertion are assumed to be the basic psychodynamics underlying pseudohomosexuality so that homosexual preoccupation, fear, panic, and so forth, are viewed merely as symbolic representations of more fundamental pathologic formations. We have found pathologic dependency to be a characteristic of the majority of homosexuals but we have also identified it in most heterosexual patients. According to our formulation, pathologic dependency forms part of the psychodynamic constellation of homosexuality, but, as pointed out, pathologic dependency appears as a secondary process. In our view, dependency and inhibited assertiveness are the *consequences* of psychologic injury and not the *causes* of it. The patients' symbolization of dependency in homosexual terms does not dispose of homosexuality as a central problem since when such symbolizations occur in dreams, fantasies, and obsessions, a homosexual *solution* is being contemplated (consciously or unconsciously) and an adaptive shift may be potential at those times.

Our findings support those of Kolb and Johnson in their emphasis upon the parental role in promoting homosexuality; those of Sullivan as to the importance of peer group relationships; those of Thompson in that heterosexuality is biologically more congenial; those of West who asserted that the participation of both parents in the molding of a male homosexual was essential. Lang found an overrepresentation of homosexual siblings in the homosexual sample he studied which is in accord with our data.

PSYCHODYNAMICS

Our study has helped us refine and extend certain concepts relevant to the etiology of male homosexuality. Certainly, the role of the parents emerged with great clarity in many detailed aspects. Severe psychopathology in the H-parent-child relationships was ubiquitous, and similar psychodynamics, attitudes, and behavioral constellations prevailed throughout most of the families of the homosexuals—which differed significantly from the C-sample. Among the H-patients who lived with a set of natural parents up to adulthood—and this was so for the entire H-sample except for fourteen cases—neither parent had a relationship with the H-son one could reasonably construe as "normal." The triangular systems were characterized by disturbed and psychopathic interactions; all H-parents apparently had severe emotional problems. Unconscious mechanisms operating in the selection of mates may bring together this combination of parents. When, through unconscious determinants, or by chance, two such individuals marry, they tend to elicit and reinforce in each other those potentials which increase the likelihood that a homosexual son will result from the union. The homosexual son becomes entrapped in the parental conflict in a role determined by the parents' unresolved problems and transferences.

Each parent had a specific type of relationship with the homosexual son which generally did not occur with other siblings. *The H-son emerged as the interactional focal point upon whom the most profound parental psychopathology was concentrated.* Hypotheses for the choice of this particular child as "victim" are offered later in this discussion.

The father played an essential and determining role in the homosexual outcome of his son. In the majority of instances the father was explicitly detached and hostile. In only a minority of cases was paternal destructiveness effected through indifference or default.

A fatherless child is deprived of the important paternal contribution to normal development; however, only few homosexuals in our sample had been fatherless children. Relative absence of the father, necessitated by occupational demands or unusual exigencies, is not in itself pathogenic. A good father-son relationship and a mother who is an affectionate, admiring wife, provide the son with the basis for a positive image of the father during periods of separation. We have come to the conclusion that a constructive, supportive, warmly related father *precludes* the possibility of a homosexual son; he acts as a neutralizing, protective agent should the mother make seductive or close-binding attempts.

The foundations of personality and psychopathology are set within the nuclear family; more specifically, within the triangular system. Parental attitudes toward a particular child are often well defined by the first year of life and after the fourth year are well established. Parental attitudes in most instances undergo little fundamental change so that the child is exposed to a continuity of relatively unchanging parental influences. When these influences are pathogenic, they create and then maintain psychopathology in the child.

In important ways, sibling relationships and parent-sibling relationships also contribute to personality formation and to psychodynamic mechanisms operant in interpersonal affairs. Siblings may "tip the scales" one way or the other; they do not set the tenuous balance. However, a good sibling relationship—in particular, one with an older male sibling—may to some extent compensate for a poor one with the parents; it may even reinforce a heterosexual adaptation in a child who might otherwise have become homosexual. A rivalrous, disturbed sibling relationship, or sibling behavior outside the family which is traumatic to the child even when not directed at him, may be the "final straw" to precipitate homosexuality. But again, it is the parents who determine the family atmosphere and the relationships that transpire within the family setting. Other events are relatively of secondary importance.

We believe that sexual development (and its vicissitudes) is a cornerstone in homosexual adaptation. We do not regard homosexuality as a nonspecific manifestation of a generalized personality disorder. Therefore we shall outline a formulation of sexual development relevant to male homosexuality.

The first manifestations of sexuality occur as an integral part of the total growth process. Intricate and complex attitudes, behavior patterns and interpersonal relationships have already evolved before significant sexual development begins. All that has preceded sexual organization plays some part in determining its course. Conversely, the sexual process will itself condition the totality of pre-existing personality attributes, interpersonal relationships, and behavior patterns.

The initial stage of heterosexual responsivity occurs between the third and sixth years of life. Differentiated reactions toward males and females are observable at this period. These reactive differences are determined by a beginning capacity to respond to sexual stimuli from heterosexual objects in the environment—parents and siblings included. The young male child not only develops the capacity to respond sexually to females but he becomes capable of exciting such responses in females, including his mother. Bieber has advanced the hypothesis that olfaction plays an important part in the initial organization of the capacity for heterosexual responsivity and differentiation; the male takes on the odor characteristic of males sometime between the third and fifth year of life. Sexual responsivity in the young male stimulates a wish to be physically close to females and, as culturally patterned, to kiss, hug, and so forth. Rivalrous feelings toward males, particularly toward the father, generally accompany the developing capacity for heterosexual responsivity. The sexual response to the mother and rivalrous feelings to the father constitute the fundamentals of the Oedipus Complex.

Sexual reactions to the mother constitute one manifestation of the male child's developing capacity for heterosexual responses. The profound relationship established with the mother during infancy and into the pre-Oedipal years becomes integrated with the emerging heterosexual responsivity toward the mother as the most prominent and accessible female in the immediate environment. The nature of the child's sexual response in no way differs from that felt toward any comparably accessible female though the singuar attachment of son to mother includes the earlier infantile dependence upon her which begins to articulate with his developing heterosexual interests. It is at this point that the incest taboo is first communicated from parent to child. Because of anxiety connected with incest, the mother will suppress her son's heterosexual responses to her. Sexual repression in concert with filial rivalry toward the father results in the son's repression of incestuous wishes.

good pt.

Parental responses to the child's emerging heterosexuality are not ordinarily emphasized in a discussion of the Oedipus Complex, yet these responses are crucial in determining the fate of the Oedipus Complex. Developmental processes in children, sexual and other, form part of a reverberating stimulus-response system with the parents. Every maturational phase of development in the child stimulates responses in the parents which, in turn, condition the original stimuli and fundamentally determine the nature of development of that specific maturational phase. We refer to the interactional response patterns involved in bowel training, walking, talking, early masturbation, and so forth.

A mother who is pleased by her son's masculinity and is comfortably related to his sexual curiosity and heterosexual responsiveness to her and other females, encourages and reinforces a masculine identification. A father who is warmly related to his son, who supports assertiveness and effectiveness, and who is not sexually competitive, provides the reality testing necessary for the resolution of the son's irrational sexual competitiveness. This type of parental behavior fosters heterosexual development which in adult life is characterized by the ability to sustain a gratifying love relationship. Parents who are capable of sexually constructive attitudes to a child usually are individuals who are capable of a love relationship with each other and provide a stable and affectionate atmosphere in the home. In the context of sexual development, a positive parental relationship provides no basis in reality for expectations of exclusive possession of the mother. Where the marital relationship is unsatisfactory, the parents may make attempts to fulfill frustrated romantic wishes through a child. In the case of the mother the child chosen for this role is usually a son. Thus, in part, she fulfills the son's unconscious incestuous wishes and she intensifies his rivalry with and fear of the father. She alienates son from father who, in turn, becomes hostile to both wife and son.

The majority of H-parents in our study had poor marital relationships. Almost half the H-mothers were dominant wives who minimized their husbands. The large majority of H-mothers had a close-binding intimate relationship with the H-son. In most cases, this son had been his mother's favorite though in a few instances an underlying CBI relationship had been concealed by a screen of maternal minimization and superficial rejection. Most H-mothers were explicitly seductive, and even where they were not, the closeness of the bond with the son appeared to be in itself sexually provocative. In about two-thirds of the cases, the mother openly preferred her H-son to her husband and allied with son against the husband. In about half the cases, the patient was the mother's confidant.

These data point to maternal attempts to fulfill frustrated marital gratifications with the homosexual son. A "romantic" attachment, short of actual physical contact (specifically, genital contact), was often acted out.

We assume that the unusually close mother-son relationship and the maternal seductiveness explicit in over half the cases had the effect of over-stimulating the sons sexually. We further assume that sexual over-stimulation promoted sexual activity rather than sexual patterns characterized by total inhibition as seen in apparent asexuality or impotence. The combination of sexual over-stimulation and intense guilt and anxiety about heterosexual behavior promote precocious and compulsive sexual activity, as was noted among H-patients. In support of these assumptions we found that homosexuals as a group began their sexual activity earlier than did the heterosexuals; the H-patients were more active sexually in preadolescence than were C-patients. The preoccupation with sexuality and sexual organs frequently observed among homosexuals appears to emerge out of an intensity of sexual urges pounding against extensive impairment of heterosexual functioning. Sexual over-stimulation together with heterosexual impairment, promotes compulsive homosexual activity. Reparative mechanisms, usually unconscious and irrational, operate to restore heterosexuality. A reparative mechanism noted among the H-patients included the selection of homosexual lovers who were quite masculine—the "large penis" type. Such a maneuver involves an attempt to identify with a powerful male through symbolic incorporation usually expressed in oral sexual pactices. Not infrequently the homosexual lover is perceived as a potent rival or as the most likely threat to heterosexual goals. The reparative aim is to divert the partner's interest from women, thus symbolically "castrating" him in the homosexual act—an irrational and magical attempt to achieve heterosexuality by eliminating an obstructive, threatening rival.

Earlier, we pointed out that one son was chosen for a particular role. Certain kinds of parental psychopathology are acted out with this son and eventuate in his becoming homosexual. We propose that the mother chooses a son whom she unconsciously identifies with her father or with a brother who has great emotional value to her—usually he is an older brother. Such an identification may be made on the basis of physical traits or other cues to which the mother reacts transferentially but which, in a fundamental sense, evolve from her wish to possess a male like her father, or both. Since the H-son is the instrument which the mother uses to act out her own anxiety-laden incestuous wishes, she is especially alert to any sexual behavior her son may express to her. Lest his behavior expose her own feelings, she suppresses all such manifestations in her son who soon learns that any act which includes an element of sexuality and virile masculinity is unwelcome to her. If her anxiety is severe enough, she attempts to demasculinize her son and will even encourage effeminate attitudes.

Most H-mothers were possessive of their sons. Because they apparently could not tolerate a romantic relationship with their own husbands, they appeared to be insecure about their ability to maintain ties with a male perceived as "valuable"; as compensation, they clung tenaciously to the H-son. In general, demasculinization by the mother serves to insure her son's continued presence; his extinguished heterosexuality then protects her against abandonment for another woman. Demasculinizing maternal behavior may also occur in those women who have been rejected by their own mothers who had preferred a male sibling. Such H-mothers have a need to dominate and control males and to hinder their effectiveness in an irrational attempt to deter further deprivation of feminine love— a female homosexual dynamic. Again, psychoanalytic experience with this type of woman leads us to hypothesize that many such mothers are burdened by deep-going homosexual problems.

It is self-evident that a man who enters into a poor marriage, and then remains in it, has serious problems. The father who is detached, hostile, and rejecting to his son in most instances is in an unsatisfactory marriage, as our data have shown. Hence, such men have a double-pronged psychopathologic interpersonal involvement —with the wife on the one hand, and with the H-son on the other. These fathers, not unlike their wives, are unable to maintain a love relationship with a spouse. Some such men attempt to fulfill those emotional goals by acting out with a daughter as their wives are acting out with a son. These fathers tend to be unusually hostile to men perceived as sexual rivals. Rejected by their wives in favor of the H-son (many of whom were openly preferred and more highly esteemed), the already existing competitive attitudes the fathers had toward males were intensified with the H-sons. Thus paternal competitive attitudes are expressed in overt hostility and rejection or in indifference. As for the son, he accurately interprets his father's behavior as sexually competitive. Fear of attack from the father coupled with the wish for his love is indeed a potent combination; it disturbs the son's own developing masculine sexuality which, he senses, is offensive to the father. Paternal preference for a daughter with expressions of love for her, which the son witnesses and envies, fosters in him the wish to be a woman; further, it interferes with a masculine identification and a heterosexual adaptation.

Much of the data of this study document the importance of the father in his son's sexual outcome. The role-fulfilling father shares supportive, organizing, and orienting behaviors with the mother. Where a father has been devaluated by a wife's contempt while the son has been elevated to a position of preference, and where the father's potentially supportive role is undermined, a highly unrealistic and anxiety-laden grandiosity is promoted in the son. To be treated as superior to the father deprives the child of having the paternal leadership he craves and the support he requires.

In the father's specific contribution to his son's psychosexual development, the father should be a male model with whom the son can identify in forming masculine patterns in a specific cultural milieu. An affectionate father through his warmth and support provides a reality denial for any retaliatory expectations the son may have for harboring sexually competitive attitudes. The father who promotes an identification with him will ordinarily intercede between his son and a wife who may be CBI, thus protecting the boy from demasculinization. Such a father does not default his paternal role out of submissiveness to his wife. Our data record only one such supportive, affectionate H-father—he was a stepfather who came upon the scene when the patient was already ten years old. This patient became exclusively heterosexual in psychoanalytic treatment.

The father who is underprotective or who singles out one or several sons for the expression of hostile attitudes and behavior is usually acting out a transference problem, generally based on difficulties had with his own father and/or a male sibling. Such a father tends to derogate his H-son and to show contempt at his failures in peer groups.

By the time the H-son has reached the preadolescent period, he has suffered a diffuse personality disorder. Maternal over-anxiety about health and injury, restriction of activities normative for the son's age and potential, interference with assertive behavior, demasculinizing attitudes, and interference with sexuality—interpenetrating with paternal rejection, hostility, and lack of support —produce an excessively fearful child, pathologically dependent upon his mother and beset by feelings of inadequacy, impotence, and self-contempt. He is reluctant to participate in boyhood activities thought to be potentially physically injurious—usually grossly over-estimated. His peer group responds with humiliating name-calling and often with physical attack which timidity tends to invite among children. His fear and shame of self, made worse by the derisive reactions of other boys, only drives him further away. Thus, he is deprived of important empathic interactions which peer groups provide. The "esprit de corps" of boyhood gang-life is missed. Having no neighborhood gang to which to belong only accentuates the feeling of difference and alienation. More than half our H-sample were, for the most part, isolates in preadolescence and adolescence, and about one-third played predominantly with girls.

Failure in the peer group, and anxieties about a masculine, heterosexual presentation of self, pave the way for the prehomosexual's initiation into the less threatening atmosphere of homosexual society, its values, and way of life. As a group, homosexuals constitute a kind of subculture with unique institutions, value systems, and communication techniques in idiom, dress, and gestures. The tendency to gravitate to large cities may also be extended to residence in particular locales and to "hangouts." Often there is a sense of identification with a minority group which has been discriminated against. Homosexual society, however, in which membership is attained through individual psychopathology, is neither "healthy" nor happy. Life within this society tends to reinforce, fixate, and add new disturbing elements to the entrenched psychopathology of its members. Although the emotional need of humans to socialize with other humans keeps many homosexuals within groups, some find the life style incompatible with other held values so that in some cases they come to prefer relative isolation.

Some homosexuals tend to seek out a single relationship, hoping to gratify all emotional needs within a one-to-one exclusive relationship. Such twosomes are usually based on unrealistic expectations, often accompanied by inordinate demands; in most instances, these pairs are caught up in a turbulent, abrasive attachment. These liaisons are characterized by initial excitement which may include exaltation and confidence in the discovery of a great love which soon alternates with anxiety, rage, and depression as magical expectations are inevitably frustrated. Gratification of magical wishes is symbolically sought in homosexual activity which is intense in the early phase of a new "affair." These relationships are generally disrupted after a period of several months to a year or so; they are generally sought anew with another partner and the cycle starts again. The depressions accompanying the dissolution of a homosexual bond and the despondency brought about by developing insight into the futility of such relationships are often precipitating circumstances motivating the undertaking of psychiatric or psychoanalytic therapy. Chronic underlying depressive states, a frequent characteristic of homosexuals, are often masked by a façade of gaiety.

A detailed study of the etiology of homosexuality in the atypical cases must await a special study of larger numbers of these subgroups than was available in the present investigation. In several instances, mothers were detached and hostile and several were detached and indifferent. Some fathers were not detached and a few were overprotective. Some homosexuals were not excessively fearful and some did not flinch from fighting; some even sought fights. Though they differed from the majority of H-patients in these aspects, they still had in common with the others highly pathologic relationships with parents and had come to fear a sustained heterosexual love relationship.

In about one-fourth of the comparison patients, evidence of severe homosexual problems was noted. None, however, had actually participated in homosexual activity in adolescence or adult life. We infer that a fragmentary homosexual adaptation had been organized and that the possibility of a homosexual shift had been considered on either a conscious or unconscious level at some time. Since a homosexual integration takes place only where there is severe anxiety regarding heterosexuality, some of these heterosexual patients were apparently tempted to escape from their fears by a flight into homosexuality. This kind of alternative to anxiety usually produces added and even more intense anxiety, since the renunciation of heterosexuality represents a serious loss to perceived self-interest; it is, in a sense, a type of castration. Secondarily, the homosexual solution is socially unacceptable and confronts the individual with unforeseen pitfalls in a new way of life. Certain heterosexuals are thus caught between the anxiety experienced in a sexual bond with a woman, and the panic and fear associated with homosexuality. We view such individuals as potentially homosexual. Only those men who have such problems are considered by us to be "latent" homosexuals, but since the concept of homosexual latency is one that assumes a universal tendency present in all men, we prefer to discard the term entirely and refer to *homosexual problems* in those patients among whom such difficulties can be identified.

The therapeutic results of our study provide reason for an optimistic outlook. Many homosexuals became exclusively heterosexual in psychoanalytic treatment. Although this change may be more easily accomplished by some than by others, in our judgment a heterosexual shift is a possibility for all homosexuals who are strongly motivated to change.

We assume that heterosexuality is the *biologic* norm and that unless interfered with all individuals are heterosexual. Homosexuals do not bypass heterosexual developmental phases and all remain potentially heterosexual.

Our findings are optimistic guideposts not only for homosexuals but for the psychoanalysts who treat them. We are firmly convinced that psychoanalysts may well orient themselves to a heterosexual objective in treating homosexual patients rather than "adjust" even the more recalcitrant patient to a homosexual destiny. A conviction based on scientific fact that a heterosexual goal is achievable helps both patient and psychoanalyst to take in stride the inevitable setbacks during psychoanalysis.

We have learned a great deal about male homosexuality, yet we are under no illusion that this is a final statement on the subject. We hope that our work will stimulate other investigators to find answers to the many questions still unanswered.

Thomas S. Szasz

[handwritten: Psychiatry is an institution to torture homo and nothing more]

The Product Conversion—
From Heresy to Illness

—*Thomas Szasz has been an outspoken rebel on questions of therapy and psychological classifications, and various other matters that some have considered satisfactorily disposed of. In this selection from his recent and controversial book,* The Manufacture of Madness, *he analyzes the concept of homosexuality and argues against several traditional modes of analysis. The Kameny article could be profitably read in conjunction with this selection.*

> The most prejudiced must admit that this religion without theology [positivism] is not chargeable with relaxation of moral restraints. On the contrary, it prodigiously exaggerates them.
> —*John Stuart Mill* [1]

In the work of Benjamin Rush, we have traced the manifestations of the great ideological conversion from theology to science. We saw how Rush had redefined sin as sickness, and moral sanction as medical treatment. In this chapter I shall analyze this process in broader terms and shall show that as the dominant social ethic changed from a religious to a secular one, the problem of heresy disappeared, and the problem of madness arose and became of great social significance. . . .

1. John Stuart Mill, *Auguste Comte and Positivism,* p. 142.

The change from a religious and moral to a social and medical conceptualization and control of personal conduct affects the entire discipline of psychiatry and allied fields. Perhaps nowhere is this transformation more evident than in the modern perspective on so-called sexual deviation, and especially on homosexuality. We shall therefore compare the concept of homosexuality as heresy, prevalent in the days of the witch-hunts, with the concept of homosexuality as mental illness, prevalent today.

Homosexual behavior—like heterosexual and autoerotic behavior —occurs among higher apes and among human beings living in a wide variety of cultural conditions. Judging by artistic, historical, and literary records, it also occurred in past ages and societies. To-day it is part of the dogma of American psychiatrically enlightened opinion that homosexuality is an illness—a form of mental illness. This is a relatively recent view. In the past, men held quite different views on homosexuality, from accepting it as a perfectly natural ac-tivity to prohibiting it as the most heinous of crimes. We shall not explore the cultural and historical aspects of homosexuality;[2] in-stead, we shall confine ourselves to a comparison of the attitude toward homosexuality during the witch-hunts and at the present time. Since late medieval and Renaissance societies were deeply imbued with the teachings of Christianity, we shall first survey the principal Biblical references to this subject.

The Bible prohibits almost every form of sexual activity other than heterosexual, genital intercourse. Homosexuality is prohibited first in Genesis, in the story of Lot. One evening, two angels come to Sodom, disguised as men. Lot meets them at the gates and invites them into his house. First, the angels refuse Lot's hospitality, offer-ing instead to spend the night in the street; but at Lot's urgings, the Old Testament tells us, "they entered his house; and he made them a feast, and baked unleavened bread, and they ate. But before they lay down, the men of the city, the men of Sodom, both young and old, all the people to the last man, surrounded the house; and they called to Lot, 'Where are the men who came to you tonight? Bring them out to us, that we may know them.' "[3]

---

2. For a classic account of homosexuality in past ages and various cultures, see Edward Westermarck, *The Origin and Development of the Moral Ideas*, Vol. II, Chapter XLIII, pp. 456–489; for a more recent exposition, see, for ex-ample, Wainright Churchill, *Homosexual Behavior Among Males*.

3. Genesis, 19: 3–5.

The men of Sodom wanted to use the travelers as sexual objects. Among the ancient Israelites, however, he who gave shelter to strangers was obligated to protect them from harm. Because of this, Lot offered his daughters as substitute objects: "Lot went out of the door to the men, shut the door after him, and said, 'I beg you, my brothers, do not act so wickedly. Behold, I have two daughters who have not known man; let me bring them out to you, and do to them as you please; only do nothing to these men, for they have come under the shelter of my roof.' " [4]

As this suggests, homosexuality was considered a serious offense. This story also makes clear the abysmal devaluation of women as human beings in the ethics of ancient Judaism. Lot values the dignity of his male guests more highly than that of his female children. The Christian ethic did not raise the worth of female life much above the Jewish; nor did the clinical ethic raise it much above the clerical. This is why most of those identified as witches by male inquisitors were women; and why most of those diagnosed as hysterics by male psychiatrists were also women.

The episode in Sodom is undoubtedly the earliest account in human history of the entrapment of homosexuals, a strategy widely practiced by the law enforcement agencies of modern Western countries, especially those of the United States. In effect, the men of Sodom were entrapped by the two strangers, who in truth were not travelers but angels, that is to say, God's plain-clothesmen. These agents of the Biblical vice-squad wasted no time punishing the offenders: ". . . they struck with blindness the men who were at the door of the house . . ." [5] The angels then warn Lot of God's plan to destroy the wicked city, giving him time to flee with his family. God's terrible punishment follows: "Then the Lord rained on Sodom and Gomorrah brimstone and fire from the Lord out of heaven; and he overthrew those cities, and all the valley, and all the inhabitants of the cities, and what grew on the ground." [6]

Homosexuality is again prohibited in Leviticus. "You shall not lie with a male as with a woman; it is an abomination." [7] Adultery, incest, and bestiality are also forbidden. The punishment for transgression is death: "If a man lies with a male as with a woman, both

4. Ibid., 19: 6–8.
5. Ibid., 19: 11.
6. Ibid., 19: 24–25.
7. Leviticus, 18: 22.

of them have committed an abomination; they shall be put to death, their blood is upon them." [8]

It is important to note that only male homosexuality is forbidden: "You shall not lie with a male as with a woman . . ." God addresses males only. He does not command woman not to lie with a female as with a man. Here by omission and implication, and elsewhere by more explicit phrasing, woman is treated as a kind of human animal, not as a full human being. The most up-to-date legal statutes of Western nations dealing with homosexuality continue to maintain this posture toward women: Though homosexual intercourse between consenting adults continues to be prohibited in many countries, nowhere does this apply to women.[9] The inference about the less-than-human status of women is inevitable. No wonder that in his morning prayer, the Orthodox Jew says, "Blessed be God . . . that He did not make me a woman," while the woman says, "Blessed be the Lord, who created me according to His will." [10]

Biblical prohibitions against homosexuality had of course a profound influence on the medieval equation of this practice with heresy; on our contemporary criminal laws and social attitudes, which regard homosexuality as a hybrid of crime and disease; and on the language we still use to describe many so-called sexually deviant acts. Sodomy is an example.

Webster's *Unabridged Dictionary* (Third Edition) defines sodomy as "The homosexual proclivities of the men of the city as narrated in Gen. 19: 1–11; carnal copulation with a member of the same sex or with an animal or unnatural carnal copulation with a member of the opposite sex; specif.: the penetration of the male organ into the mouth or anus of another." This definition is pragmatically correct. In both psychiatric and literary works, the term "sodomy" is used to describe sexual activity involving contact between penis

8. Ibid., 20: 13. For further Biblical references to homosexuality, condemning it in essentially similar terms, see Judges 1: 22–30; 1 Kings 22: 46; 2 Kings 23: 7; Romans 1: 27; 1 Corinthians 6: 9; and 1 Timothy 1: 10.

9. Kinsey and his coworkers have fully documented the differential social treatment, throughout the ages, of male and female homosexual acts. The Talmud, they observe, is relatively lenient regarding women, classifying female homosexual activity as a "mere obscenity," disqualifying the offender from marrying a rabbi. (Alfred C. Kinsey, Wardell B. Pomeroy, Clyde E. Martin, and Paul Gebhard, *Sexual Behavior in the Human Female*, p. 484.) "In medieval European history there are abundant records of death imposed upon males for sexual activity with other males, but very few recorded cases of similar action against females." (Ibid.)

10. Quoted in Simone de Beauvoir, *The Second Sex*, p. xxi.

and mouth or anus, regardless of whether the "passive" partner is male or female. Fellatio is thus a type of sodomy. Because human beings frequently engage in these and other nongenital sexual acts, Kinsey correctly emphasized that there are few Americans who, in their everyday sexual lives, do not violate both the religious prohibitions of their faith and the criminal laws of their country.[11]

In short, the Church opposed homosexuality not only, or even primarily, because it was "abnormal" or "unnatural," but rather because it satisfied carnal lust and yielded bodily pleasure. This condemnation of homosexuality, says Rattray Taylor, "was merely an aspect of the general condemnation of sexual pleasure and indeed of sexual activity not directly necessary to ensure the continuation of the race. Even within marriage, sexual activity was severely restricted, virginity was declared a more blessed state than matrimony." [12] It is no accident, then, that carnal lust, leading to nonprocreative sexual practices and pleasure of all kinds, was a characteristic passion of witches. They were supposed to satisfy their cravings by copulating with the Devil, a male figure of superhuman masculinity, equipped with a "forked penis," enabling him to penetrate the woman at once vaginally and anally.[13]

As we turn to a consideration of the Church's attitudes toward sex during the witch-hunts, we discover a concrete connection between notions of religious deviance and sexual offense: Heresy and homosexuality become one and the same thing.[14] For centuries, no penological distinction is made between religious unorthodoxy and sexual misbehavior, especially homosexuality. "During the Middle Ages," says Westermarck, "heretics were accused of unnatural vice [homosexuality] as a matter of course. . . . In medieval laws sodomy was also repeatedly mentioned together with heresy, and the punishment was the same for both." [15]

In thirteenth-century Spain, the penalty for homosexuality was castration and "lapidation" [execution by stoning].[16] Ferdinand and

11. Alfred C. Kinsey, Wardell B. Pomeroy, and Clyde E. Martin, *Sexual Behavior in the Human Male,* pp. 659–666.

12. Gordon Rattray Taylor, Historical and Mythological Aspects of Homosexuality, in Judd Marmor (Ed.), *Sexual Inversion,* pp. 140–164; pp. 145–146.

13. Ibid., p. 145.

14. The concept of evil, especially in so far as it functions mainly as a rhetorical device justifying the expulsion of the source of danger, absorbs many cognitive distinctions. Thus, in the Middle Ages, heretic, sorcerer, sodomist, and witch were often subsumed under a single category.

15. Westermarck, p. 489.

16. Henry Charles Lea, *A History of the Inquisition of Spain,* Vol. 4, p. 362.

Isabella changed this, in 1479, to "burning alive and confiscation, irrespective of the station of the culprit." [17] In other words, then the crime was subject to punishment by both secular and ecclesiastic courts—just as now it is subject to punishment by both penal and psychiatric sanctions. In 1451, Nicholas V empowered the Inquisition to deal with it. "When the institution [Inquisition] was founded in Spain," Lea writes, ". . . the Seville tribunal made it [homosexuality] the subject of a special inquest; there were many arrests and many fugitives, and twelve convicts were duly burnt." [18] The Spanish Inquisition, whose principal enemies . . . were Judaizers and Moriscoes, was thus also hard on homosexuals.[19]

In Portugal, too, the Spanish prohibitions against homosexuality were strictly enforced. "In 1640, the Regulations prescribe that the offence is to be tried like heresy, and the punishment is to be either relaxation [burning] or scourging [flogging] and the galleys. In a case occurring in the Lisbon *auto* of 1723, the sentence was scourging and ten years of galley-service." [20]

In Valencia, the usual punishment for homosexuality was burning at the stake. There was, however, some disinclination to inflict this penalty because these offenders ". . . could not escape, as heretics could, by confession and conversion." [21] In this connection it is interesting to note that homosexual clerics were treated more leniently than laymen exhibiting the same conduct. "Many authorities . . . ," says Lea, "held that clerics were not to be subjected to the rigor of the law for this offense, and it was common opinion that incorrigibility was required to justify the ordinary penalty." [22]

17. Ibid.

18. Ibid.

19. This was not true of the Roman Inquisition, whose principal enemies were witches and Protestants. ". . . throughout Italy," Lea tells us, "the crime was everywhere treated with a leniency wholly inadequate to its atrocity. The Roman Inquisition, moreover, took no cognizance of it." This tolerance, indeed approval, of homosexuality in Italy is attested to by the fact that, in 1664, some Conventual Franciscans actually "rendered themselves conspicuous by sounding the praises of the practice . . ." (Lea, *A History of the Inquisition of Spain,* p. 365.)

20. Lea, Vol. 4, pp. 365–366.

21. Ibid., p. 367.

22. Ibid., p. 368. Physicians now enjoy similar lenience with respect to such typical psychiatric "offenses" as depression and the threat of suicide. Laymen are severely punished for such conduct: they are hospitalized and treated against their will. Although the incidence of suicide is higher in physicians than in any other group—and is highest among psychiatrists—medical men exhibiting such conduct are rarely punished for it with involuntary mental hospitalization and treatment.

Crossroads—Christopher and Gay Streets, New York City.

Two gay young men on Christopher Street.

Jim Owles (right), president of Gay Activists Alliance,
with friend.

Members of Gay Youth on New York's Forty-second Street during the October
1970 moratorium.

Malcolm (Marcia Johnson) with lover.

Love in Nelson Rockefeller's office.

The frequency of prosecutions for homosexuality in Spain was appreciable. From 1780 to 1820, Lea records, "the total number of cases coming before the three tribunals [in Valencia] was exactly one hundred." [23]

In English-speaking countries, the connection between heresy and homosexuality is expressed through the use of a single word to denote both concepts: buggery. The double meaning of this word persists to this day. Webster's *Unabridged Dictionary* (Third Edition) defines "buggery" as "heresy, sodomy"; and "bugger" as "heretic, sodomite." The word is derived from the medieval Latin *Bugarus* and *Bulgarus,* literally Bulgarian, "from the adherence of the Bulgarians to the Eastern Church considered heretical."

This connection, at once semantic and conceptual, between unorthodoxy and sodomy, was firmly established during the late Middle Ages, and has never been severed. It is as strong today as it was six hundred years ago. To be stigmatized as a heretic or bugger in the fourteenth century was to be cast out of society. Since the dominant ideology was theological, religious deviance was considered so grave an offense as to render the individual a nonperson. Whatever redeeming qualities he might have had counted for nought. The sin of heresy eclipsed all contradictory, personal characteristics, just as the teachings of God and the Church eclipsed all contradictory, empirical observations. The disease called "mental illness"—and its subspecies "homosexuality"—plays the same role today. The late Senator Joseph McCarthy thus equated the social sin of Communism with the sexual sin of homosexuality and used the two labels as if they were synonymous. He could not have done this had there been no general belief that, like medieval heretics, men labeled "homosexual" are somehow totally bad. They can have no compensating or redeeming features: They cannot be talented writers or patriotic Americans. Given this premise—which McCarthy did not invent, but only appropriated for his use—it follows that homosexuals must also be politically deviant, that is, Communists. The same logic applies in reverse. If Communists are the modern, secular incarnations of the Devil—political incubi and succubi, as it were—then it follows that they, too, can have no redeeming features. They must be completely bad. They must be homosexuals.[24]

23. Ibid., p. 371.

24. In using the term "mental illness" (and its variants) we follow the same principle. When we call men like Ezra Pound or Lee Harvey Oswald mad, we establish, by ascription, a characteristic of that person which overshadows with

We are ready now to consider the problem of homosexuality in its contemporary form: that is, is homosexuality a disease? In a recent authoritative volume on "sexual inversion," Judd Marmor, the editor, raises this question, and answers that "Most of the psychoanalysts in this volume, except Szasz, are of the opinion that homosexuality is definitely an illness to be treated and *corrected*." [25] (Italics added.) The correctional zeal of the modern psychiatric therapist shows itself here in a way that cannot be mistaken. Disease as a biological condition and as a social role are confused. Cancer of the bladder is a disease; but whether it is treated or not depends on the person who has the disease, not on the physician who makes the diagnosis! [26] Marmor, like so many contemporary psychiatrists, forgets or ignores this distinction. There is, to be sure, good reason why he, and other "mental health workers," do so: By pretending that convention is Nature, that disobeying a personal prohibition is a medical illness, they establish themselves as agents of social control and at the same time disguise their punitive interventions in the semantic and social trappings of medical practice.

René Guyon, a French student of sexual customs, has recognized this characteristic tendency of modern psychiatry to brand as sick that which is merely unconventional. "The trouble to which the psychiatrists have gone," he observes, "to explain . . . nature in terms of convention, health in terms of mental disease, is scarcely to be believed. . . . The distinctive method of its system is that every time it comes across a natural act that is contrary to the prevailing conventions, it brands this act as a symptom of mental derangement or abnormality." [27]

---

transcendent badness the individual whom it is supposed to describe. Once the characterization is accepted, it negates the individual's other human—especially good—qualities. He is thus degraded and dehumanized. We then no longer worry about him as a person with rights and talents. If he is a poet, we can dismiss him as an artist; if he is an accused criminal, we can ignore his guilt or innocence; and if he is a suspected presidential assassin, murdered in jail, we can simplify a hopelessly unresolved event with far-reaching political and international implications by attributing everything about it to the madness of a single, virtually unknown, individual. In short, psychiatric heresy, like religious heresy, is a functional concept. It is useful for the society that employs it; were it not so, the concept would never have evolved and would not continue to receive popular support.

25. Marmor, p. 15.

26. In this connection, see Thomas S. Szasz, Scientific method and social role in medicine and psychiatry, *A.M.A. Arch. Int. Med.*, 101: 228–238 (Feb.), 1958; and Alcoholism: A socioethical perspective, *Western Med.* 7: 15–21 (Dec.), 1966.

27. René Guyon, *The Ethics of Sexual Acts*, pp. 270–271.

The question of whether or not homosexuality is an illness is therefore a pseudo problem. If by disease we mean deviation from an anatomical or physiological norm—as in the case of a fractured leg or diabetes—then homosexuality is clearly not an illness. Still, it may be asked if there is a genetic predisposition to homosexuality, as there is to a stocky body build; or is it entirely a learned pattern of behavior? This question cannot be answered with assurance. At present, the evidence for such predisposition is slim, if any. The biologically oriented person may argue, however, that more evidence for it might be discovered in the future. Perhaps so. But even if homosexuals were proven to have certain sexual preferences because of their nature, rather than nurture, what would that prove? People who are prematurely bald are sick, in a stricter sense of this word, than homosexuals could possibly be. What of it? Clearly, the question that is really being posed for us is not whether a given person manifests deviations from an anatomical and physiological norm, but what moral and social significance society attaches to his behavior—whether it be due to infectious illness (as was the case with leprosy in the past), or to learned preference (as is the case with homosexuality today).

Psychiatric preoccupation with the disease concept of homosexuality—as with the disease concept of all so-called mental illnesses, such as alcoholism, drug addiction, or suicide—conceals the fact that homosexuals are a group of medically stigmatized and socially persecuted individuals. The noise generated by their persecution and their anguished cries of protest are drowned out by the rhetoric of therapy—just as the rhetoric of salvation drowned out the noise generated by the persecution of heretics and their anguished cries of protest. It is a heartless hypocrisy to pretend that physicians, psychiatrists, or "normal" laymen for that matter, really care about the welfare of the mentally ill in general, or the homosexual in particular. If they did, they would stop torturing him while claiming to help him. But this is just what reformers—whether theological or medical—refuse to do.[28]

The idea that the homosexual is "sick" only in the sense that he is so categorized by others, and himself accepts this categorization,

---

28. For many decades, but especially since the days of Senator Joseph McCarthy, the insinuation of homosexuality about one's adversaries has become an accepted strategy in American political life. If homosexuality is an illness—"like any other"—then why do psychiatrists not protest its use as a means of social degradation and political disqualification?

goes back at least to André Gide's autobiographical work, *Corydon*, and perhaps earlier. First published anonymously in 1911, the narrative is set in the form of a series of dialogues between the author and his younger friend Corydon. The following excerpt illustrates Gide's conception of the homosexual as a victim of an overzealously heterosexual society.

"I am . . . preparing a fairly important study on the subject [of homosexuality]" [says the author].

"Aren't the works of Moll, Krafft-Ebing, and Raffalovitch enough for you?" [replies Corydon].

"They are not satisfactory. I would like to approach it differently. . . . I am writing a *Defense of Homosexuality*."

"Why not a *Eulogy*, while you are about it?"

"Because such a title would force my ideas. I am afraid people will find even the word '*Defense*' too provocative . . . the cause lacks martyrs."

"Don't use such big words."

"I use the words needed. We have had Wilde, Krupp, Macdonald, Eulenburg . . . Oh, victims! Victims as many as you please. But not a single martyr. They all deny it; they always will deny it."

"There you are! They all feel ashamed and retract as soon as they are faced with public opinion, the press, or the courtroom."

". . . Yes, you are right. To try to establish one's innocence by disavowing one's life is to yield to public opinion. How strange! One has the courage of one's opinions, but not of one's habits. One can accept suffering, but not dishonor." [29]

Here Gide unmasks homosexuality as a socially stigmatized role, like witch or Jew, which, under the pressure of public opinion, its bearer is likely to disavow and repudiate. The homosexual is a scapegoat who evokes no sympathy. Hence, he can be only a victim, never a martyr. This is as true today in the United States as it was in France a half century ago. The same applies, moreover, to the mentally ill; he, too, can only be a victim, never a martyr.

The next excerpt illustrates Gide's penetrating insight into the disease concept of sexual inversion, and, *mutatis mutandis*, into mental illness generally.

29. André Gide, *Corydon*, pp. 8–10.

"If you had been aware of it [homosexual inclination], what would you have done?" [asks Corydon].

"I believe I would have cured the boy" [replies the author].

"You said a moment ago that it was incurable . . ."

"I could have cured him as I cured myself. . . . By persuading him he was not sick . . . that there was nothing unnatural in his deviation."

"And if he had persisted, you would naturally have yielded to it."

"Ah! That is an entirely different question. When the physiological problem is resolved, the moral problem begins." [30]

Gide thus shows that the "diagnosis" of homosexuality is in actuality a stigmatizing label which, to protect his authentic identity, the subject must reject. To escape from medical control, the homosexual must repudiate the diagnosis ascribed to him by the physician. In other words, homosexuality is an illness in the same sense as we have seen Negritude described as an illness. Benjamin Rush claimed that Negroes had black skin because they were ill; and he proposed to use their illness as a justification for their social control. Rush's modern follower asserts that men whose sexual conduct he disapproves of are ill; and he uses their illness as a justification for their social control.

Only in our day have Negroes been able to escape from the semantic and social trap in which white men have held them fast after their legal shackles had been cast off a century ago. So-called mental patients, whose fetters—forged of commitment papers, asylum walls, and fiendish tortures passed off as "medical treatments"—have a strangle hold on their bodies and souls are only now learning how to properly abase themselves before their psychiatric masters. It seems probable that many more people will have to be injured by means of psychiatric labeling and its social consequences than have been so far, before men will recognize, and protect themselves from, the dangers of Institutional Psychiatry. This, at least, is the lesson which the history of witchcraft suggests.

So long as men could denounce others as witches—so that the witch could always be considered the Other, never the Self—witchcraft remained an easily exploitable concept and the Inquisition a flourishing institution. Only loss of faith in the authority of the

30. Ibid., pp. 20–21.

inquisitors and their religious mission brought an end to this practice of symbolic cannibalism. Similarly, so long as men can denounce
each other as mentally sick (homosexual, addicted, insane, and so
forth)—so that the madman can always be considered the Other,
never the Self—mental illness will remain an easily exploitable concept, and Coercive Psychiatry a flourishing institution. If this is so,
only loss of faith in the authority of institutional psychiatrists and
their medical mission will bring an end to the Psychiatric Inquisition. This day is not imminent.

My contention that the psychiatric perspective on homosexuality
is but a thinly disguised replica of the religious perspective which
it displaced, and that efforts to "treat" this kind of conduct medically
are but thinly disguised methods for suppressing it, may be verified
by examining any contemporary psychiatric account of homosexuality. The handling of the subject by Karl Menninger, widely recognized as the most "liberal" and "progressive" of modern psychiatrists,
is illustrative. In *The Vital Balance*, Menninger discusses homosexuality under the general rubric of "A Second Order of Dyscontrol
and Dysorganization," immediately following an analysis of "Per-
verse Sexual Modalities." [31] "We cannot, like Gide, extol homosexuality," writes Menninger. "We do not, like some, *condone* it.
We regard it as a *symptom* with all the functions of other symptoms
—aggression, indulgence, self-punishment, and the effort to forestall
something worse." [32] (Italics added.) Menninger, like other medical
writers on moral topics, gives himself away by the choice of his
words: If homosexuality is a "symptom," what is there to "condone"
or not "condone"? Menninger would not speak of "condoning or
not condoning" the fever of pneumonia or the jaundice of biliary
obstruction—but he does speak of "not condoning" a psychiatric
"symptom." His "therapeutic" recommendations for homosexuality
bear out the suspicion that his medical role is but a cloak for that of
the moralist and social engineer.

A "married man, a church member, a director of a bank, the
father of three children"—in short, a pillar of the community—
consults Menninger and confides his secret to him: He is a homosexual. The man asks: "But what can I do?" Menninger's answer:
"Of course one thing he could do would be to live continently; there
are millions of heterosexually inclined people who are continent for
one reason or another, and this should be no more difficult for a

31. Karl Menninger, *The Vital Balance*, pp. 195–198.
32. Ibid., p. 198.

homosexually inclined individual." [33] True. But would not the possibility of sexual continence have occurred to a man who is the successful director of a bank? [34]

Menninger's second recommendation is "to get treatment for the condition. Treatment can be efficacious if the afflicted one is not too strongly entrenched in despair or in the rationalizations that there was something wrong with his hereditary genes, that he is condemned to be this way and must make the best of it." [35] To Menninger, the "treatment" can have only one goal: to convert the heretic to the true faith, to transform the homosexual into a heterosexual. The possibility of helping the client accept his existing inclinations with greater equanimity, to help him value his own authentic selfhood more than his society's judgment of it—these therapeutic alternatives are not even mentioned by Menninger. Indeed, he castigates the homosexual by reversing an old accusation against him: Only a few years ago—after giving up the "theory" that homosexuality was caused by masturbation, which was standard psychiatric dogma toward the end of the nineteenth century—psychiatrists insisted that sexual inversion was a genetic disease; it was due to "bad heredity." Despite this, Menninger flatly accuses the homosexual of "rationalizing" if he believes that heredity may have something to do with the nature of his sexual interests, and is not eager to change them in the direction approved by society. Perhaps one reason for Menninger's intellectual intransigence is that he has no doubt that he knows what homosexuality—its "essence"—really is: It is "aggression"—the psychiatric name for Satan. "But the fact remains," he writes, "that as we see homosexuality *clinically* and *officially* it nearly always betrays its *essentially* aggressive nature." [36] (Italics added.) Of course, when Menninger looks at any other sexual or social behavior "clinically and officially [sic]," he sees their "essence" also in aggression.[37] Like the devout theologian seeing the Devil lurking

---

33. Ibid., p. 196.

34. In this connection, see Guyon, who writes: "Finally, the medical profession, prostituting science to the service of taboo (and taking the latter for granted), has endeavored to show that it is possible to forgo the sexual act without injury to health . . ." (René Guyon, *The Ethics of Sexual Acts,* p. 204.) Guyon is here referring to heterosexual acts, but, *mutatis mutandis,* the same also applies to homosexual and autoerotic acts.

35. Ibid.

36. Ibid., p. 197.

37. Menninger offers the same explanation for masturbation: ". . . in the unconscious mind it [masturbation] always represents an aggression against some one." (Karl Menninger, *Man Against Himself,* p. 69.)

everywhere, Menninger, the devout Freudian, sees aggression and the death instinct.

Occasionally, however, Menninger forgets his clinical lines and speaks in explicitly clerical terms. In his Introduction to *The Wolfenden Report,* for example, he asserts that "Prostitution and homosexuality rank high in the kingdom of evils" [38]—surely a remarkable statement from a leading psychiatrist in the second half of the twentieth century. Nor does calling prostitution and homosexuality grave sins prevent Menninger from regarding these activities as mental illnesses as well. "From the standpoint of the psychiatrist," he writes, "both homosexuality and prostitution—and add to this the use of prostitutes—constitutes evidence of immature sexuality and either arrested psychological development or regression. Whatever it be called by the public, there is no question [sic] in the minds of psychiatrists regarding the abnormality of such behavior." [39] Menninger seems to believe that entertaining no doubts about one's opinions is a special virtue, a sure sign of psychiatric grace.[40]

Contemporary psychiatrists will not admit to the possibility that they might be wrong in categorizing sexual inversion as an illness. "In a discussion of homosexuality, psychiatrists would probably agree unanimously on at least one point: the belief that the homosexual is a sick person." [41] This statement appears in the introduction to a pamphlet on homosexuality, distributed free to the profession by Roche Laboratories, one of the principal manufacturers of so-called psychopharmacologic drugs. Like the inquisitor, the psychiatrist defines, and thereby authenticates, his own existential position by what he opposes—as heresy or illness. In stubbornly insisting that the homosexual is sick, the psychiatrist is merely pleading to be accepted as a physician.[42]

38. Karl Menninger, Introduction, in *The Wolfenden Report,* pp. 5-7; p. 5.
39. Ibid., p. 6.
40. The righteous convictions of mankind's self-appointed benefactors has moved Russell to observe that "Most of the greatest evils that man has inflicted upon man have come through people feeling quite certain about something which, in fact, was false." (Bertrand Russell, *Unpopular Essays,* p. 162.)
41. *Crosscurrents of Psychiatric Thought Today,* p. 1.
42. Since true belief—whether in the mythologies of Christianity or of Psychiatry—is difficult to establish, especially to the satisfaction of a skeptical judge, hostility against the heretic becomes the hallmark of the genuineness of belief. Speaking through Sancho Panza, Cervantes puts it this way: "Yet the historians ought to take pity on me and treat me kindly in their writings, if only because I've always believed in God and all the tenets of the Holy Roman Catholic Church, and because I am a mortal enemy to the Jews." (Miguel de Cervantes Saavedra, *The Adventures of Don Quixote,* p. 516.) In other words, as the

As befits the ministrations of a modern inquisitor, the persecutory practices of the institutional psychiatrist are couched in the vocabulary of medicine. Pretending to be diagnosing a measles-like illness during its incubation period in order the better to treat it, the psychiatrist actually imposes pseudomedical labels on society's scapegoats in order the better to handicap, reject, and destroy them. Not satisfied with diagnosing overt homosexuals as "sick," psychiatrists claim to be able to discover the presence of this supposed disease (in its "latent" form, of course), in persons who show no outward sign of it. They also claim to be able to diagnose homosexuality during childhood, while it is incubating, as it were. "We have noted," write Holemon and Winokur, "that this [effeminate behavior] often antedated homosexual orientation and homosexual relations. In these patients effeminacy seems to be the primary problem and the sexual behavior is secondary. From this one should be able to predict which children will develop effeminate homosexuality by selecting those with objective signs of effeminacy." [43] In a similar vein, Shearer declares that "excessive clinging to the parent of the opposite sex, especially between father and daughter, should also alert the physician to the possibility of homosexuality." [44] What constitutes "excessive clinging"? How much affection between child and parent of the opposite sex is permitted without it signifying the presence of the dread disease, homosexuality?

From the foregoing we may safely conclude that psychiatric opinion about homosexuals is not a scientific proposition but a medical prejudice.[45] It is pertinent to recall here that the more attention the inquisitors paid to witchcraft, the more the witches multiplied. The

---

faithful Spaniard living at the height of the Inquisition proved his religious orthodoxy by hating Jews, so the scientific psychiatrist living today proves his medical orthodoxy by hating mental illness.

43. [*Crosscurrents of Psychiatric Thought Today*], p. 13.

44. Ibid., p. 14.

45. In one of those ironic reversals of roles which occur every so often in human history, the homosexual is now persecuted by physicians, and defended by clergymen. In an article published in the influential *National Catholic Reporter*, Father Henri Nouwen of Utrecht, in the Netherlands, recasts the problem of homosexuality in the light of modern Christian and phenomenological teaching. His essential thesis is that homosexuality is neither a sin nor a disease, but a medical, and especially psychiatric, prejudice. "If a man has chosen the homosexual way of life, prefers homosexual circles and homosexual friends, and does not show any desire or willingness to change," writes Father Nouwen, "it does not make any sense to punish him or try to change him." (Henri J. M. Nouwen, Homosexuality: Prejudice or mental illness? *Nat. Cath. Rep.*, Nov. 29, 1967, p. 8.) See also Lars Ullerstam, *The Erotic Minorities*, especially p. 24.

same principle applies to mental illness in general, and to homosexuality in particular. Zealous efforts to eradicate and prevent such
"disorders" actually create the conditions in which the assumption
and ascription of such roles flourish.

With the penetrating insight of the literary artist, William S.
Burroughs has described just this process—that is, the manufacture
of madness through a "medical examination" for the "early detec-
tion" of homosexuality. An episode in *Naked Lunch*, called "The
Examination," begins with Carl Pederson finding "a postcard in his
box requesting him to report for a ten o'clock appointment with
Doctor Benway in the Ministry of Mental Hygiene and Prophy-
laxis . . ." [46] As the examination gets underway, Pederson realizes
that he is being tested for "sexual deviation." The doctor explains
that homosexuality is "a sickness . . . certainly nothing to be
censored or uh sanctioned any more than say . . . tuberculo-
sis. . . ." [47] However, since it is a contagious disorder, it must be
treated compulsorily, if necessary. " 'Treatment of these disorders
[says Doctor Benway] is, at the present time, hurmph symptomatic.'
The doctor suddenly threw himself back in his chair and burst into
peals of metallic laughter. . . . 'Don't look so frightened young
man. Just a professional joke. To say treatment is symptomatic
means there is none . . .' " [48] After subjecting Pederson to a series
of humiliating "tests," the doctor finally says, "And so Carl will you
please oblige to tell me how many times and under what circumstances you have uh indulged in homosexual acts???" [49] As the scene
ends, Pederson is going mad: "The doctor's voice was barely audible.
The whole room was exploding out into space." [50]

It is clear that psychiatrists have a vested interest in diagnosing
as mentally ill as many people as possible, just as inquisitors had
in branding them as heretics. The "conscientious" psychiatrist authenticates himself as a competent medical man by holding that
sexual deviants (and all kinds of other people, perhaps all of mankind, as Karl Menninger would have it) are mentally ill, just as the
"conscientious" inquisitor authenticated himself as a faithful Christian by holding that homosexuals (and all kinds of other people)
were heretics. We must realize that in situations of this kind we are

46. William S. Burroughs, *Naked Lunch*, pp. 186–197; p. 186.
47. Ibid., p. 188.
48. Ibid., p. 189.
49. Ibid., p. 196.
50. Ibid., p. 197.

confronted, not with scientific problems to be solved, but with social roles to be confirmed.[51] Inquisitor and witch, psychiatrist and mental patient, create each other and authenticate each other's roles. For an inquisitor to have maintained that witches were not heretics and that their souls required no special effort at salvation would have amounted to asserting that there was no need for witch-hunters. Similarly, for a psychopathologist to maintain that homosexuals are not patients and that neither their bodies nor their minds require special efforts at cure would amount to asserting that there is no need for coercive psychiatrists.

It is necessary to keep in mind here that most people diagnosed as physically ill *feel* sick and *consider themselves* sick; whereas most people diagnosed as mentally ill *do not feel* sick and *do not consider themselves* sick. Consider again the homosexual. As a rule, he neither feels ill, nor considers himself ill. Hence, he usually does not seek the help of a physician or psychiatrist. All this, as we have seen, parallels the situation of the witch. As a rule, she, too, neither felt sinful, nor considered herself a witch. Hence, she did not seek the help of the inquisitor. If, then, a psychiatrist is to have a patient of this kind, or a priest such a parishioner, each must have the power to impose his "care" on an unwilling subject. The State gives this power to the psychiatrist, just as the Church gave it to the inquisitor.

But these are not the only possible, or indeed actually existing, relationships between psychiatrists and patients, or priests and parishioners. Some of their relationships are, and were, wholly voluntary and mutually consensual. The discussion about the disease concept of homosexuality (and mental illness generally) narrows down to two questions, and our answers to them. First, should psychiatrists have the right to consider homosexuality a disease (however defined)? I say: Of course they should. If that concept helps

51. One prominent psychiatric expert on homosexuality classifies bachelorhood itself as a form of mental illness. "Failure to marry in either sex is the consequence of the fear of it," says Irving Bieber. "There is increasing recognition that bachelorhood is symptomatic of psychopathology . . ." (*Time,* Sept. 15, 1967, p. 27.) While failure to marry may, of course, be due to fear of the other sex or of marriage as a social institution, the urge to marry may be due to fear of loneliness or of homosexuality. To Bieber, bachelorhood signifies psychopathology. To me, his widely shared view signifies the intense dread of a sexual role frowned upon by society. In contemporary America, the urge for social acceptance as normally heterosexual is as strong as was the urge, in Renaissance Spain, for acceptance as faithfully Catholic. Playing the former role requires, in Bieber's judgment, that one classify bachelorhood and homosexuality as diseases, just as playing the latter role required, in the judgment of earlier experts, that one classify Judaism and Mohammedanism as heresies.

them, they will be wealthier; if it helps their patients, the patients will be happier. Second, should psychiatrists have the power, through alliance with the State, to impose their definition of homosexuality as a disease on unwilling clients? I say: Of course they should not. I have presented my reasons for this opinion elsewhere.[52]

Psychiatrists and others who like, and plead for the adoption of, the disease concept of homosexuality (and of other types of human behavior) often seem to be talking about the first question—that is, what kind of disease the alleged "patient" has. But, as a rule, consciously or unwittingly, they are concerned with the second question—that is, how to control or "correct" (to use Marmor's term) the patient's alleged "sickness." The president of the Mattachine Society, the nation's largest organization of homosexuals, rightly warns that "when doctors rush into print with wild claims of 'cures' for homosexuality they are not serving the homosexual. Indeed, they are doing just the opposite; they are increasing social pressure on him. . . . A 'cure' would be a sort of 'final solution' to the homosexual problem." [53]

Our position on the disease concept of homosexuality and its social control through medicine could be vastly clarified were we to apply to it our experience with the heresy concept of homosexuality and its social control through religion. Indeed, the parallels between these two sets of theoretical concepts and social sanctions need to be extended only to include one additional consideration— the legitimacy or illegitimacy of combining religious and medical *ideas* and *practices* with political *power*.

If it is true that God rewards faithful Christians with eternal bliss

52. See especially Thomas S. Szasz, Scientific method and social role; Alcoholism: A socioethical perspective; and *Law, Liberty, and Psychiatry*. I do not claim originality for my position on homosexuality. Nor is it held by me alone. Robert Lindner, a well-known nonmedical psychoanalyst writes: ". . . when the veneer of our contemporary system of defenses against the age-old conflict over sex is stripped away, there is to be discovered the same hostility for the invert and his way of life and the same abhorrence of him as a person that have been traditional in Western society. That we now employ such terms as 'sick' or 'maladjusted' to the homosexual appears to me to make little difference so far as basic attitudes and feelings are concerned. As a matter of fact, I suggest that precisely these designations reveal the ugly truth of our actual animus toward homosexuals and the sham of modern social-sexual pretensions; for in the current lexicon such words reflect the nonconformism of their referents—and nonconformism is the major, perhaps the only, sin of our time." (Robert Lindner, *Must You Conform?*, pp. 32–33.)

53. Dick Leitsch, The psychotherapy of homosexuality: "Let's forget Jocasta and her little boy, *Psychiat. Opin.*, 4: 28–35 (June), 1967: p. 35.

in a life hereafter, is this not inducement enough to insure true belief? Why should the State use its police power to impose religious faith on nonbelievers, when, if left alone, such heretics are sure to suffer eternal damnation? In the past, the zealous Christian countered this challenge by affirming his boundless love for his "misguided" brother whom it was his duty to "save" from his horrible fate. Since the heathen could usually not be saved by persuasion alone, the use of force—justified by the lofty theological goal—was in order.

Witnessing the tragic consequences of this logic translated into everyday life, the Founders of the American Republic reasserted the classic distinction between truth and power, and sought to embody this distinction in appropriate political institutions. The Founding Fathers thus reasoned that if the Christian religions were "true" (as many of them believed they were), then their value (or the value of other religions) ought to become manifest to rational men (and they treated men generally as rational). Entertaining the possibility of religious falsehood, they refused to endorse any particular faith as the only true one. In short, they held that should there be error in religion, men should be left unhampered to discover it for themselves and to act freely on their discoveries. The upshot was the uniquely American concept of religious freedom and pluralism, based on a separation of Church and State. This concept, which depends wholly on the blocking of the official guardians of religious dogma from access to the police power of the State, is embodied in the First Amendment to the Constitution, which states that "Congress shall make no law respecting an establishment of religion, or prohibiting the free exercise thereof . . ."

Inasmuch as the ideology that now threatens individual liberties is not religious but medical, the individual needs protection not from priests but from physicians. Logic thus dictates—however much expediency and "common sense" make this seem absurd—that the traditional constitutional protections from oppression by a State-recognized and supported Church be extended to protections from oppression by a State-recognized and supported Medicine. The justification now for a separation of Medicine and State is similar to that which obtained formerly for a separation of Church and State.

As the Christian concept of sin carries with it its own deterrent of suffering in hell, so the scientific concept of disease carries with it its own deterrent of suffering on earth. Moreover, if it is true that nature rewards faithful believers in medicine (and especially those who seek prompt and properly authorized medical care for their illnesses) with a long and healthy life, is this not inducement enough to insure true belief? Why should the State use its police power to impose medical dogma on nonbelievers, when, if left alone, such heretics are sure to suffer the ravages of bodily and mental deterioration? Today, the zealous psychiatrist counters this challenge by affirming his limitless medical obligation to his "sick" brother whom it is his duty to "treat" for his dread disease. Since the madman cannot usually be cured by persuasion alone, the use of force—justified by the lofty therapeutic goal—is in order.

Witnessing the tragic consequences of this logic translated into everyday life, we ought to emulate the wisdom and the courage of our forebears and trust men to know what is in their own best medical interests. If we truly value medical healing and refuse to confuse it with therapeutic oppression—as they truly valued religious faith and refused to confuse it with theological oppression—then we ought to let each man seek his own medical salvation and erect an invisible but impenetrable wall separating Medicine and the State.[54]

54. A new Constitutional Amendment, extending the guarantees of the First Amendment to medicine, would have to state that "Congress shall make no law respecting an establishment of medicine, or prohibiting the free exercise thereof . . ." At this time in our history, anything even remotely resembling such a declaration would seem to be quite impossible, for Organized Medicine is now as much a part of the American government as Organized Religion had been of the government of fifteenth-century Spain. Still, a small beginning in this direction might perhaps be made.

Martin Hoffman

Homosexuals and the Law

—Martin Hoffman, in this particular selection, presents a forceful argument for the necessity of changing the existing laws in the U.S.A. Except for several states, homosexuals are penalized by light to extremely heavy penalties for engaging in sexual relations, whether between consenting adults practicing in private or not. However, Hoffman argues for radical changes in the law so that a true homosexual law reform can take place. The Curzon selection could also be profitably read in conjunction with this selection.

One evening, while talking to a young man in a San Francisco gay bar, I heard him complain about some aspects of his life and then say, "Maybe I'll go to Chicago. Gay kids are legal in Illinois." He was referring to the fact that in 1961 the Illinois legislature removed the laws governing sexual relations between consenting adults in private from the statute books, but he was also expressing here a common misunderstanding, the notion that homosexuality *per se* is illegal. This is incorrect; nowhere is it against the law to be homosexual, to be sexually attracted to members of one's own sex. What is illegal are certain acts, and the law does not discriminate in regard to the sex of the individuals who perform these acts, which are illegal in both a homosexual and a heterosexual context. This is due to a combination of factors, one of them being the fact that the law traditionally does not prohibit states of mind, but only proscribes certain forms of behavior. Another reason for this seeming anomaly is the fact that the statutes themselves are very ill-defined. It is certainly not clear from reading them, and sometimes it is not even clear to appellate courts, just

From *The Gay World* by Martin Hoffman (New York: Basic Books, Inc., 1968). © 1968 by Basic Books, Inc., Publishers. Reprinted by permission.

exactly what they prohibit. This is obviously a result of the great reticence of the law-making bodies and courts which have enacted and enforced these statutes to discuss openly the matter of homosexual acts. As Morris Ploscowe pointed out, judges are very uneasy when they have to deal with cases involving abnormal sexual behavior. One court wrote, "We regret that the importance of this question [whether oral-genital contact, fellatio, is a crime against nature] renders it necessary to soil the pages of our reports with a discussion of a subject so loathsome and disgusting as the one confronting us" (Ploscowe, 1962, p. 183). The statutes themselves share the same reticence to describe the actual acts which they are prohibiting. In many states they merely prohibit "the crime against nature with man or beast," or "sodomy with man or beast." In the following chapter we will discuss in some detail the phrase "crime against nature," for in order to understand this term properly it is necessary to examine the concept of nature itself. Here we wish to point out that these statutes, which derive from the time of Henry VIII, traditionally include only anal intercourse; they do not include oral-genital relations, either fellatio or cunnilingus. In prohibiting anal intercourse, the prohibition applies *equally to heterosexual and to homosexual acts.* Therefore, we have a curious paradox: the law which is supposed to prohibit homosexuality is in reality a law which prohibits only one kind of homosexual act and is written so that it covers a good deal of what goes on in the bedrooms of heterosexually married couples as well. Under this law, a man who performs anal intercourse with his wife is guilty of sodomy, whereas a homosexual pair in the next apartment who are performing mutual fellatio are not doing anything illegal.

As a result of these confusions, the court has not known quite what to do with oral-genital relations, and there have been a number of differing interpretations by various courts in different jurisdictions. Some courts have redefined the sodomy laws to include fellatio or cunnilingus, whereas others have explicitly stated that the statute cannot cover these acts. In 1897 a California court held that the sodomy statute did not include fellatio or cunnilingus; therefore a separate statute (California Penal Code, Section 288a) was enacted to outlaw oral copulation. It should be emphasized that this California statute prohibits heterosexual as well as homosexual oral-genital relations. This kind of legislative resolution of the problem has been adopted in a number of states.

The statutes against certain sexual acts do not, by any means, exhaust the laws which are used against homosexuals. There are a number of very vaguely worded misdemeanor statutes that can be used by the authorities against behavior occurring in public places, which account for the majority of arrests for homosexual behavior. In California, there are three main categories: outrageous conduct, lewd and lascivious behavior, and the vagrancy laws. An example of these is California Penal Code, Section 650½: "A person who willfully and wrongfully commits any act which seriously injures the person or property of another, or which seriously disturbs or endangers the public peace or health, or which openly outrages public decency . . . for which no other punishment is expressly prescribed by this code, is guilty of a misdemeanor." The vagrancy laws in the United States appear to be derivative from English laws which were originally enacted to keep farm workers at work on the land and therefore prohibited individuals from wandering about. These laws prohibiting wandering or vagrancy are so vague that they can cover a great deal of homosexual behavior in public places, providing the authorities wish to interpret them in this fashion. For example, homosexuals who cruise parks or rest rooms can be arrested under any number of statutes. If they are actually found committing a homosexual act, they can be arrested under the sodomy or oral copulation laws; if they are engaged in solicitation or in physical contact with the partner short of a sexual act, they can be arrested for outrageous conduct or lewd and lascivious behavior; and if they are merely loitering around a men's room in a manner which the police consider to be for the purpose of eventual homosexual contact, they might be arrested under the vagrancy laws.

AN ENCOUNTER WITH THE POLICE

Richard is a 35-year-old photographic equipment salesman who has the habit of visiting a well-known men's room in a public building not far from where he works. I interviewed him on the morning after he had been arrested. He said he was charged with indecent exposure. On the night of the arrest he said that he acted more aggressively in the men's room than he habitually does because, as he said, "I was unusually horny." He stayed in the john for 30 to 35 minutes. One of the men in the room was masturbating, but Richard was not interested in him because he did not find him sufficiently attractive. He went into one of the booths and was sexually excited by the sight of the foot and pants leg of the person in the stall next to him. This individual, whom he imagined was an attractive young man, was wearing Levis and tennis sneakers. He tried to attract him by foot-tapping, but did not seem to be able to get a response. Finally, he got up and went to the area near the urinals where he exposed his genitals to a young man who had just walked through the door. This did not bring any sign of sexual interest from the man, so Richard finally became discouraged and left the men's room. As soon as he walked out the door he was arrested by the individual to whom he had exposed himself, who was a police officer. Another individual, whom he had seen leaving the john at the time he originally came in—at least half an hour before—turned out to be the officer's associate.

This pattern of behavior is typical of that in which many homosexuals engage. Obviously, it is quite risky, and especially in view of the fact that Richard and his fellow john-cruisers usually have sex *right in the lavatory* after they make a successful contact, it is no surprise that a number of them run into legal trouble as a result of these practices. What is surprising, rather, is that many of them apparently engage in these practices for years *without* an arrest.

A STUDY OF HOMOSEXUAL LAW ENFORCEMENT

My own observations about the relationships between homosexuals and the law have been based on my interviews of individuals who have generally not had any difficulty with the law. Thus, while I had some general impressions about the problem, I was not able to support these with what might be regarded as sufficient empirical data. Fortunately, however, a very excellent study done by the staff of the U.C.L.A. *Law Review* was published in March, 1966, entitled *The Consenting Adult Homosexual and the Law: An Empirical Study of Enforcement and Administration in Los Angeles County.* Their documented conclusions fully support my own general observations on the problem. Since this report is a somewhat technical study of approximately 200 pages, it is not, I think, beside the point to make a brief summary of some of the more important findings here.

The most widely used provisions for punishing homosexuals are in the disorderly conduct statute, which is Section 647 of the California Penal Code: "Every person who commits any of the following acts shall be guilty of disorderly conduct, a misdemeanor: (a) Who solicits anyone to engage in or who in any public place or in any place open to the public or exposed to public view engages in lewd or dissolute conduct. . . . (d) Who loiters in or about any toilet open to the public for the purpose of engaging in or soliciting any lewd or lascivious or any unlawful act."

This law was enacted in 1961 after the California legislature repealed the old Section 647 which defined vagrancy. This was the result of many years of criticism directed at the old statute for being much too vague, not requiring proof of any criminal act, and providing the possibility that a conviction could be based on events which happened some time before the arrest was made. According to interviews with 15 law enforcement agencies in the Los Angeles area, it appears that approximately 90 to 95 percent of all homosexual arrests are for violations of California Penal Code, Section 647(a). Of perhaps even greater interest is that the large majority of these arrests result from solicitation of decoys by homosexuals.

What are decoys? Decoys are law enforcement officers who intentionally provide homosexuals with the opportunity to make a proscribed solicitation. They are, very often, young and attractive and dress in the kind of clothing which would appeal to the homosexual male, such as tight-fitting Levis. They usually work with a fellow officer who keeps out of sight, but appears on the scene when the arrest is made.

Most convictions under 647(a) are based exclusively on the arresting officer's allegation that the defendant has made an oral solicitation for a lewd act. Usually the decoy's partner cannot get close enough to witness either the solicitation or the occasionally lewd touching.

Homosexuals frequently accuse the police of engaging in "entrapment." Actually, in the use of decoys the law makes a fine distinction between entrapment and "enticement." The distinction hinges on whether the intent to commit the crime originated in the mind of the defendant or in the mind of the officer. If the defendant has a pre-existing criminal intent, the officer's intent is irrelevant and there is no entrapment. It is permissible to entice the suspect who is engaged in criminal activity or who has a predisposition to commit the crime. Illegal inducement occurs only when it would be sufficient to lead the innocent into a criminal act.

There are really two issues involved here. The first is: do the police sometimes, or often, engage in behavior which actually constitutes illegal entrapment? For example, do they lead the defendant on by conversation which cannot be documented in court and in which the ultimate legal disposition revolves around the defendant's word against the officer's? The second question is: even if police were *never* to engage in any illegal entrapment devices, is it desirable that police manpower be used for this kind of activity? The first question is an empirical one, and a good deal of debate can be generated by asking homosexuals and police agencies to state their differing views on the subject. Police agencies maintain that their officers are well trained to avoid entrapment, and homosexuals claim that the police, in fact, do entrap them all the time. Since I have no evidence on this matter and the U.C.L.A. study presents none, I shall leave it here, except to point out that the answer to question number one hinges in part on our attitude toward question number two. This is because, obviously, abuses occur in any social system and, thus, in any law enforcement system. Hence police, when on actual duty and regardless of their training, sometimes do things which they are not supposed to do. Consequently, if their work depends on a very fine distinction between entrapment and enticement, it is to be expected that on some occasions they overstep the bounds. The question then becomes: is the behavior which they are out to stop of such a nature that it requires (a) the manpower involved in order to apprehend the offenders, and (b) the loss of individual rights which might occur if law enforcement officers are overzealous and overstep the strict legal criteria which are supposed to govern their activity? On this matter, let me quote from the conclusions and recommendations of the U.C.L.A. *Law Review* study:

> Empirical data indicate that utilization of police manpower for decoy enforcement is not justified. Societal interests are infringed only when a solicitation to engage in a homosexual act creates a reasonable risk of offending public decency. The incidence of such solicitations is statistically insignificant. The majority of homosexual solicitations are made only if the other individual appears responsive and are ordinarily accomplished by quiet conversation and the use of gestures and signals having significance only to other homosexuals. Such unobtrusive solicitations do not involve an element of public outrage. The rare indiscriminate solicitations of the general public do not justify the commitment of police resources to suppress such behavior. It is accordingly recommended that operation

of suspected homosexuals by police decoys be eliminated and that routine patrol of bars, public toilets and parks by plainclothes and uniformed officers be utilized to suppress offensive homosexual conduct. (Pp. 795–96.)

I need only add that I am in complete agreement with the conclusions as stated. As a matter of fact, I would argue further that putting out as decoys police officers who are young, attractive, and seductively dressed, and who engage in enticing conversations with homosexuals, is itself an outrage to public decency. Since practically no homosexual arrests involve complaints from anyone, it is a very good question just why public funds are being expended for this purpose.

LOCATION OF ARRESTS

It is very clear from interviewing homosexuals that there is no real fear that they will be arrested for sexual behavior occurring in the privacy of their own homes. Those men in my sample who have been arrested have all been arrested in public places. The U.C.L.A. study found that of their 493 felony arrest cases, only 24 acts took place in a private residence. All others were in public or semi-public places. Two hundred seventy-four were in rest rooms, 108 were in cars, 18 in jails, 17 in parks, 15 in the baths, and 11 on the beach. Of the 475 misdemeanor arrests, only six occurred in private locales (homes, hotels, apartments). One hundred thirty-nine were in rest rooms, 98 were in cars, 83 in parks, 62 in theaters, 49 in bars, 14 in streets, and five in the baths (pp. 707–8). It is virtually impossible to arrest individuals for private homosexual activity without exceeding the search-and-seizure limitations. Thus there is no real attempt made to enforce against sexual relations between consenting adults in private.

It is very interesting in this regard to note that of the 493 felony arrests, 457 were for oral copulation. This is clearly because oral copulation is much the preferred activity in the kind of public place that would be visited by the police, particularly rest rooms, parks, theaters, and automobiles. Participants in anal intercourse usually want to engage in this activity where a bed is available, and thus they usually adjourn to private quarters. Fellatio, however, can occur without too much mechanical difficulty in any number of public places, such as the stall in a public toilet, the back of a movie theater, or in a park where one of the participants is standing up against a tree.

Homosexuals sometimes allege that police officers will arrest them and then either make a deal with the homosexual in which he has the choice of either orally copulating the officer or being arrested, or, more diabolically, will entice the homosexual into orally copulating him before revealing his identity, and then will arrest him anyway. This cannot, in general, be documented, but it is interesting to note that in 1927, in the case of People vs. Spaulding (81 Cal. App. 615, 254 Pac. 614), a conviction for oral copulation was affirmed, even though one of the arresting officers allowed himself to be orally copulated by the defendant before the arrest was made. Hence there is evidence that abuses do occur. However, the question is not really whether we can stop abuses by more efficient administration by law enforcement agencies, but, rather, whether the present system of decoy operation is basically justifiable. I think it is not.

While I agree with the recommendations of the U.C.L.A. *Law Review* on the subject of decoys, I do not question the necessity for patrolling of public places by uniformed police officers. Public sexual activity—both homosexual and heterosexual—in which there is very heavy petting, or genital display or contact, is simply too offensive to too many people to be permitted. There is no question that there are many homosexuals who engage in overt sexual behavior in public places. As a matter of fact, some of them will admit that they do so *because* the fact that they might be arrested is itself sexually exciting to them. There is simply no way of preventing these individuals from engaging in activity that would, under any circumstances conceivable at the present time, outrage passers-by. Hence it seems to me that the police cannot be blamed when an individual who has been caught sucking the penis of another man in a park or public lavatory finds himself in court. I have interviewed a sufficient number of adult male homosexuals who are highly intelligent and occupy respectable and even prestigious occupational positions to assert that a substantial portion of these men—though not the majority—cruise johns and parks and engage in sexual acts *in* the johns and parks. Thus, some kind of police surveillance of these public places would appear to be necessary.

THE HOMOSEXUAL IN COURT

After talking with homosexuals who have found their way into the arms of the law and after looking over the results of the Los Angeles study, I have the distinct impression that the participants in the courtroom drama, both the judge and the defendant, and in very many cases the prosecutor also, are all somewhat embarrassed by the whole affair and wish to get it over with as quickly as possible. Of the 493 felony arrests in the Los Angeles study, only 11 of the defendants asked for a jury trial. Clearly, the main desire of the defendant is to avoid publicity. This is very important to note, because the fact is that knowledge in the community that one is homosexual is much more damaging to a man's life than any sentence which is likely to be imposed by the court.

But what about the incredibly long prison sentences for sodomy that are written down in the statute books? Isn't it true that it is possible to get 10 or 15 years for a single homosexual act? Of course, it is *possible,* and these figures do appear in the statutes, but the Los Angeles study shows in very clear terms that this is not the kind of thing that happens. A comparison of the sentences imposed in the felony cases and in the misdemeanor cases shows quite similar outcomes. The defendant is fined, is given a jail sentence which is then immediately suspended, and is placed on probation. As a result of the 457 felony convictions, only three men went to prison. Furthermore, over 95 percent of the felony convictions are converted to misdemeanors by judicial action. This is possible in California because the judge can convert a conviction for oral copulation (though not for anal intercourse) from the status of a felony to a misdemeanor. As we noted, 457 of the 493 felony arrests were for oral copulation.

Hence, the likelihood of an individual who is arrested for a homosexual act going to prison is very low. What the defendant is really afraid of is that the people in the community will find out about his sexual proclivity, and it is this rather than the fear of legal penalties which makes him most upset when he is arrested. Probably he would prefer to have been arrested for income-tax evasion. So in this sense there is an analogy between present times and those times past when judges did not soil the court records with discussions of abominations against nature. The difference is that today, as Ploscowe noted from his own interviews, judges agree that homosexuality is not really deterrable. There are approximately 6,000,000 acts for every 20 convictions. The judges continue to feel that the *public* acts can be reduced by legal sanctions. Yet their feelings about middle-class men who are arrested in public places seem to be not generally indignation or a wish to punish, but rather, "Why did an intelligent man do a crazy thing like this?" The trials are handled without publicity, with great dispatch, and the sentences are very much lighter than a reading of the statute books would lead one to believe. . . . The judges realize that putting a homosexual into prison is like trying to cure obesity by incarceration in a candy shop. We know that there is a great deal of homosexual behavior in prison and that the incidence is much higher than in the general population, since prisons are by definition one-sexed environments. Also, insofar as the judges have adopted a psychiatric view of homosexuality they feel that the men they see before them are mentally ill and that no purpose would be served by sending them to prison. The only reason, then, for sending a man to prison would be if he is a danger to the community, and the consenting adult homosexual is clearly no danger to anyone.

REGISTRATION OF HOMOSEXUALS

In the State of California, any person convicted of anal intercourse, oral copulation, soliciting or engaging in lewd conduct, loitering to engage in or solicit lewd conduct, or indecent exposure must, within 30 days of his coming into the city or county in which he resides, register with the chief of police of the city, or the sheriff of the county. According to the Los Angeles study, law enforcement officials are very adamant in their desire to have homosexuals registered and are annoyed when the courts allow defendants to plead to a non-registerable lesser included offense. They say they favor registration because of their belief that homosexuals are prone to commit crimes against children and violent crimes (pp. 737–38).

It is a matter of empirical fact that the consenting adult homosexual who gets in trouble with the law is *not* prone to commit violent crimes or crimes against children. Homosexuals are no more prone to seduce young boys than are heterosexual males to seduce young girls. There is, indeed, an accent on youth in the male homosexual world, but this is hardly the same as pedophilia. The

age of the male homosexual's ideal love object would be somewhere in the early 20's, but this is the same, after all, for heterosexual men, as a perusal of *Playboy* magazine will readily reveal.
Those men who prefer young boys form a very special and distinct
group, just as do those who prefer young girls, and they are a very
small minority of the adult male population.

In 1965, the Institute for Sex Research at Indiana University
(founded by the late Alfred C. Kinsey) published a massive volume
on sex offenders (Gebhard *et al.*, 1965). Interviewers from the
Institute personally talked with over 1,500 men convicted for a
wide variety of sex offenses. It was necessary for them to subdivide
their sample into various categories.

> On a priori grounds it is evident that for the majority of sex of-
> fenses there are three independent variables: (1) whether the of-
> fense involved a member of the same or opposite sex, i.e., whether
> the offense was homosexual or heterosexual in nature, (2) whether
> the sexual activity was consented to (consensual) or whether force
> or threat was involved, and (3) whether the object of the offense
> was a child, minor, or adult. (P. 11.)

The authors then go on to make a very significant statement, one
which should forever dispose of the myth that homosexuals are
prone to violence: "These three variables combine to form 12 types
of sex offenses, which we reduced to nine because the use of force is
rare in homosexual activity" (p. 11). The use of violence is thus
seen to be a prerogative mainly of heterosexuals; it appears certain that homosexuals are actually *less* violent than heterosexuals.
This point is worth emphasizing because a number of writers, with
credentials that might indicate they ought to know better, have
tried to promulgate the idea that homosexuals are unusually violent.

In this study, one of the categories in which offenders were
classified was those who made homosexual overtures to, or had
sexual contact with, boys under 12. If we examine the kind of
sexual relations which went on between the two males involved,
I think we can form a theory as to why force or violence would
not be a factor. In 45 percent of the cases, masturbation was the
technique, and in 38 percent of the cases, fellatio was performed on
the boy. Anal intercourse occurred in only 4 percent of the cases.
Masturbation or fellation of a boy involves producing an erection
on his part and bringing him to orgasm. I think it is not difficult

to see that this can only be done with the cooperation of the boy. In other words, these sexual techniques are not susceptible to force or violence. One cannot bring a boy to orgasm unless he is a consenting partner. Thus, while it is theoretically possible that there could be a category for homosexual offenses which would be analogous to heterosexual rape, this would only apply to anal intercourse, and this is not a technique which seems to be of very much interest to those homosexual adults who have sexual relations with boys under 12. The kind of thing that they want to do when they get the boy alone is something which is not possible to achieve by the use of compulsion.

Again, we should emphasize that those adult males who engage in sexual acts with young boys represent only a small fraction of the total adult male homosexual population. As a matter of fact, as the Kinsey Institute study pointed out, those individuals who were arrested for sexual offenses with boys under 12 are the least oriented toward their own sex of all males arrested for homosexual acts. They are generally bisexual; of those who had sex with boys under 12, ultimately nearly two-thirds will marry. Of those who had sexual relations with boys between the ages of 12 and 15 slightly more than half will marry. Of those men who had sexual relations with males over age 16, about 40 percent will ultimately marry. In other words, it is fair to say that the younger the male partner of the sex offender, the more likely he is to be bisexual *rather than exclusively homosexual.* As this study shows, most adult males who have sexual relations with boys under 12 also show a relative predisposition toward heterosexual offenses with girls under 16. "In brief, most of them are interested sexually in young people, preferably but not necessarily male, and their minimum age limit is quite elastic and can be stretched to suit the immediate circumstances" (Gebhard *et al.,* p. 272). . . .

The point of this discussion is to show two things: first, because of the kind of sexual act they want to engage in, those adult males who have sexual relations with small boys would not be able to use force even if they wanted to, and there is no evidence that they want to. The second point is that the exclusive male homosexual is *not* the characteristic sex offender against children. He is much more likely to be a man who has been or will be married and who also has a tendency to want sex relations with young girls. The average adult male homosexual who goes to the gay bars or to the baths is no more likely to molest little boys than is the average male heterosexual likely to molest small girls. Hence the suggestion, made by police officials, that the consenting adult homosexual, who is arrested is a potential danger to children or is prone to violence is simply not true. While I do not wish to deny that there are indeed child molesters, it must be made clear that they are a separate class of persons and are not the men about whom this book is written.

HOMOSEXUAL LAW REFORM

In 1955 the American Law Institute and in 1957 the English Committee on Homosexual Offenses and Prostitution (known as the Wolfenden Committee after its chairman, Sir John Wolfenden) both concluded that homosexual behavior between consenting adults in private should be removed from the jurisdiction of the criminal law. In 1961 the State of Illinois revised its entire penal code, and since the recommendation of the American Law Institute was embodied in that Institute's Model Penal Code, the Illinois legislature simply adopted the recommendation. This was done without significant public debate, in contrast to the procedure adopted in England where the recommendation of the Wolfenden Committee took ten years to finally be enacted into law. These recommendations, and subsequent actions by parliamentary bodies, are landmarks in the history of Anglo-Saxon sexual jurisprudence. At the time of this writing, none of the other 49 American states has changed its statutes to incorporate this recommendation of the American Law Institute.

Before making any further remarks, I want to state quite clearly and emphatically that I am in complete agreement with these recommendations. Sexual relations which occur between consenting adults in private places are simply no business of the law, and the present statutes which cover them should be removed from the books. But it is important to ask this question: what effect would this change in the law have on current relations between homosexuals and the courts? The evidence presented in this chapter makes it quite clear what effect this change would have. *It would have no effect.* We have already seen that while an arrest will occasionally be made, under these statutes, in a private place, by and large these laws are already a dead letter. The vast majority of homosexual acts never come to the attention of law enforcement agencies, and the vast majority of those which do come to the

attention of these agencies do so because of activity which goes on
in public places. One of the reasons an august legal body, such as
the American Law Institute, can advocate such a change in the
law is that the legal profession already knows that these laws are
dead. It knows that they are not enforced to any significant extent,
and that they cannot be enforced because of the search-and-seizure
provisions of the Constitution. Nor would anybody want them enforced, because if they were fully enforced, literally millions of
citizens would be arrested, including a very large number of married couples.

My point is simply this: it is quite desirable that these laws be
removed from the books. They *are* unjust, and unjust statutes
should be abolished even if they are not currently being enforced.
The very existence on the statute books of unjust and unenforceable
laws is discrediting to our entire legal system, as a number of
writers have pointed out. But while this is a desirable aim, let it
be made clear that such a change would have no significant effect
on the life of the American male homosexual. The problems which
he faces are, basically, not legal problems. They are *social* problems of a much more subtle kind, and in order for these problems
to be solved, fundamental changes in the public attitude toward
homosexuality will have to occur. If the proposed changes in the
law are to represent a first step toward a significant change in
public attitude, then they are intelligently conceived. If, on the
other hand, they are to take place in the absence of any further
changes on the part of the larger society in its attitude toward
homosexuality, then they will accomplish nothing.

This view of homosexual law reform is not just a speculation.
It has been corroborated by a series of interviews I have conducted
with homosexuals who live or have lived in Chicago. Since Chicago
has been, for well over five years, free from laws prohibiting homosexual relations between consenting adults in private, we must ask
the question, has any significant change in the texture of homosexual life occurred in that city since the law was put into effect?
The answer to this question is, clearly, no. On the basis of this
special effort which I made to interview homosexuals in the city
of Chicago and those who formerly lived there but have come out
to the West Coast, I find that the general problems of the homosexual are exactly the same as they are in California. All the de-
scriptive and theoretical statements contained in this book apply
with the same degree of accuracy to Chicago as they do to San

Francisco or Los Angeles. As a matter of fact, one can go further: homosexuals in Chicago have had somewhat *more* trouble with the law *since the enactment of the new penal code* than have homosexuals in San Francisco during the same period of time. One of the leading baths in Chicago and several of the more prominent gay bars were raided during that period and a number of respectable citizens were arrested during these raids. This has not happened in San Francisco during this same time period. Of course, one can say that these raids and arrests were not made under the provisions of the law that we are talking about. But this is precisely the point. The police do not generally use the sodomy laws against homosexual behavior in private as a means for arresting homosexuals in any state. They use provisions such as disorderly conduct, lewd and lascivious behavior, solicitation, etc., for purposes of arrest. When individuals *are* charged with violation of the sodomy laws (or oral copulation laws) it is because of behavior in public places. Licenses of bars and baths can be revoked by state administrative agencies on the grounds that a number of such arrests have occurred on the premises. The statutes prohibiting homosexual acts between consenting adults in private are simply not an issue in such legal encounters. Hence we do not expect that their abolition would have any effect on homosexual life and, as we have seen in Chicago, it has had no effect.

Let us be clear about what we are doing. Homosexual law reform must mean something more than merely the abolition of the sodomy laws, or it will mean nothing. It must go further than simply the elimination of an unenforced law from the statute books, or else it will go nowhere. Its ultimate aim must be to bring about substantial changes in the larger society—changes which will go much further than those legal alterations recommended by the American Law Institute. If it does not do this, a movement for homosexual law reform will be as moribund as the law which it seeks to abolish.

SOLICITATION AND THE MODEL PENAL CODE

A sad fact about the American Law Institute's Model Penal Code is that it contains a provision which reads as follows:

Section 251.3. Loitering to Solicit Deviate Sexual Relations.
A person is guilty of a petty misdemeanor if he loiters in or near

any public place for the purpose of soliciting or being solicited to engage in deviate sexual relations.

It is not at all clear from reading the text of the Code whether or not "public place" includes bars. More importantly, this Section does not distinguish solicitation which would offend ordinary persons, who were in an ordinary "public place" in the usual course of their day, from harmless inquiry by one homosexual to another as to his interest in a mutual sexual experience.

Does it make any sense to "legalize" homosexual acts if it is still illegal for one man to invite another to participate in such a newly legalized act? One sometimes wonders to what extent the American Law Institute was really interested in changing the wrongness of the current attitude toward homosexuality or whether it was simply interested in getting an unenforced law off the books, in order to make the statutory provisions conform more to current police practice. If the latter was their aim, the Model Penal Code is written admirably. However, especially since we know that the sodomy laws are currently a dead letter, Section 251.3 perpetuates a very bad aspect of current policy, one that really counts heavily in the lives of very many homosexual men.

Joseph A. McCaffrey

Homosexuality: The Stereotype, the Real

—In this article the author argues that a gulf has been cre-
ated between heterosexuals and homosexuals and that part
of this is due to the mechanism of stereotyping, which can
effectively block any possible substantial understanding. In
addition, he argues that there must be a radical distinction
drawn between those characteristics that are essential to sex-
uality and those that are incidental.

Stereotyping has had an interesting history, much like war. Its mother is ignorance raped by prejudice, and there is no doubt about the progeny of such a union. Its swath through the annals of man is highly visible and so also its cursed effects. Several classical examples indicate the variety and resultant savagery of this particular mode of conceptualizing.

The first Christians came across stereotyping rather quickly (defenseless and anormal groups usually do). They were soon branded as having an assortment of vicious and traitorous characteristics. Thus, early Christian apologists were defending the Church against such charges as cannibalism, atheism, and incest. It is no wonder that so many Romans equated the lion's teeth with the gavel of justice. Stereotypes, after all, make reality a simpler commodity to deal with, because they frequently make the real unreal.

Stereotyping did not disappear with Christian domination over the remnants of the Roman Empire. In fact, this hardy strain continued to nourish itself on the various gyrations that the history of man was to go through. Some usages of stereotyping appear not to have been malicious *in intent* although they always have been malicious *in fact*. Probably the most egregious example of the stereotype, since it not only had the burden of ignorance and prejudice but also malice, was the Nazi stereotyping of the Jews. We are all too familiar with this horrendous perversity and the cynicism and brutality that marked its occurrence.

It is not difficult to show the illogical features of any usage of the stereotype. It is difficult, however, to show someone that he or she indulges in the use of the stereotype. And yet, if we examine ourselves we find that at least occasionally, at some points of our thinking processes, we fall prey to this mode of thinking.

A stereotype need not be of only one variety. This is especially true of the stereotyping of the homosexual, either as it is manufactured by the "straight" world or the "gay" world. It is important to realize that stereotyping frequently leads to counter-stereotyping. Thus, one tarnished image reflects still another. This dismal state of affairs complicates the question of the stereotype and its relationship to the homosexual.

There are two relatively standard heterosexual stereotypes of the male homosexual. (There are others, but these two will serve to indicate the problem involved.) I will call these: (1) the "loner-sneak" stereotype and (2) the "promiscuous-belligerent" stereotype. These are not mutually exclusive categorizations; thus, one can blend into the other and there can be a combination of sorts. In addition, the irony of this labeling, of course, is that one tends to stereotype the mind that stereotypes.

1. *The loner-sneak stereotype.* There is some basis in reality for this stereotype. Some straights (heterosexuals) seize on the partial fact that some homosexuals live in an extreme state of alienation, anxiety and loneliness. Because the condition of homosexuality is abnormal in terms of what the heterosexual believes the proper sexual response to be and, subsequently, because the idea of a man making love to another man is repulsive and "sick," it is only "logical" to assume that such a pervert should in fact feel alienated, anxious, desperate, and lonely—the ways of evil are punished. Also, if we feel that people should be a certain way we then conspire to engender in reality such an effect or seize upon such an effect if it is at all manifested, claiming that as a universal ingredient for any such condition. This is a "fulfilling prophecy" for the heterosexual who uses the loner-sneak stereotype.

Thus, the homosexual is depressed and lonely, or so goes the reasoning. He compulsively retreats into himself and away from all other meaningful human relations. His sole and perpetual pursuit is the orgasm, a momentary physical satisfaction which relieves the tremendous emptiness of his life. His life is built around the eternally destructive antagonism of these two forces, i.e., loneliness and the other-directed although contextually bankrupt orgasm. This ugly picture can be enhanced further by adding various details to it, e.g., the sterile one-room lodgings; the greasy and insipid meals at the local hub of despair; the possible dependency on alcohol or perhaps drugs; the regular voyeuristic fare of pictures of men's genitals and the imaginary masturbatory and seductive rummagings of a man incapable of breaking the chains that cut and bind him; and finally, for now, the pronounced and omnipresent temptation to suicide that creates havoc in the castrated "self" that is the homosexual.

An exaggeration? I suggest not, nor is the picture complete yet. He is the man who stalks public toilets and gives the despairing and beseeching look to those unfortunate or compassionate enough to understand eyes. He sits in toilet stalls and signals with his feet, hoping for someone as desperate as he who will reach out to him. The face is meaningless, frequently it is not even seen; what counts is the delivery system—the mechanism, the cherished and hopefully grandiose penis. He is the man who steals "love." One further color, however, must be added to this already bizarre portrait. He persistently preys on the unsuspecting, not the adult, but the child or young man. He is sometimes spotted on the playground area with candy, pornographic material, or perhaps drugs. A look of childlike anticipation conceals the furtiveness of this despicable and sordid activity. This man proselytizes others to enter into his life of despair, a Satanic exercise to say the least—a depraved sneak to say more.

Does the stereotype fit? Yes—there probably are homosexuals who fit this description, not completely one would hope, but close enough to make one shudder. But, there are many, many "straights" who use this loner-sneak model as their primary vehicle of analysis and as their "covering philosophy" in their confrontation with homosexuals, *few of whom could be said to conform to this stereotype.* From their initial repulsion and further cultural reinforcement the rest flows easily and smoothly. One wonders whose "soul," however, is really lost in this warped vision of the homosexual—

the stereotyper or the stereotyped, but that is another question for another time. This belief pattern is not held by all, however, some of whom are far more attached to the promiscuous-belligerent stereotype. Only some straights are sophisticated enough to accept more than one stereotype—i.e., that homosexuals can be either one of the two, or a combination of them, or possess characteristics not even mentioned here.

2. *The promiscuous-belligerent stereotype.* Everyone knows, or so goes the reasoning, that homosexuals are flighty and superficial people. There have been many nationally publicized magazine and newspaper articles that have attested to the "fact" that homosexuals apparently cannot have sustained relations (a "marriage" or an "affair"). This inability is due to the fact that they are immoral, rootless, and intemperate perverts. No wonder homosexuals are promiscuous, flitting from one sex delivery system to another, perhaps questing for an unreachable goal—the eternal union that will bring everlasting happiness.

This promiscuity is marked with cynicism and hatred for the sex partner. The hatred comes from the constant reminder of the ever-changing penis, which proves that the homosexual has unstable, useless, and incoherent wishes. Since male identification is not really possible for these men (if they are at all honest), it is an only too familiar occurrence, the reasoning continues, to see a strong feminine identification indicated by such follies as limp wrists, lisping, mincing, and various other signs that spell out their caricatured and absurd version of how a woman acts. In addition, they are frequently known by their professions; thus, it is no secret that they are often hair stylists, interior decorators, fashion designers, stage actors, male nurses, artists, and also serve in various other professions that need the "feminine touch." Here, again, we see the crippling progress of this argument quickly turning into a solid and deadly stereotype.

This attack on the integrity and autonomy of the homosexual personality is not nearly complete. To the heterosexual, probably the most galling characteristic of the promiscuous types is that they also have a chip on their shoulder: they are belligerent. This stereotype is obviously influenced by the increasingly vocal and ever-heightened visibility of the gay world and its erratic stepchild the Gay Liberation Front. Homosexuals weren't always belligerent, but they have changed, and so has the dialectical nature of stereotyping —that ever-shifting instrument that continually evolves and thus survives. Accordingly, with political and social activism on the part of a group already intensely hated, there is a head-on confrontation.

These homosexuals flaunt their perversion. Their entire life style revolves around sex and you had better beware when in their company since seduction of a straight is a prime and critical ego booster. These homosexuals are self-protective and frequently, when in a position of power (such as employment administrator), rule out the qualified heterosexual if a homosexual is also available. They are selfish, narcissistic, and grossly unfair. In fact, they parade their sickness with a belligerence and audacity that would put a matador to shame. They say that their own life style is equal, if not superior, to the heterosexual's and have taken to the political arena to force their way of life upon an unsuspecting majority by asking for the legalization of their heinous crimes against nature. These promiscuous and belligerent homosexuals should be seen as what they are—dangerous and destructive members of a society already substantially weakened by its unthinking and odious capitulation to all manners and varieties of vice.

This stereotype doesn't end here. But it is developed enough to indicate the extent to which a stereotype can be taken. Again, there probably are some homosexuals who do come fairly close to this vivid picture. That they exist in the numbers that some heterosexual stereotypers indicate is surely untrue and without doubt reflects a wish to break down undesirable realities into easily digestible tablets.

So far, then, we have seen the gnarled products of two popular homosexual stereotypes. Two other phenomena should be included. These can be called the prostereotype and the counterstereotype. The former is what some *homosexuals* portray as the typical homosexual in contrast to that entertained by the straight world; the latter is one rather common stereotype held by some homosexuals concerning the "typical straight." We shall call these respectively: (1) the gifted-liberated stereotype, and (2) the brute-fool stereotype.

1. *The gifted-liberated stereotype.* It is said, or known, that such diverse personalities as Plato, Alexander the Great, Julius Caesar, Francis Bacon, William Shakespeare, Michelangelo, Leonardo Da Vinci, Oscar Wilde, André Gide, Jean Genet, and countless others who have helped create the history of mankind have been homosexuals. Some advocates of the homosexual life don't view this with the slightest surprise. It is well known, the reasoning goes, that homosexuals are artistic and gifted souls, far more involved in the

arts than any statistical calculation would indicate. Witness the plaintive cries of Broadway critics that male-female relationships have had their clearest and frequently most damaging expression set forth by homosexuals. This is because talent, if allowed to express itself on an open and competitive market, will reach the top of the heap. The homosexual, by the fact of his condition and due to his special insights, transcends the majority of mankind and reaches limits of artistic and related expression granted to none but a few heterosexuals. The homosexual occupies a privileged situation which allows him to possess experiences and knowledge that straights just cannot have and will not ever have.

But this self-portrait is still sketchy. There is also the concept of liberation. The liberation of the homosexual personality takes place on many fronts, sex and attitudes toward sex being only some of them, though of immense importance in the liberation process. Homosexual relationships have a built-in protection against those pursuits that heterosexuals have wasted much energy upon: marriage, children, longevity, property, divorce, and alimony. All of these tend to militate against true and honest sexual expression, which, by its nature (because desire and its fulfillment are usually equivalent to sexual happiness), is not limited to one partner nor must it be distorted by time dimensions. In other words, the homosexual is not burdened beyond the natural capacity of man. Thus he can function as a free sexual agent and take from life and the goodness of others all that there is to be had, and he returns it in like dimensions. He enjoys a fuller existence than the straight; for this reason and also because he is part of a minority group that will no longer bow to the heterosexual party line, he is surely a liberated individual. Again, and this cannot be emphasized enough, some homosexuals do in fact enjoy a creative existence far beyond that of most men, and some do exist in a framework of sexual liberation as defined above. But to mistake this sometimes coincidental factor as a standard is to blunder as badly as those who have presented the other vicious and nonsensical stereotypes we have seen.

2. *The brute-fool stereotype.* For one reason or another, heterosexuals have dominated the development of Western civilization—perhaps this is why civilization has turned out as it has, some homosexuals reason. After all, when men hate each other instead of loving each other, war, social evils, and injustice become common commodities. This hate is carried over into the war between the

sexes where brutish and vulgar attitudes are too often the only way heterosexual men are capable of relating to women. Only now are women seriously beginning to see how oppressed they have been through the centuries. The heterosexual man is crude and dominated by the real center of a woman's power (since women are not allowed to function as equals)—that which lies between her legs. Heterosexuals know this and tend to hate the very thing that draws them. For this reason, and others, he retaliates with harshness and brutality. He has neither respect nor love for the opposite sex—a situation where manipulation and disdain is the primary driving force.

The woman's sexuality is what captures the male, and because he falls for this tender trap he is also made a supreme fool. He is imprisoned in the greatest dungeon of all—marriage and all the consequences that follow from it. Heterosexuals from then on are forced to lead a life of petty nuisances and, if extramarital relations are attempted, a life of lies.

It is because of this and the extreme jealousy that heterosexuals have of liberated homosexuals that there are harsh laws and stupid, biased attitudes concerning the homosexual. It is no wonder, then, that heterosexuals should be more pitied than hated by the homosexual. It is surprising that the heterosexual doesn't see what is taking place and defect to a life style and mode of sex not only more becoming to the male but also much more rewarding in terms of self-liberation.

This is just one of an array of stereotypes that some homosexuals harbor. And it is true that some heterosexual men do and can relate to women only with vulgarity and brutishness and that this way of relating is dominated by a hatred for women. Also, marriage can be an entrapping and ugly situation that sometimes leaves the husband feeling the fool and slave—no doubt of this. That it is ascribed as a standard by some homosexuals indicates the tension between the homosexual and heterosexual and the almost total breakdown in one's perception of the other.

Thus, we stand in an arena of misunderstanding and asinine hatred. Stereotyping renders its services to any civilization or nation ready to accept them. America has been all too willing. However, there is little to be gained in ascertaining who is the more guilty and who is the less guilty—the heterosexual or the homosexual. There is much to be gained, however, when all of those responsible look squarely at the results of their endeavors and see the essential insanity of stereotyping.

So, I have tried to present these stereotypes in as sharp and, perhaps, as brazen a fashion as possible. They can be far more subtle, but harmful nonetheless, especially since these stereotypes speak to some aspect of reality, though in exaggerated and oversimplified form.

Finally, stereotypy blocks or closes off alternatives in the mind, thus ruining the chance for any deep understanding of the other person. The result is animosity, lack of caring, and the closing off of avenues to the other person, avenues which do not and need not include the sexual. The essential in man is sexuality and not its form of expression whether homosexual, heterosexual, or bisexual. Making love to another man is incidental to the *capacity for making love*. It should be endowed with those other capacities which are inextricably bound up with it. Thus the capacities for love, caring, and fellowship, among others, blend and create the essential in man—the human. Misuse of the capacity for love is not a function of the sex of the other person but depends on how the other is approached—whether human meets human, nonhuman meets human, or nonhuman meets nonhuman. A solution to the moral, psychological, pastoral, and legal problems of the homosexual cannot be had by consulting Kinsey or, worse still, consulting the popular stereotypes of the day, whether conjured up by the homosexual or the heterosexual. Sexuality grants no special privileges to any of us except one—it enables us to receive the call as to what we are: human beings. A rejection of that call is a violation of our nature or essence.

Evelyn Hooker, Chairman

Final Report of the Task Force on Homosexuality

—In 1954 the British Government appointed a committee to report on the questions of homosexuality and prostitution. The subsequently far-reaching document of this committee became known as the Wolfenden Report *(1957). Thirteen years later, the Director of the National Institute of Mental Health appointed a committee to do very much the same thing in the U.S.A. on the question of homosexuality. Like the British report, this report also has had some far-reaching effects and may eventually serve as a springboard for some major changes in attitude toward homosexuality on the part of the American people and their institutions.*

In September 1967, a Task Force on Homosexuality was appointed by Dr. Stanley F. Yolles, Director of the National Institute of Mental Health. This group consisted of outstanding behavioral, medical, social and legal scientists. . . . Each member has had extensive research and study experience in the areas of sexuality and sexual deviation. The mandate of the Task Force was to review carefully the current state of knowledge regarding homosexuality in its mental health aspects and to make recommendations for Institute programming in this area. . . .

The members of the Task Force were unanimous in their support of the recommendations made. . . . . [However] three members of the Task Force, Drs. Ford, Riecken and Wallace expressed reservations with respect to the recommendations on social policy. . . .

From *Final Report of the Task Force on Homosexuality: National Institute of Mental Health,* Evelyn Hooker, Chairman. (Bethesda, Maryland: N.I.M.H., 1969).

INTRODUCTION

Human sexuality encompasses a broad range of behavior within which lie both the exclusive heterosexual and the exclusive and confirmed homosexual. Between these two exclusive extremes, there are individuals in whom a heterosexual preference is predominant but who will, under certain circumstances (such as imprisonment) become involved in homosexual behavior, and persons whose main erotic attraction is to members of their own sex but who will occasionally seek out heterosexual experiences. The internal and social forces motivating sexual behavior are likewise varied, and may range from strivings for warmth and closeness to the expression of anger and aggression. Homosexuality is not a unitary phenomenon, but rather represents a variety of phenomena which take in a wide spectrum of overt behaviors and psychological experiences. Homosexual individuals can be found in all walks of life, at all socioeconomic levels, among all cultural groups within American society, and in rural as well as urban areas. Contrary to the frequently held notion that all homosexuals are alike, they are in fact very heterogeneous.

Homosexual individuals vary widely in terms of their emotional and social adjustments. Some persons who engage in homosexual behavior function well in everyday life; others are severely maladjusted or disturbed in their functioning. There are those whose total life is dominated by homosexual impulses and those whose sexual behavior is just one component in their total life experience.

There also is wide diversity among homosexual individuals in terms of their sense of responsibility. The individual who engages in sexual behavior only with another consenting adult in private must be viewed differently from the one whose sexual behavior is with children and adolescents or who otherwise violates public decency.

Homosexuality presents a major problem for our society largely because of the amount of injustice and suffering entailed in it not only for the homosexual but also for those concerned about him. Although estimates of the prevalence of homosexuality are only tentatively established, it is believed that there are currently at least three or four million adults in the United States who are predominantly homosexual and many more individuals in whose lives homosexual tendencies or behavior play a significant role. Individual homosexuals suffer in being isolated from much of society and from the fact that they live in a culture in which homosexuality is considered maladaptive and opprobrious. Their families suffer in feeling responsible and in adjusting to the problem. Society at large inevitably loses in a number of ways—loss of manpower, economic costs, human costs, etc. For these reasons (among others), efforts must be made at both the individual and social levels to deal with the problems associated with homosexuality.

RECOMMENDATIONS

The detailed recommendations which follow are subsumed under the more general recommendation for the establishment of an NIMH Center for the Study of Sexual Behavior. The functions of this Center would include involvement in programs concerned with:

1. Research
2. Training and Education
3. Prevention
4. Treatment
5. Social Policy

It is the consensus of this Task Force that for the development of a meaningful program it is essential that the study of homosexuality be placed within the context of the study of the broad range of sexuality, both normal and deviant. It is therefore strongly recommended that there be established within NIMH a Center for the Study of Sexual Behavior. We urge that the program of the Center be comprehensive so as to include research, training, demonstration and services. It should be a multidisciplinary effort with representation from relevant disciplines and professions. . . .

Dissemination of current knowledge in the field would be a further function of the Center. . . . Among prime targets toward which to direct information would be community mental health centers, inasmuch as they are appropriate agencies to disseminate educational materials to schools, civic groups, etc., and they can reach children and adolescents and their families at periods which are critical in psychosexual maturation. Work with other health, welfare, educational, legal and other organizations (public and private) would also be essential. Under NIMH sponsorship, effective programs (such as workshops) could be launched which would serve to orient key personnel to effective means for dealing with the social and individual problems associated with sexual behavior and development.

In summary, some of the primary goals of the NIMH Center for Study of Sexual Behavior should be to develop knowledge, generate and disseminate information, mollify taboos and myths, provide rational bases for intervention, and provide data to policymakers for use in their efforts to frame rational social policy. Some of the specific recommendations to follow will be specific to sexual deviation, while others will relate to the general area of sexuality.

1. *Research*

We recommend that basic and applied research activities in the area of homosexuality be given high priority and that the following issues, here briefly outlined and presented roughly in order of priority, are most urgently in need of investigation:

(A) *Taxonomy* of homosexual experiences and behavior with special emphasis on the development of better sampling methods to cover the total range of homosexual phenomena. This range should include homosexual individuals who do not come into contact with medical, legal or other social control or treatment sources and who therefore have been least studied.

(B) *Incidence and epidemiology* of homosexual experience and behavior. Present estimates are based on data which are inadequate and out of date. Because it is widely believed that the incidence of homosexuality is related to sociocultural factors, samplings should include studies of demographically differentiated sub-groups, such as a range of ethnic and income groups.

(C) *Review of the procedures employed by various control agencies* (police, courts, probation officers, etc.) in dealing with homosexual individuals. Laws and regulations against homosexual behavior are the major official means by which society attempts to control it. We know relatively little about their actual operation or effects. There is evidence to indicate that entrapment is not uncommon, that existing laws are selectively enforced and that serious injustice often results. The possible abridgement of civil rights in cases involving homosexuality should be reviewed. These processes should be studied to estimate their effectiveness in decreasing overt manifestations of homosexuality, as well as their direct and indirect effects on homosexuals and on society.

(D) *Research on the job history and occupational performance* of homosexuals, especially of non-patient populations. The effects of homosexuality on working relationships with fellow employees should also be evaluated. In addition, the impact of discriminatory employment practices on the occupational aspirations and achievement of homosexuals should be investigated.

(E) *Studies of cultural factors in homosexuality in the United States.* Investigations are needed of the institutionalized system of values and patterns of behavior concerning sex and the relation of these values to social and economic factors. The effects of the portrayal of homosexual behavior, attitudes and values in literature and drama, and the public's responses to such portrayal are in need of study. The taboo on homosexuality has a variety of functions linking it not only with values concerning heterosexual behavior, but also with other aspects of the social system, and these functions may directly include both the maintenance of a certain level of homosexuality and of the social arrangements of homosexuals.

(F) *Investigation of informational and attitudinal patterns* that provide the social climate within which homosexuality develops and exists. This should include studies of social mores and value systems, communication media, and attitudes of various agencies of social influence and control, including peer groups, parents, judges, probation officers, clergy, medical doctors and police.

(G) *Cross-cultural studies* to clarify the significance of family structure, role differentiation, child training, economic organization, values, religion, and ideology in relation to sex and sexual deviation. These should also include studies across different cultures as well as among different segments of society in terms of social class, ethnicity, age, education, etc.

(H) *Comparative studies of male and female homosexuality* in relation to all of the problems cited above. That so few studies of female homosexuals have been carried out is of concern because this is a significant population in terms of numbers alone and one which merits better understanding. In addition, the striking differences in societal attitudes toward male and female homosexuals must inevitably result in different adaptational patterns that ought to be studied.

(I) *Studies of homosexual social organizations* including the networks of one-to-one relationships and clique structures, as well as collective patterns within formal and informal social organizations.

These relationships and groups play an important role in the adult socialization of homosexuals and in shaping and influencing homosexual careers and life patterns.

(J) *Studies of family dynamics and complications.* Special emphasis should be placed on some of the least studied aspects of the problem, especially non-patient populations, the bisexual spouse, the effects on the family of having a homosexual member, etc.

(K) *Biologic and genetic factors* possibly related to the development of sexual behavior are seriously in need of further research. Although animal studies in this area show promise, the study of larger samples and more careful attention to research design is required to obtain meaningful answers at the human level.

(L) *Studies of personality factors in homosexuality* focusing on intrapsychic elements, and personality dimensions that characterize homosexual, in contrast to non-homosexual individuals.

(M) *Problems of etiology and determinants* of homosexuality must be an ultimate concern. Present evidence is inconclusive, although it does suggest that homosexuality has multiple etiologic roots. Progress in this complex area will depend in large part on the results of studies outlined in the sections above.

2. Training and Education

We recommend that education and training programs be provided in the following areas, with all approaches being of great immediate importance.

(A) *Training of mental health professionals* in the area of human sexuality. Such training is currently woefully inadequate, with poor transmission of currently available information and frequent fragmentation of training efforts. . . .

(B) *Broader programs in sex education.* Information about homosexuality should be included in such programs in the schools as well as for the public at large. Efforts should also be made to educate the general public because among many segments of the population homosexuality remains a taboo topic and an area in which much misinformation abounds. As such, it can create pervasive anxieties as well as condemnatory and punitive attitudes which could be prevented or alleviated if valid information about homosexuality were disseminated.

(C) Special training for *all law enforcement personnel* who come in contact with homosexual issues or problems, and for *guidance and caretaking personnel.* Target groups for such training should include teachers, ministers, lawyers, health educators, and youth group counselors. Homosexuality is often viewed with either disgust or anxiety, emotions which interfere with an objective understanding of the problem. Special efforts should be made to modify these attitudes. . . .

(D) *Collection and dissemination of information on sexuality.* A "clearinghouse for sex information" should be established within the National Clearinghouse for Mental Health Information to make available knowledge now widely scattered in many professional areas and journals.

3. Prevention

For most workers in the field, the prevention of the development of a homosexual orientation in an individual child or adolescent is seen as one of the most important goals. In light of this, intensive effort should be made to understand better the factors involved in effective primary prevention. It is obvious that research in a number of the areas described above, including parental relationships, childhood peer activities, endocrine, genetic and biological elements, effects of early trauma, the role of social class mores, and developmental crises, will have a direct bearing on the design of preventive programs.

4. Treatment

The NIMH Center would be concerned with the dissemination of information relating to various aspects of the treatment process. At the outset it is important to distinguish between an individual's "homosexuality" and his overall level of functioning and discomfort.

In general, the goal of treatment for homosexual patients as for others must be the decrease of discomfort and increase in productive functioning.

(A) Expansions of efforts to develop *new therapies* and to *improve the efficiency of current therapeutic procedures* (relating both directly to change in sexual orientation and to adaptation in general) which are often very time-consuming and limited in their effectiveness.

(B) Support of *treatment centers* (for example, community mental health centers and student health centers) in order to enable them to render service to a greater number of persons with homosexual problems and their families. With respect to change in homosexual orientation, the current literature suggests that perhaps one-fifth of those exclusively homosexual individuals who present themselves for treatment are enabled to achieve some heterosexual interests and competence if they are motivated to do so; that a much higher percentage (perhaps 50%) of predominantly homosexual persons having some heterosexual orientation and who present themselves for treatment can be helped to become predominantly heterosexual; but that in court-referred or parent-referred cases where motivation to change is often lacking and cannot be engendered, treatment is much less successful.

While it cannot be assumed that a large proportion of homosexuals will go into treatment (or will have the facilities available should they wish treatment), the Task Force endorses efforts directed toward the treatment for some individuals, especially adolescents and bisexuals. We consider it important to counteract the sense of hopelessness and inevitability prevalent among many homosexuals, and to improve the insufficiency of treatment facilities. We hope and expect that as treatment methods improve and expand, more and more persons will seek treatment voluntarily. For those whose behavior is presently held to require the application of legal sanctions, the Task Force urges that preference be given to rehabilitation, rather than imprisonment.

One specific purpose of all these efforts would be to help reduce the taboo against asking for help for sexual problems. Anxiety produced by this taboo now discourages many individuals from seeking help and frequently prevents mental heath professionals from giving effective help.

A point which needs continual re-emphasis is the need for careful evaluation of all therapeutic programs. It is essential from both practical and scientific points of view to have studies of validity and effectiveness an integral part of these programs from their very beginning.

5. Social Policy

Although recommendations relating to social policies are not the primary focus of the activities of NIMH, nonetheless much of the Institute's function in many areas serves to provide support for researches and analyses which in themselves will be of use to policymakers in the framing of rational and socially beneficial measures.

Much of the homosexuality research that is needed relates directly to issues of public policy and for this reason we urge that policy-related research be an important component of the Center's work. Some of the areas of investigation mentioned above (under Research)—particularly taxonomy, incidence and epidemiology, informational and attitudinal patterns, processes used by various control agencies, and job histories and occupational performances of homosexuals—are especially pertinent from this standpoint.

Systematic studies in these areas will fill many of the gaps in our present knowledge of homosexuality and may well prove to have a direct bearing on the future formulation of specific public policy measures. Meanwhile, however, public policies are in force and the majority of this Task Force considers that it would be remiss if it did not express its serious misgivings about certain policy measures currently employed with respect to homosexual behavior. We believe that most professionals working in this area—on the basis of their collective research and clinical experience and the present overall knowledge of the subject—are strongly convinced that the extreme opprobrium that our society has attached to homosexual behavior, by way of criminal statutes and restrictive employment practices, has done more social harm than good and goes beyond what is necessary for the maintenance of public order and human decency. Accordingly, these recommendations are offered with the full awareness that findings from further research must provide a more firm basis for continuing critical re-evaluation of policy measures in this area.

Changes in social policy can be discussed under two headings, namely *legal changes* and *changes in employment policies and practices*.

(A) *Legal changes.* Although many people continue to regard homosexual activities with repugnance, there is evidence that public attitudes are changing. Discreet homosexuality, together with many other aspects of human sexual behavior, is being recognized more and more as the private business of the individual rather than a subject for public regulation through statute. Many homosexuals are good citizens, holding regular jobs and leading productive lives. The existence of legal penalties relating to homosexual acts means that the mental health problems of homosexuals are exacerbated by the need for concealment and the emotional stresses arising from this need and from the opprobrium of being in violation of the law. On the other hand, there is no evidence suggesting that legal penalties are effective in preventing or reducing the incidence of homosexual acts in private between consenting adults. In the

United States such persons are so seldom brought to trial that to all intents and purposes such laws are dead letters, and their repeal would merely officially confirm a situation that already exists. It should be emphasized that the repeal of such laws would in no way affect existing legal sanctions against sexual behavior which violates public decency or involves the seduction of minors, whether such behavior be homosexual or heterosexual. A number of eminent bodies—the British Wolfenden Commission, the Ninth International Congress on Criminal Law, and the American Law Institute in its Model Penal Code have all recommended, after extensive studies, that statutes covering sexual acts be recast in such a way as to remove legal penalties against acts in private among consenting adults. A majority of this Task Force accepts and concurs with this recommendation and urges that the NIMH support ongoing studies of the legal and societal implications of such a change with respect to both homosexual and heterosexual behavior.

We believe that such a change would reduce the emotional stresses upon the parties involved and thereby contribute to an improvement in their mental health. Furthermore, such a change in the law would also encourage revisions in certain governmental regulations which now make homosexual acts a bar to employment or a cause for dismissal. By helping thereby to remove a source of anxiety over being discovered, this would make an indirect contribution to the mental health of the homosexual population. It would also serve to reduce the possibilities for blackmail, which are a constant hazard to the homosexual under present conditions. To be sure, full equality in employment, full security and full acceptance by the society for homosexuals will not be achieved by changes in the law alone, but such changes may help to facilitate the recasting of public attitudes that is ultimately needed.

(B) *Employment Policies and Practices.* It is recommended that there be a reassessment of current employment practices and policy relating to the employment of homosexual individuals with a view toward making needed changes. Discrimination in employment can lead to economic disenfranchisement, thus engendering anxiety and frustrating legitimate achievement motivation.

Present employment policies generally deal with the homosexual individual as if homosexuality were a specific and homogeneous category of behavior, and tend to ignore the wide range of variation that exists. We recognize that some homosexuals, like some heterosexuals, may be unsuitable employees in some situations because they do not exercise reasonable control over their sexual tendencies or activities. Second, in highly sensitive positions, the possibility that a homosexual may be subject to blackmail or undue influence may affect the suitability of a homosexual individual for such employment, although changes in our present laws concerning homosexuality may ultimately eliminate this.

CONCLUSION

In conclusion, we wish to stress once more the fact that the mental health implications related to healthy and aberrant sexual behavior are enormous. Many people believe that we are currently undergoing a revolution in sexual mores and behaviors. The interest on the part of NIMH in the study of sexual behavior is both timely and in the best tradition of its basic concern with improving the mental health of the nation.

MEMBERS OF THE TASK FORCE:

Evelyn Hooker, Chairman

Judd Marmor

Edward Auer

David L. Bazelon*

Clelland Ford

Jerome D. Frank

Paul Gebhard

Seward Hiltner

Robert Katz

John Money

Morris Ploscowe

Henry W. Riecken

Edwin M. Schur

Anthony F. C. Wallace

Stanton Wheeler

* Resigned, June 3, 1969.

Carl Wittman

Refugees from Amerika: A Gay Manifesto

> —*Wittman's persuasive article has been referred to by some as the bible of the Gay Liberation Movement. The author carefully solidifies his argument that the homosexual is a viciously persecuted individual. In effect, this piece constitutes an elementary "bill of rights" for homosexuals—both male and female.*

San Francisco is a refugee camp for homosexuals. We have fled here from every part of the nation, and like refugees elsewhere, we came not because it is so great here, but because it was so bad there. By the tens of thousands, we fled small towns where to be ourselves would endanger our jobs and any hope of a decent life; we have fled from blackmailing cops, from families who disowned or "tolerated" us; we have been drummed out of the armed services, thrown out of schools, fired from jobs, beaten by punks and policemen.

And we have formed a ghetto, out of self protection. It is a ghetto, rather than a free territory, because it is still theirs. Straight cops patrol us, straight legislators make our laws, straight employers keep us in line, straight money exploits us. And we have pretended everything is OK, because we haven't been able to see how to change it—we've been afraid.

From *San Francisco Free Press* (December 22–January 7, 1970).

In the past year, there has been an awakening of gay liberation ideas and energy. How it began we don't know: perhaps we were inspired by black people and their liberation movement; we learned how to stop pretending from the hip revolution. Amerika in all its ugliness has surfaced with the war and our national leaders. And we are revulsed by the quality of our ghetto life.

Where once there was frustration, alienation, and cynicism, there are new traits among liberated gays: we are full of love for each other and are showing it; we are full of anger at what has been done to us. And as we recall all the self-censorship and repression for so many years, a reservoir of tears pours out of our eyes. And we are euphoric, high, with the initial flourish of a movement.

We want to make ourselves clear; our first job is to liberate ourselves, and that means clearing our heads of the garbage that's been poured into them. This pamphlet is an attempt at raising a number of issues, and present some ideas to replace the old ones. It is primarily for ourselves—a starting point for discussion. If straight people of good will find it useful in understanding what gay liberation is about, so much the better.

It should also be clear that these ideas reflect the perspective of one person, and are determined not only by my homosexuality, but my being white, male, and middle class. It is my individual consciousness. Our group consciousness will evolve as we get ourselves together—we are only at the beginning.

I. ON ORIENTATION

1. WHAT HOMOSEXUALITY IS: Nature leaves undefined the object of sexual desire. The gender of that object has been imposed socially. Humans originally put a taboo on homosexuality because they needed every bit of energy to produce and raise children— survival of the species was a priority. With overpopulation and technological change, that taboo is absurd and continues only to exploit us and enslave us.

As kids, we refused to capitulate to demands that we smother our feeling toward each other. Somewhere we found the strength to resist being indoctrinated, and we should count that among our assets. We have to realize that our loving each other is a good thing, not an unfortunate thing, and that we have a lot to teach straights about sex, love, strength, and resistance.

Homosexuality is NOT a lot of things. It is not a makeshift in the absence of the opposite sex; it is not hatred or rejection of the opposite sex; it is genetic; it is not the result of broken homes (except inasmuch as we could see the sham of American marriage). HOMOSEXUALITY IS THE CAPACITY TO LOVE SOMEONE OF THE SAME SEX.

2. BISEXUALITY: Bisexuality is good; it is the capacity to love people of either sex. The reason so few of us are bisexual is because society made such a big stink about homosexuality that we got forced into seeing ourselves as either straight or nonstraight. Also, many gays got turned off to the ways men are supposed to relate to women and vice-versa, which is pretty fucked up. Gays will begin to get turned onto women when 1) it's something that we do because we want to, and not because we should; 2) when women's liberation has changed the nature of heterosexual relationships.

We continue to call ourselves homosexual, rather than bisexual, even if we do make it with the opposite sex also, because saying "Oh, I'm Bi" is a cop out for a gay. We get told it's ok to sleep with guys as long as we sleep with women, too, and that's still putting homosexuality down. We'll be gay until everyone has forgotten that it's an issue. Then we'll begin to be complete people.

3. HETEROSEXUALITY: Exclusive heterosexuality is fucked up; it is a fear of people of the same sex, it is anti-homosexual, and it is fraught with frustrations. Heterosexual sex is fucked up, too; talk to women's liberation about what straight guys are like in bed. Sex is aggression for the male chauvinist; sex is obligation for the traditional woman. And among the young, the modern, the hip, it's only a subtle version of the same. For us to become heterosexual in the sense that our straight brothers and sisters are is not a cure, it is a disease to cop out.

II. ON WOMEN

1. LESBIANISM: It's been a male dominated society for too long, and that has warped both men and women. So gay women are going to see things differently from gay men; they are going to feel oppression as women, too. Their liberation is tied up with both gay liberation and women's liberation.

This paper speaks from the gay male point of view. Although some of the ideas in it may be equally relevant to gay women, it would be arrogant to presume this to be a manifesto for lesbians.

We look forward to the emergence of a lesbian liberation voice. The existence of a lesbian caucus within the New York Gay Liberation Front has been very helpful in challenging male chauvinism among gay guys and anti-gay feelings among women's lib.

2. MALE CHAUVINISM: All men are infected with male chauvinism—we were brought up that way. It means we assume that women play subordinate roles and are less human than ourselves. (At an early gay liberation meeting, one guy said, "Why don't we invite women's liberation, and they can bring sandwiches and coffee.") It is no wonder that so few gay women have become active in our groups.

Male chauvinism, however, is not central to us. We can junk it much more easily than straight men can. For we understand oppression. We have largely opted out of a system which oppresses women daily—our egos are not built on putting women down and having them build us up. Also, living in a mostly male world, we have become used to playing different roles and doing our own shit-work. And finally, we have a common enemy: the big male chauvinists are also the big anti-gays.

But we need to purge male chauvinist behavior and thought among us. Chick equals nigger equals queer. Think about it.

3. WOMEN'S LIBERATION: They are assuming their equality and dignity, and in doing so are challenging the same things we are: the insufferable roles, the exploitation of minorities by capitalism, the arrogance of straight white male middle class Amerika. They are our sisters in struggle.

Problems and differences will become clearer when we begin to work together. One major problem is our own male chauvinism. Another is the uptightness and hostility to homosexuality that many women have—that is the straight in them. A third problem is differing views on sex: sex for them has meant oppression, while it has been the symbol of our freedom. We must come to understand each other's style, jargon and humor.

We want to begin more intensive discussions with women's liberation. And in any case we must support their demands and understand their viewpoint.

III. ON ROLES

1. MIMICRY OF STRAIGHT SOCIETY: We are children of a straight society. We will think straight, and that is part of our oppression. One of the most fucked up of straight concepts is inequality. Straight (also white, English, male, capitalist) thinking sees things always in terms of order and comparison. A is before B, B is after A; 1st is higher than second is higher than 3rd; there is no room for equality. This idea gets extended to male/female, on top/on bottom, spouse/nonspouse, heterosexual/homosexual; boss/worker, rich/poor, white/black. Our social institutions cause and reflect this verbal heirarchy. This is Amerika.

We have lived in these institutions all our lives, so naturally we mimic the roles. For a long time we mimicked these roles to protect ourselves—a survival mechanism. Now we are becoming free enough to shed these roles which we've picked up from the institutions which have imprisoned us.

Stop mimicking straights, stop censoring ourselves.

2. MARRIAGE: Marriage is a prime example of a straight institution fraught with role playing. Traditional marriage is a rotten, oppressive institution. Those of us who have been in heterosexual marriages too often have blamed our gayness on the breakup of the marriages. No. They broke up because marriage is a contract which smothers both people, denies needs, and places impossible demands on both people. And we had the strength, again, to refuse to capitulate to the roles which were demanded of us.

Gay people must stop measuring their self respect by how well they mimic straight marriages. Gay marriages will have the same problems as straight ones, except in burlesque. For the usual legitimacy and pressures which keep straight marriages together are absent—kids, what will parents think, what will neighbors think.

To accept the idea that happiness comes through finding a nice spouse and settling down, showing the world that "We're just the same as you" is avoiding the real issues, and is an expression of self hatred.

3. ALTERNATIVES TO MARRIAGE: People want to get married for lots of good reasons, although marriage doesn't meet those

needs. We're all looking for security, a flow of love, a feeling of belonging and being needed.

These needs can be met through any number of social relationships and living situations. The things we want to get away from are: 1. exclusiveness, propertied attitudes toward each other, a mutual pact against the rest of the world; 2. promises about the future, which we have no right to make and which prevent us from, or make us feel guilty about, growing; 3. inflexible roles, roles which do not reflect us at the moment but are inherited through mimicry and inability to define equalitarian relationships.

We have to define for ourselves a new pluralistic, role-free social structure for ourselves. It must contain both the physical space and spiritual freedom for people to live alone, live together for a while, live together for a long time, either as couples or in larger numbers; and the ability to flow easily from one of these states to another as our needs change.

Liberation for gay people is to define for ourselves how and with whom we live, instead of measuring our relationships by straight values.

4. GAY "STEREOTYPE" ROLES. The straight's image of the gay community is defined largely by those of us who have violated straight roles. There is a tendency among "homophile" groups to deplore gays who play visible roles—the queens and the nellies. As liberated gays, we must take a clear stand: 1) gays who stand out have been the most courageous among us; they came out and withstood straight disapproval before the rest of us. They are our first martyrs; 2) if they have suffered from being open, it is straight society whom we blame for that suffering.

5. CLOSET QUEENS: This phrase is becoming the equivalent to "uncle Tom." To pretend to be straight sexually, or to pretend to be straight socially, is probably the most damaging pattern of behavior in the ghetto. It has many forms—the married guy who makes it on the side secretly; the guy who will go to bed once but who won't develop any gay relationships; the pretender at work or school or home who changes the gender of the friend he's talking about; the guy who'll suck cock in the bushes but who won't come home with you.

Closet queenery must end. If we are liberated, we are open with our sexuality. Come out. Come out. Come out.

BUT: in saying come out, we have to have our heads together about a few things: 1) closet queens are our brothers; they are to be defended against attacks by straight people. 2) Our fear of coming out is not totally paranoid: the stakes are high—loss of family ties, loss of job, loss of straight friends—these are all real risks. Each of us has to make the steps toward openness at our own speed and on our own impulses. Being open is the foundation of liberation, and it has to be built solidly. 3) Closet queen is a blanket term covering a multitude of patterns of defense, self-hatred, lack of strength, and habit. We are all closet queens in one way or another, and all of us had to come out—very few of us were "flagrant" at the age of seven! We must afford our brothers and sisters the same patience we afforded ourselves. And while their closetness is part of our oppression, it's more a part of their oppression; they alone can decide WHEN and HOW.

IV. ON OPPRESSION

It is important to catalog and understand the different facets of our oppression. There is no future in arguing about degrees of oppression. A lot of "movement" types come on with a line of shit about homosexuals not being oppressed as much as blacks or Vietnamese or workers or women. We don't happen to fit into their ideas of class (or caste). Bull—when people feel oppressed, they act on that feeling. And we feel oppressed. Talk about the priority of black liberation or ending imperialism over our "problem" is just antigay propaganda.

1. PHYSICAL ATTACKS: We are attacked, beaten, castrated and left dead over and over again. There are half a dozen known unsolved slayings in San Francisco parks in the last few years. Punks, often minority group members who look around for someone under them socially, feel encouraged to beat up on queers, and cops look the other way. If we recall, that used to be called lynching.

Cops in most cities have harassed our meeting places—bars, baths, parks. They set up entrapment squads. A Berkeley brother was murdered by a cop this spring when he tried to split after finding out that the trick who was making advances to him was a cop. Cities set up "pervert" registration, which if nothing else scares our brothers into the closet.

One of the most vicious slurs on us is to blame us for prison "gang rapes." These rapes are invariably done by people who consider themselves straight, and the objects of these rapes are us and other straights who can't defend themselves. The press campaign to link prison rapes with homosexuality is an attempt to make straights fear and despise us, so they can oppress us more. And it is typical of the fucked-up straight mind to think that homosexual sex means tying a guy down and fucking him. That's aggression, not sex—and if that's what sex is for a lot of straight people, that's their problem, not ours.

2. PSYCHOLOGICAL WARFARE: Right from the beginning we have been subjected to a barrage of straight propaganda. Since our parents don't know any homosexuals, we grow up thinking that we're all alone and different and perverted. Our school friends identify "queer" with any nonconformist or bad behavior. Our elementary school teachers tell us not to talk to strangers or accept rides in cars. The television, billboards and magazines pour forth an unreal idealization of male/female relationships, and make us wish we were different, we were "in." In family living classes we're taught how we're supposed to turn out. And all along, the best we hear, if anything, about homosexuality is that it's an unfortunate problem.

3. SELF OPPRESSION: As gay liberation grows, we will find our up tight brothers and sisters, particularly those who are making a buck off our ghetto, coming on strong to defend the status quo. This is self-oppression: "don't rock the boat"; "things in SF are ok"; "gay people just aren't together"; "I'm not oppressed." These lines are right out of the mouths of the straight establishment. A large part of our oppression would end if we would stop putting ourselves and our pride down.

4. INSTITUTIONAL: Discrimination against gays is blatant, if we open our eyes. Homosexual relationships are illegal, and even if these laws are not regularly enforced, they play the role of encouraging closet queenery. The vast bulk of the social work/psychiatric field looks upon homosexuality as a problem, and treats us as sick. Employers, particularly big business and (with some exceptions) government, let it be known that our skills are acceptable only as long as our sexuality is hidden.

The discrimination in the draft and armed services is a major pillar of the general attitude toward gays. If we are willing to label ourselves publicly not only as homosexual, but as sick, we can qualify for deferment; and if we're not "discreet" (read dishonest) we get drummed out of the service. Hell no, we won't go—of course—but we can't continue to stand back and let the army fuck us over this way, either.

V. ON SEX

1. WHAT SEX IS: Sex is both creative expression and communication: good when it is either, and better when it is both. Sex can also be aggression—and usually is when those involved do not see each other as equals; and it can also be perfunctory, when we are distracted or preoccupied. These uses of sex spoil what is good about it.

I like to think of good sex in terms of playing the violin—(on one level) with both people seeing the other's body as an object of producing beauty as long as they play it well; and on another level the players communicating through their mutual production and appreciation of a thing of beauty. As in good music, you get totally into it—and coming back out of that state of consciousness is like finishing a work of art, or coming back from an episode of an acid or mescaline trip. And to press the analogy further: the variety of music is infinite and varied, depending on the capabilities of the players, both as subjects and as objects. Solos, duets, quartets (symphonies, even, if you happen to dig Romantic music!) are possible. And the variations in gender, response, and bodies are like different instruments. And perhaps what we have called sexual "orientation" probably just means that we have learned to play certain kinds of music well, and have not yet turned on to other music.

2. OBJECTIFICATION: In this scheme of things, people are sexual objectives, but they are also subjects, and are human beings who appreciate themselves as object and subject. This use of human bodies as objects is legitimate (not harmful) only as long as it is reciprocal. If one person is always the object and the other the subject, it stifles the human being in both of them. Objectification must also be open and frank. By silence we often assume or let the other person assume that sex means commitments: if it does, ok, but if it doesn't, say so. (Of course, it's not all that simple: our capabilities for manipulation are unfathomed—all we can do is try.)

Gay liberation people must understand that women have been treated EXCLUSIVELY and DISHONESTLY as sexual objects. It is a major part of their liberation to play down sexual objectification and begin to develop other aspects of themselves which have been stifled so long. We respect this. We also understand that many liberated women will, for a while, be appalled or disgusted at the open and prominent place that we put sex in our lives—and while this is a natural response from their experience, they must learn what it means for us.

For us, sexual objectification is a focal point of our liberation. Sex is precisely that which we are not supposed to have with each other. And to learn how to be open and good with each other sexually is part of our liberation. And one major distinction is obvious: objectification of sex for us is something we choose to do among us, while for women it is imposed by their oppressors.

3. ON POSITIONS AND ROLES: Much of our sexuality has been perverted through mimicry of straights, and through warping from self-hatred. These sexual perversions are basically anti-gay:
   "I like to make it with straight guys"
   "I'm not gay, but I like to be 'done' "
   "I like to fuck, but don't want to be fucked"
   "I don't like to be touched above the neck"
This is role playing at its worst; we must transcend these roles— we strive for democratic, mutual, reciprocal sex. This doesn't mean that we are all mirror images of each other in bed, but that we break away from roles which enslave us. We already do better in bed than straights do, and we can do even better.

4. ON CHICKENS AND STUDS: Face it, nice bodies, and young bodies, are attributes, they're groovy. They are inspiration for art, for spiritual elevation, for good sex. The problem arises only in the inability to relate to people of the same age, or people who do not fit the plastic stereotypes of the good body. At that point, objectification eclipses people, and is an expression of self-hatred: "I don't like gay people, and I don't like my own sexuality, but if a stud (or chicken) will go to bed with me, I can pretend I'm not me."

A footnote on exploitation of children: kids can take care of themselves, and are sexual beings way earlier than we'd like to admit. Those of us who began cruising in our early teens know this, and we were doing cruising, not being debauched by our elders.

Scandals such as that in Boise, Idaho about homosexuals perverting the youth are dirty lies: the high school kids were exploiting gay people who were too scared to express the fullness of their homosexuality. And as for child molesting, the overwhelming amount is done by straight guys to little girls: it is not particularly a gay problem, and is a function of an antisex puritanism and its resulting frustrations.

5. PERVERSION: We've been called perverts enough to be automatically suspicious of this word. Still many of us shrink from the idea of certain kinds of sex: with animals, sado/masochism, "dirty" sex (involving piss and shit). Right off, even before we take the time to learn any more, there are some things to get straight: a) we shouldn't be apologetic to straights about gay people whose sex lives we don't understand or share; b) it's not particularly a gay issue, except that gays probably are less hung up about sexual experimentation; c) let's get some perspective—even if we were to get into the game of deciding what's good for someone else, the harm done to people in these "perversions" is undoubtedly less dangerous or unhealthy than is tobacco or alcohol. d) While they can be reflections of neurotic or self-hating patterns, they may also be enactments of spiritual or important things: e.g. sex with animals may be the beginning of interspecies communication: some dolphin-human breakthroughs have been made on the sexual level; e.g. one guy who says he digs eating shit during sex occasionally says it's not the taste or texture or role, but just a symbol that he's so far into the sex that those things no longer bother him; e.g. s/m, when consensual, can be described as highly developed artistic endeavor, a ballet the constraints of which are threshholds of pain and pleasure.

VI. ON OUR GHETTO

We are refugees from Amerika. So we came to the ghetto—and as other ghettos, it has its negative and positive aspects. Refugee camps are better than what preceded them, or people never would have come. But they are still enslaving, inasmuch as we are limited to being ourselves there and only there.

Ghettos breed self-hatred. We stagnate here, accepting the status quo. And the status quo is rotten. We are all warped by our oppression, and in the helplessness of the ghetto we blame ourselves rather than our oppressors.

Ghettos breed exploitation: Landlords realize they can charge exorbitant rents and get away with it, because there is a limited area which is safe to live in. The Mafia control of bars and baths in New York is only an extreme example of outside money controlling our institutions for their profit. In San Francisco, the Tavern Guild is in favor of maintaining the ghetto, because it is through the ghetto culture that they make a buck. We crowd their bars not because of their merit, but because of the absence of any other social institutions. And the Guild has refused to let us collect defense funds or pass out literature in their bars—need we ask why?

Police or con men who shake down the straight gays in return for not revealing them; the bookstores and movie makers who get away with outrageous prices because they are the only outlet for pornography; the heads of "modeling" agencies, and other pimps, who exploit both the hustlers and the customers—these are the parasites who flourish in the ghetto.

SAN FRANCISCO—GHETTO OR FREE TERRITORY: Our ghetto certainly is more beautiful, larger, and more diverse and freer than most ghettos, and certainly more than Amerika—that's why we're here. But it is not ours—capitalists make money off us, police patrol us, the government tolerates us as long as we shut up, and daily we work for and pay taxes to those who oppress us.

To be a free territory, we must govern ourselves, set up our own institutions, defend ourselves, and use our own energies to improve our lives. The emergence of gay liberation communes and our own paper is a good start. The talk about a gay liberation coffeeshop-dance hall, should be followed through. Rural retreats, political offices, food retail cooperatives, free school, unalienated gay bars and afterhours places—they must be developed if we are to have even the shadow of a free territory.

VII. ON COALITION

Right now the bulk of our work has to be among ourselves—selfeducating, fending off attacks, and building our free territory. Thus basically we have to have a gay/straight vision of the world, until the oppression of gays is ended.

But two problems exist with that as a total vision: 1) we can't change Amerika alone, we need coalition with other oppressed groups at some point; 2) many of us have "mixed" identities—we are gay, and also we are part of another group trying to free itself —women, blacks, other minority groups; we may also have taken on identities which are vital to us: dopers, ecologists, radicals.

Whom do we look to for coalition?

1. WOMEN'S LIBERATION: Without repeating earlier statements, 1) they are our closest ally—we have to try hard to get together with them; 2) a lesbian caucus is probably the easiest way to deal with gay guys' male chauvinism, and challenge the straightness of women's liberation; 3) we as males must be sensitive to their developing identities as women, and respect that; if we know what our liberation consists of, they certainly know what's best for them.

2. BLACK LIBERATION: This is tenuous right now, because of the uptightness and supermasculinity of many black males (which is understandable). Notwithstanding, we must support their movement and demands; we must show that we mean business; and we must figure out which our common enemies are: police, city hall, capitalism.

And they need us too: In New York, where blacks and whites are in a stalemate about community control of schools and police, a solid support from the very large gay population can make the difference between justice or continuing racism.

3. CHICANOS: Basically the same problem as with blacks: trying to overcome mutual animosity and fear, and finding ways to support their movement. The extra problem of superuptightness and machismo among Latin cultures, and the traditional pattern of Mexican "punks" beating on homosexuals, can be overcome: we're both oppressed, and by the same people at the top.

4. WHITE RADICALS AND IDEOLOGUES: We're not, as a group, Marxist or communist—we haven't figured out what kind of economic-political structure is good for us as gays. Nobody—capitalist or communist—has treated us as anything other than shit so far.

But we know we are radical, in the same sense that we know the system we're living under is the direct source of oppression, and it's not just a question of sharing the pie. The pie is rotten.

We can look forward to coalition and mutual inspiration with white radical groups if they are able to transcend their antigay and male chauvinist patterns. We must support radical and militant demands as they come up, e.g. Moratorium, People's Park; but only as a group; we can't compromise our gay identity.

Problems: because radicals are mostly doing somebody else's thing, they are likely to want to avoid issues which affect them directly, and may see us as jeopardizing their "work" with workers, blacks. Some years ago, a dignitary of SDS at the onset of a community organization project announced at an initial staff meeting that there would be no homosexuality (or dope) on the project. And recently in NYC, a movement group which had a coffeehouse get together after a political rally, told the gays to leave when they started dancing together.

Perhaps it would be useful to approach them by helping them free the homosexual within them.

5. HIP AND STREET PEOPLE: Perhaps the major dynamic of recent gay lib sentiment is the hip revolution within the gay community. Emphasis on love, drop out, be honest, stop dressing drably, hair, smoke dope. Those who are the least vulnerable to attack by the establishment are the freest to express themselves.

We can make a direct appeal to young people, who are increasingly not so up tight about homosexuality. One kid, after having his first sex with a man, said "I don't know what all the fuss is all about, it's not that different from making it with a girl!"

The hip/street culture has led people into a lot of other things: encounter/sensitivity, the quest for reality, liberating territory for the people, ecological consciousness, communes. These are real points of agreement.

6. HOMOPHILE GROUPS: 1) Reformist and pokey as they might sometimes be, they are our brothers. They will grow just as we have grown and will grow. Don't attack them, particularly in straight or mixed company. 2) Ignore their attacks on us. 3) Cooperate where cooperation is possible without essential compromise of our identity.

CONCLUSION: AN OUTLINE OF IMPERATIVES FOR GAY LIBERATION

1. Free ourselves: come out, everywhere; initiate self-defense and political activity; initiate community institutions; think

2. Turn other gay people on: talk all the time; understand, accept, forgive.

3. Free the homosexual in everyone: we'll be getting a lot of shit from threatened latents: be gentle and keep talking and acting free.

4. We've been playing an act for a long time: we're consummate actors. Now we can begin TO BE, and it'll be a good show!

Ted Pankey

Gay Lib

—*Pankey is just one of many homosexuals who have put together a philosophy of life for themselves and who have decided to present this philosophy in a public medium such as an underground newspaper. His argument, though not radical in itself, is nevertheless radical according to society's traditional approach to homosexuality. In addition, it is a manifestation of still another phenomenon—homosexuals organizing on various campuses (in this case Southern Illinois University) across the country (e.g., Columbia, Minnesota, and UCLA).*

In a society in which sex, a natural human process, no more or less than eating, growing, dying, is blown up to astronomical proportions and in a world that has always demanded uniformity to the norm, it is little wonder that the position of the homosexual today is spotlighted for criticism. And yet while today's criticism is so great, there is always a very hushed atmosphere about it. One can feel the sense of embarrassment and misunderstanding above the roar of a gang beating up on a Gay and then disappearing, above the chaos of the raid on the bar, and above the jeer of schoolmates who recognize that Johnny is just a little bit "funny." The established society of today has simply never been ready for what they fear may be lurking within those who are "different." And it is just because of this avoidance-of-the-issue attitude that the homosexual has been pushed into corners of dirty, dark little rooms and willfully ignored. I don't find it too surprising to have heard a woman comment recently after having read of the arrest of two Gays, "Oh, are there homosexuals in this town?" It is this same kind of misunderstanding and oppression which has created the lost and hope-

From *Big Muddy Gazette* (Carbondale, Ill.: "Late April," 1971). Reprinted by permission of the author and publisher.

less attitudes prevalent among so many Gays today trying to play the game and make it in the Straight world.

From the beginning, from the minute you are born, your indoctrination begins. You are immediately classified as male or female and are expected thereafter to fulfill the role which established society prescribes for you: blue for boys and pink for girls. Girls play girls' games and boys play those meant for boys. Girls learn to help in the kitchen while boys are trained to do men's work. You know the rest of how that goes. But then comes the day of sexual awakening. It is a period in which experimental relations occur, many of which are homosexual. Remember those days? I'll even bet there wasn't too much guilt over it either, except for the indoctrination which you had already had drilled into you that sex, in general, was dirty. But after a while you learned to direct your sexual activity exclusively toward the opposite sex (if you were allowed to believe that sex is beautiful at all), for that is, after all the arrangement society recognizes. And he whom the same indoctrination does not reach, who continues on the most natural form of sexual expression he has ever known is harassed and labeled sick and perverted until he retreats into his own dirty, dark little room and shuts the closet door behind. "We, ever since we became aware of being Gay, have each day been forced to internalize the labels: 'I am a pervert, a dyke, a fag.' And the days pass, until we look out at the Straight world from our homosexual bodies, bodies that have become synonomous with homosexuality, bodies that are no longer bodies but labels."

OUT OF THE CLOSETS AND INTO THE STREETS. This is the motto of modern Gay Liberation, challenging the worn-out stereotypes which Gays have been forced to assume, questioning the old labels of "sick" and "perverted," reminding everyone Gay, Straight, or whatever, that we are all ultimately people, people of diverse capacities. The homosexual is no less among them.

So here we are at last. SIU Gay Lib stands up willingly to discuss ourselves freely and openly, reaching out to offer an alternative to the up-tight Gay who has locked himself in his closet believing he is alone, unequal to his oppressors, or unworthy of any kind of beauty.

There are those who argue that homosexuality is unnatural due to two bodies not being adapted to each other. To this we can only reply that a woman's breasts do not fit into a man's chest. Or for those of you who contend the Gay "world" is full of prostitution and one-night stands, I will remind you only to look at yourselves and find among heterosexuals the same conditions present among any people who are deprived of sexual happiness. I feel I may quote here from Carl Wittman's Gay Manifesto: "Homosexuality is not a makeshift in the absence of the opposite sex; it is not hatred or rejection of the opposite sex; it is not the result of broken homes except in as much as we could see the sham of American marriages. Homosexuality is the capacity to love someone of the same sex . . . for us to become heterosexual in the same sense that our Straight brothers and sisters are, is not a cure, it is a disease."

We of SIU Gay Lib, therefore, render our services to the Carbondale and University community with the following objectives in mind: (1) Liberation of the homosexual from himself. It is the hate for ourselves which must be overcome before we can ever hope to love anyone else. (2) Promotion of mutual understanding between Gays and Straights. It is not enough for us merely to tolerate each other. (3) Reform of laws discriminating against Gays.

As for the straights who do not believe the causes of Gay Lib are necessarily their concern—I will let you remember that you can never really be rid of us, for we reproduce ourselves out of your bodies—and out of your minds. We are one with you. Your child may after all be homosexual. We must all strive to unite ourselves in a world where we are all free to love or further whatever the cause without fear or shame.

Paul Goodman

Memoirs of an Ancient Activist

—*Paul Goodman, a trenchant social and educational critic, does something in this article that ten years ago would have been virtually inconceivable—he professes his homosexual proclivities. While this is still fairly uncommon, it is noteworthy that several highly placed personalities have done likewise in the past few years. It is still another sign that either homosexuals have perceived a thawing of heterosexual attitudes, or, and perhaps more likely, that a more virulent dialectic between homosexuals and heterosexuals is about to take place.*

In essential ways, homosexual needs have made me a nigger. I have of course been subject to arbitrary insult and brutality from citizens and the police. But except for being occasionally knocked down, I have gotten off lightly in this department, since I have a good flair for incipient trouble and I used to be nimble on my feet. What is much more niggerizing is being debased and abashed when it is not taken for granted that my out-going impulse is my right; so I often, and maybe habitually, have the feeling that it is not my street. I don't mean that my passes are not accepted, nobody has a right to that; but that I'm not put down for making them. It is painful to be frustrated, yet there is a way of rejecting someone that accords him his right to exist and is the next best thing to accepting him; but I have rarely enjoyed this treatment.

Allen Ginsberg and I once pointed out to Stokely Carmichael how we were niggers but he blandly put us down by saying that we could always conceal our dispositions and pass. That is, he accorded to us the same lack of imagination that one accords to niggers; we

From *Memoirs of an Ancient Activist* by Paul Goodman (WIN, 11/15/69). From *WIN Magazine*, V (November 15, 1969), 4–7. Reprinted by permission.

did not really exist for him. Interestingly, this dialogue was taking place on national TV, that haven of secrecy.

In general, in America, being a queer nigger is economically and professionally less disadvantageous than being a black nigger, except for a few areas like government service, where there is considerable fear and furtiveness. (In more puritanic regimes, like present-day Cuba, being queer is professionally and civilly a bad deal.) But my own experience has been very mixed. I have been fired three times because of my queer behavior or my claim to the right to it—and these are the only times I have been fired. I was fired from the University of Chicago during the early years of Hutchins, from Manumit School (an offshoot of A. J. Muste's Brookwood Labor College), and from Black Mountain College. These were highly liberal and progressive institutions, and two of them were communitarian. Frankly, my experience of radical community is that it does not tolerate my freedom. Nevertheless, I am all for community because it is a human thing, only I seem doomed to be left out.

On the other hand, my homosexual acts and the overt claim to the right to commit them have never disadvantaged me much, so far as I know, in more square institutions. I have taught at half a dozen State universities. I am continually invited, often as chief speaker, to conferences of junior high school superintendents, boards of Regents, guidance counsellors, task forces on delinquency, etc., etc. I say what I think right, I make passes if there is occasion—I have even made out, which is more than I can say for conferences of SDS or Resistance. Maybe such company is so square that it does not believe, or dare to notice, my behavior; or more likely, such professional square people are more worldly and couldn't care less what you do, so long as they do not have to face anxious parents and yellow press.

On the whole, although I was desperately poor up to a dozen years ago—I brought up a family on the income of a share-cropper —I do not attribute this to being queer but to my pervasive ineptitude, truculence, and bad luck. In 1944, even the Army rejected me as "Not Military Material" (they had such a stamp), not because I was queer but because I made a nuisance of myself with pacifist action at the examination center and also had bad eyes and piles.

Curiously, however, I have been told by Harold Rosenberg and the late Willie Poster, that my sexual behavior used to do me damage in precisely the New York literary world; it kept me from being invited to advantageous parties. I don't know. What I observed in the 30's and 40's was that I was excluded from the profitable literary circles dominated by Marxists and ex-Marxists, because I was kind of an anarchist. For example, I was never invited to PEN or the Committee for Cultural Freedom. Shucks! (When CCF finally got around to me at the end of the 50's, I had to turn them down because they were patently CIA.)

To stay morally alive, a nigger uses various kinds of spite, the vitality of the powerless. He can be randomly destructive; he feels he has little to lose and maybe he can prevent the others from enjoying what they have. Or he can become an in-group fanatic, feeling that only his own kind are authentic and have soul. There are queers and blacks belonging to both these parties. Queers are "artists," blacks have "soul"—this is the kind of theory which, I am afraid, is self-disproving, like trying to prove you have a sense of humor. In my own case, however, being a nigger seems to inspire me to want a more elementary humanity, wilder, less structured, more variegated, and where people have some heart for one another and pay attention to distress. That is, my plight has given energy to my anarchism, utopianism, and Gandhianism. There are blacks in this party too.

My actual political attitude is a willed reaction-formation to being a nigger. I act that "the society I live in is mine," the title of one of my books. I regard the President as my public servant whom I pay, and I berate him as a lousy worker. I am more constitutional than the supreme court.

In their in-group band, Gay Society, homosexuals can get to be fantastically snobbish and a-political or reactionary, and they put on being silly like a costume. This is an understandable ego-defense: "You gotta be better than somebody," but its payoff is very limited. When I give occasional talks to the Mattachine Society, my invariable pitch is to ally with all other libertarian groups and liberation movements, since freedom is indivisible. What is needed is not defiant pride and self-consciousness, but social space to live and breathe.

In my observation and experience, queer life has some remarkable political values. It can be profoundly democratizing, throwing together every class and group more than heterosexuality does. Its promiscuity can be a beautiful thing (but be prudent about VD). I myself have cruised rich, poor, middle class, and petit bourgeois; black, white, yellow, and brown; scholars, jocks, and dropouts; farmers, seamen, railroad men, heavy industry, light manufacturing, communications, business, and finance; civilians, soldiers, and sailors, and once or twice cops. There is a kind of political meaning, I guess, in the fact that there are so many types of attractive human beings; but what is more significant is that the many functions in which I am professionally and economically engaged are not altogether cut and dried but retain a certain animation and sensuality. HEW in Washington and IS 210 in Harlem are not total wastes, though I talk to the wall in both. I have something to occupy me on trains and buses and during the increasingly long waits at airports. I have something to do at peace demonstrations—I am not inspirited by guitar music—though no doubt the TV files and the FBI with their little cameras have probably caught pictures of me groping somebody. For Oedipal reasons, I am usually sexually antisemitic, which is a drag, since there are so many fine Jews. The human characteristics which are finally important to me and can win my lasting friendship are quite simple: health, honesty, not being cruel or resentful, being willing to come across, having either sweetness or character on the face. As I reflect on it, only gross stupidity, obsessional cleanliness, racial prejudice, insanity, and being drunk or high really put me off.

In most human societies, of course, the sexual drive has been one more occasion for injustice, the rich buying the poor, males abusing females, sahibs using niggers, the adults exploiting the young. But I think this is neurotic and does not give the best satisfaction. It is normal to befriend what gives you pleasure. St. Thomas, who was a grand moral philosopher though a poor metaphysician, says that the chief human use of sex (as distinguished from the natural law of procreation) is to get to know other persons intimately, and that has been my experience.

A criticism of homosexual promiscuity is that, rather than democracy, there is an appalling superficiality of human contact, so that it is a kind of model of the mass inanity of modern urban life. I don't know if this is generally the case; just as, of the crowds who go to art-galleries, I don't know who are being spoken to by the art and who are being bewildered further. "Is he interested in me or just in my skin? If I have sex with him, he will regard me as nothing"— I think this distinction is meaningless and disastrous; in fact, I follow up in exactly the opposite way, and many of my lifelong personal loyalties had sexual beginnings; but is this the rule or the exception? Given the usual coldness and fragmentation of community life at present, I have a hunch that homosexual promiscuity enriches more lives than it desensitizes. Naturally, if we had better community, we'd have better sexuality.

Sometimes it is sexual hunting first of all that brings me to a place where I meet people—e.g., I used to haunt bars on the waterfront; sometimes I am in a place for another reason and incidentally hunt—e.g., I call on my publisher and make a pass at a stock-boy; sometimes these are both of a piece—e.g., I like to play handball and I am sexually interested in fellows who play handball. But these all come to the same thing, for in all situations I think, speak, and act pretty much the same. Apart from ordinary courteous adjustments of vocabulary—but not of syntax—I say the same say and do not wear different masks or find myself with a different personality. Perhaps there are two opposite reasons why I can maintain my integrity: on the one hand, I have a strong enough intellect to see how people are for real in our only world, and to be able to get in touch with them despite differences in background; on the other hand, I am likely so shut in my own preconceptions that I don't even notice glaring real obstacles that prevent communication.

How I do come on hasn't made for much success. Since I don't use my wits to manipulate, I rarely get what I want; since I don't betray my own values, I am not ingratiating; and my aristocratic egalitarianism puts people off unless they are secure enough to be aristocratically egalitarian themselves. Yet the fact that I am not phony or manipulative has also kept people from disliking or resenting me, and I usually have a good conscience. If I happen to get on with someone, there is not a lot of lies and bullshit to clear away.

Becoming a celebrity in the past few years seems to have hurt me sexually rather than helped me. For instance, decent young collegians who might like me and used to seek me out, now keep a respectful distance from the distinguished man—perhaps they are now sure that I *must* be interested in their skin, not in them. And the others who seek me out just because I am well known seem to panic when it becomes clear that I don't care about that at all and I come on as myself. Of course, a simpler explanation of my worsening luck is that I'm growing older every day, probably uglier, and certainly too tired to try hard.

As a rule I don't believe in poverty and suffering as means of education, but in my case the hardship and starvation of my inept queer life have usefully simplified my notions of what a good society is. As with any other addict who cannot get an easy fix, they have kept me in close touch with material hunger. So I cannot take the

GNP very seriously, nor the status and credentials, nor grandiose technological solutions, nor ideological politics, including ideological liberation movements. For a starving person, the world has got to come across in kind. It doesn't. I have learned to have very modest goals for society and myself, things like clean air and water, green grass, children with bright eyes, not being pushed around, useful work that suits one's abilities, plain tasty food, and occasional satisfactory nookie.

A happy property of sexual acts, and perhaps especially of homosexual acts, is that they are dirty, like life: as Augustine said, *Inter urinas et feces nascimur.* In a society as middle class, orderly, and technological as ours, it is essential to break down squeamishness, which is an important factor in what is called racism, as well as in cruelty to children and the sterile putting away of the sick and aged. Also, the illegal and catch-as-catch-can nature of many homosexual acts at present breaks down other conventional attitudes. Although I wish I could have had many a party with less apprehension and more unhurriedly—we would have enjoyed them more —yet it has been an advantage to learn that the ends of docks, the backs of trucks, back alleys, behind the stairs, abandoned bunkers on the beach, and the washrooms of trains are all adequate samples of all the space there is. For both good and bad, homosexual behavior retains some of the alarm and excitement of childish sexuality.

It is damaging for societies to check any spontaneous vitality. Sometimes it is necessary, but rarely; and certainly not homosexual acts which, so far as I have heard, have never done any harm to anybody. A part of the hostility, paranoia, and automatic competitiveness of our society comes from the inhibition of body contact. But in a very specific way, the ban on homosexuality damages and depersonalizes the educational system. The teacher-student relation is almost always erotic; if there is a fear and to-do that it might turn into overt sex, it either lapses or becomes sick and cruel. And it is a loss that we do not have the pedagogic sexual friendships that have starred other cultures. Needless to say, a functional sexuality is incompatible with our mass school systems. This is one among many reasons why they should be dismantled.

I recall when *Growing Up Absurd* had had a number of glowing reviews, finally one irritated critic, Alfred Kazin, darkly hinted that I wrote about my Puerto Rican delinquents because I was queer for them. Naturally. How could I write a perceptive book if I didn't pay attention, and why should I pay attention to something unless, for some reason, it interested me? The motivation of most sociology, whatever it is, tends to produce worse books. I doubt that anybody would say that my observations of delinquent adolescents or of collegians in the Movement has been betrayed by infatuation. But I do care for them. (Of course, *they* might say, "With such a friend, who needs enemies?")

An evil of the hardship and danger of queer life in our society, however, as with any situation of scarcity and starvation, is that we become obsessional about it. I myself have spent far too many anxious hours of my life fruitlessly cruising, which I might have spent sauntering for nobler purposes or for nothing at all, pasturing my soul. Yet I think I have had the stamina, or stubbornness, not to let my obsession cloud my honesty. I have never praised a young fellow's bad poem because he was attractive, though of course I am then especially pleased if it is good. Best of all, of course, if he is my lover and he shows me something that I can be proud of and push. Yes, since I began this article on a bitter note, let me end it with a happy poem I like, from *Hawkweed*:

> We have a crazy love affair,
> it is wanting each other to be happy.
> Since nobody else cares for that
> we try to see to it ourselves.
>
> Since everybody knows that sex
> is part of love, we make love;
> when that's over we return
> to shrewdly plotting the other's advantage.
>
> Today you gazed at me, that spell
> is why I choose to live on.
> God bless you who remind me simply
> of the earth and sky and Adam.
>
> I think of such things more than most
> but you remind me simply. Man,
> you make me proud to be a workman
> of the Six Days, practical.

Franklin E. Kameny

Gay Liberation and Psychiatry

—*Franklin Kameny, who coined the phrase "gay is good" and who has been one of the major driving forces in the move for homosexual freedom in the U.S.A., tackles one of the most conspicuous groups of "oppressors" in the eyes of many homosexuals—the psychiatric community. With the increased self-awareness and pride felt by many homosexuals, it stands to reason that all assumptions held by "straight" society about them will be put to serious challenge. The Kameny article is a fine example of this tendency.*

Increasingly since the summer of 1969, stories involving Gay Liberation as a concept and the Gay Liberation Front or organizations of similar name have appeared in the media, to the extent that the phrase "gay liberation" has almost become a household term. Beyond ideas of its involvement with homosexuality, militancy, and demonstrations, however, little of accuracy—in fact, little at all—is known about the movement by most people. In particular, the relationship between Gay Liberation and psychiatry, the approaches of Gay Liberation to psychiatry, and the possible impact of Gay Liberation on psychiatry—all taken here and below in the narrow context of psychiatry vis-à-vis homosexuality—have been little discussed in print.

While this article will deal nominally with Gay Liberation, it will deal more broadly with the whole homophile movement and its approaches to psychiatry and related matters, and still more broadly with trends in the homosexual community (a community to the very existence of which psychiatry seems not only to give negligible recognition, but the existence of which psychiatry seems

"Gay Liberation and Psychiatry" by Franklin E. Kameny, from *Psychiatric Opinion*, VIII (February, 1971), 18–27. Reprinted by permission of the author and publisher, Opinion Publications, Inc.

actively to resist and to resent). It will touch only in passing on some other collateral political and sociological aspects of Gay Liberation, and it will not attempt a complete analysis of the Gay Liberation organizations, their ideologies, structure, or operation. It is written by and from the viewpoint of a homosexual, a scientist (a non-psychiatrist) who has long been active with the homophile movement and works closely with a number of homophile organizations including one of the more active Gay Liberation Front groups.

Gay Liberation, as a formal entity, had its birth in a riot by homosexuals in late June, 1969, at a gay bar called the Stonewall, on Christopher Street in Greenwich Village.

The details of the riot, the incidents which precipitated it (police harassment of the management of the bar), or its merits are not important. The time was ripe, the homosexual community was ready, and if the riot had not occurred at the Stonewall at that time, it would soon have occurred elsewhere. What is important is the message conveyed by the riot—probably the first ever staged by homosexuals. That message was:

> *We have been shoved around for some 3,000 years. We're fed up with it and we're starting to shove back. If we don't get our rights and the decent treatment as full human beings which we deserve, and get them NOW, there's going to be a lot more shoving back.*

Implicit in this is an uncompromising insistence on the moral right of homosexuals to become, to be and to remain homosexual, as expressed in a formal statement adopted in approximately the following form by the North American Conference of Homophile Organizations in August, 1968:

> In our pluralistic society the homosexual has a moral right to be a homosexual, and being a homosexual, has a moral right to live his homosexuality fully, freely and openly, free of arrogant and insolent pressures to convert to the prevailing heterosexuality, and free of penalties, disabilities or disadvantages of any kind, public or private, official or unofficial, for his nonconformity.
>
> By parallel and by analogy, the homosexual in our pluralistic society has the same moral rights as do the Catholic and the Jew to be Catholics and to be Jews, and being so, to live their religions fully, freely and openly, free of arrogant and insolent pressures to convert to the prevailing Protestant Christianity and free of penalty, disability or disadvantage of any kind for their nonconformity.

Immediately following the riot, the first Gay Liberation Front group was organized in New York City. In the ensuing 18 months or so, such groups have sprung up in the country all over, and are continuing to do so at a rapid rate. An estimate of their number is difficult to obtain. Perhaps 50 might be somewhere near the truth at the moment.

Two points must be kept in mind from an organizational viewpoint. First, although there is extensive communication and co-operation and some nationally based meetings have occurred, there is no national Gay Liberation Front. Each organization is a separate entity. Second, Gay Liberation Front organizations, as a class, have little necessarily in common with each other except their name (which has great charisma) and the fact that they were all formed since June of 1969. They cover the range from conservative (moderately) to radical (very); from traditionally structured groups with constitution and officers to resolutely unstructured ones; from "change the System" to "smash the System"; from groups confining themselves narrowly to issues involving homosexuals and homosexuality to groups crossing lines into a variety of other issues and causes.

Nevertheless, statistically there are certain features which tend to characterize Gay Liberation Front groups, although with many differences from group to group. They tend to have minimal internal organizational structure and informal membership; they tend to be activist and militant; they tend to be political and being so, to be to the left; and they tend to form alliances in both ideology and in activity with the causes of other minority groups, particularly blacks and women. There tends to be a strong feeling that the abuses and oppressions afflicting such groups—racism, sexism, etc.—in our society are unitary in nature and are closely interrelated: "No one is free until every one is free." There tends to be a feeling that much of the dehumanizing of minority groups in our society is intrinsic to the existing system and is inherent in the basic structure of our society, requiring, therefore, changes of a radical nature often achievable only by radical methods.

As the underlying theme of the Gay Liberation approach to homosexuality, as of the entire homophile movement for many years, are two basic precepts: (1) That homosexuals are fully the equal of heterosexuals, and (2) (related but distinct) that homosexuality is fully the equal of heterosexuality. With the first goes the full bid for equality in employment, civil rights, decent treatment, etc.; it usually raises little demur from psychiatrists and others and, in fact, is usually warmly endorsed. The second raises greater problems for many people and is much the more controversial, psychiatrically and otherwise; it is insisted upon quite uncompromisingly. Where many of the Gay Liberation groups tend, often mildly, to part company on these precepts from the remainder of the homophile movement is in the degree to which they care to make the compromises implied in the word *equal*. Tending to feel themselves to be in the more alienated segments of society, there is an inclination simply to consider homosexuals and homosexuality as affirmatively good on an absolute basis in comparison with the remainder of society, and its preferences and practices considered irrelevant.

That word *irrelevant* leads from this brief and necessarily somewhat superficial and simplistic general survey of Gay Liberation to discussion of the implications to psychiatry not only of Gay Liberation but of general trends within the homosexual community.

The homophile movement can be considered to have existed with some continuity for about two decades. The movement can be defined as one created to better the lives of homosexuals *as homosexuals*. During that period, the movement has evolved from small, hesitant beginnings to its present large, diversified, multifaceted and highly and increasingly militant state. A persistent theme, stated tentatively at first but uncompromisingly over the past decade, has been an absolute rejection of the notion that homosexuality is pathological in any sense or is a symptom of pathology of any kind. The basis for this approach deserves some examination.

In past eras when society wished to condemn a group of people, it termed them sinful, and their departures from the norm were called heresies. Sin is no longer very meaningful to many people, heresy carries little weight in a society which places a high positive value on intellectual freedom and dissent and the high priests of former days have been replaced by the high priests of the present day—the psychiatrists and psychoanalysts. So now homosexuals are called sick. An allegation of sickness, however, has to be substantiated by those making it, not refuted by those against whom it is made. A reading of the psychiatric literature demonstrates how abysmally psychiatry fails to make its case. The failure comes on three prime counts:

1. *Inadequate definitions of such terms as pathology, sickness, disorder, neurosis, etc., in this context.* These terms, when defined at all, are defined as persistent nonconformity in a matter of which society makes an issue. In an era when all of society's basic premises

are being subjected to searching questions and frequent outright rejection, and when it is being increasingly realized that society exists solely for the benefit of its members and not vice versa, an exaltation and deification of society to the status of the prime referent and an unexamined assumption that the goals of therapy should be adjustment to society seem singularly misplaced. Many definitions of pathology are teleological and represent fundamentalistic theology in thinly disguised form. Theology has its place, but pathology is a scientific concept which cannot be defined or determined in theological or teleological terms. Other definitions are objectionable in that, by a pseudo-biological functionalism, they seem to make of people mere appendages of their genital organs rather than the other way round.

There is a tendency, too, to take a monolithic view of humankind; to adopt an implicit assumption that all people are turned out of the same mould, like so many faceless robots; that there is *one* prescribed course of psychosexual development, *one* proper way of enjoying sexual activity, *one* pattern of intimate affectional relationship, and that any others are indications of pathology. To those who believe in the richness, pluralism and diversity of humanity and consider it one of our greatest glories, and who believe in the very welcome "do your own thing" philosophy, such narrowness of view is an affront.

2. *Poor use of scientific method, particularly poor sampling techniques.* Virtually the entire literature is based upon studies of psychiatric patients—hardly a representative subgroup from which to draw valid conclusions as to the pathology or condition of the larger group. There are other flagrant violations of basic scientific method—lack of control groups, inept statistical analysis, multiple variables and non-separation of variables, etc.

3. *Poor logic and unclear thinking.* Repeatedly, assumptions of pathology are fed into one end of a study, only to be plucked out unchanged at the other end as conclusions. Studies of the causes of homosexuality are made which assume, as starting hypotheses, ONLY something defective or disturbed in the individual's background, leading obviously to theories of causation based solely upon an assumption of something having gone awry. The causes of *hetero*sexuality are never explored.

A perfect example of the unclear thinking which abounds in this regard occurred during a conversation between me and a psychiatrist prominent in this field on a recent Baltimore television program. The psychiatrist asserts that our society suffers from "homoerotophobia"—a phobia against homosexuality. I quite agree. He then defines homosexuality as pathological because it represents a departure from, or maladjustment to, the standards of our society. Keeping in mind that a phobia is a pathological fear, this psychiatrist is thus saying that homosexuals are sick because a sick society says they are sick. Apparently he has never heard of the old adage, beloved of grammarians but applicable here, that two negatives equal a positive. His fuzzy thinking is typical of his profession on this subject.

I speak with outrage and indignation as a scientist when I say that this entire "sickness theory" of homosexuality is shabby, shoddy, slipshod, slovenly, sleazy, and just-plain-bad science.

We have been *defined* into sickness by a mixture of cultural, theological, moral and sociological value judgments camouflaged in the language of science.

In view of the inordinate weight carried by psychiatrists in our society, the person who could give a good course in science, scientific method and logic and could persuade large numbers of psychiatrists and psychoanalysts to take it in order that they could learn to recognize bad science and practice good science would be a major benefactor of mankind.

It is for these reasons that some homophile organizations have adopted formal statements of position phrased approximately:

> *In the absence of valid scientific evidence to the contrary, homosexuality cannot properly be considered a sickness, illness, disturbance, disorder, neurosis or other pathology of any kind, nor as a symptom of any of those, but must properly be considered as a preference, orientation or propensity not different in kind from heterosexuality and fully on par with it.*

Basically, what the situation seems to boil down to is that medicine—and especially psychiatry—has a pathologic psychological need for sexual hobgoblins. For well over a century that hobgoblin was masturbation. Although many doctors still do not accept masturbation with complete equanimity—doctors not being noted for being members of the intellectual avant-garde—apparently medicine has largely recovered from its masturbation aberration. It has now substituted another hobgoblin: homosexuality. Actually, it is not homosexuality which is pathological in this context, it is the entire discipline of psychiatry.

If it were only a matter of a number of sick doctors making a pack of damned fools of themselves on these subjects, there would be no great loss. But when they impose their aberrations on countless poor people who are misguided enough to consider these doctors authorities, thereby ruining their lives and producing endless needless misery, then those doctors bear a heavy burden of guilt indeed. They have not thus far demonstrated much of a sense of responsibility or remorse for the evil they have done.

With the allegation of sickness disposed of, it is possible to see the question of homosexuality from the perspective of Gay Liberation and the remainder of the homophile movement.

Because homosexuality is most certainly a psychological condition, there has been a tendency to look to psychiatry and psychology and their practitioners as THE authorities on homosexuality and also as the sole or prime sources of information on the subject and of solutions to the problems which accompany it.

This makes as little sense as to say that because skin color is a biological condition we should look to biologists, geneticists and dermatologists for authoritative information on racism and for solutions to the problems of the ghetto. If we did, we would not even get a realistic or adequate formulation of the problems, much less solutions to them. We do no better by going to psychiatrists and psychoanalysts for formulations of, or solutions to, the real problems of real homosexuals.

Accordingly, it is about time that this entire subject were taken off the psychoanalyst's couch and out of the psychiatrist's office and the psychologist's laboratory and approached as what it is: A *sociological* problem in prejudice, discrimination, and bigotry, directed against a minority group not different in kind from others of our sociological minority groups. It is society which is defective and at fault and needs our attention, not the homosexual.

At this point, psychiatry, psychoanalysis, medicine, and their practitioners become totally irrelevant to the concerns of the great majority of homosexuals whose problems are not the medical ones of an emotional nature which they are usually taken to be, but are more likely to be sociological and related to employment. As with other minority groups, these problems are not of the homosexual's own making.

Thus, the homophile movement and Gay Liberation explicitly reject concern with those twin obsessions of psychiatry: cause and "cure." (The very use of the term "cure" is rejected as being inapplicable, since homosexuality is not a sickness; "change" is a preferred term.)

More than that, however, psychiatry is taken strongly to task as not only an adversary, but as THE archenemy.

Psychiatrists seem to be singularly obtuse and insensitive to the effects of their position on this question of pathology. An allegation of mental illness—which IS what is being made here, all the suave sophistries and semantics notwithstanding—is a crippling accusation in our society, even when termed merely a "neurosis." It is not one to be made lightly or without full and incontrovertible substantiation. That psychiatry and psychoanalysis and their practitioners consistently characterize homosexuality in this way, without adequate basis, can be looked upon only as unethical, irresponsible, and self-serving.

A single, pointed, if perhaps minor, example of the effects of the characterization of homosexuality as an illness is the denial of security clearances to homosexuals, even in instances where the government grants that they are not vulnerable to blackmail on the grounds that because psychiatrists term homosexuality a sickness, all homosexuals are unstable (an argument which has been formally advanced by the Federal government and has been formally accepted by a Federal court).

The unproven allegation that homosexuality is pathological (in any of its semantic guises—a disturbance, a disorder, a neurosis, etc.—or a symptom of any of these) is recognized as not only destructive to the self-respect, self-esteem, self-confidence, and self-image of the homosexual (thereby, in self-fulfilling fashion, helping to produce some of the very symptoms which psychiatrists claim to find in their homosexual patients and in all homosexuals) but as perhaps the major supportive factor currently (now that organized religion is coming around) behind the negative attitudes of society at large. These attitudes inculcate into the homosexual (as into the black in ways which are different in detail but identical in essence and result) a feeling of inferiority and of second-rateness. Thus psychiatry wreaks major violence upon the psyche of the homosexual, both first hand and through the aid which it offers to the maintenance of societal bigotry.

Deeply resented, too, is the tendency not only of psychiatry, but of moralists, theologians, lawyers and jurists to treat homosexuals as patients, specimens, and things—to talk *about* or *to* homosexuals instead of *with* us. We have been made a passive battlefield across which conflicting, self-appointed authorities of dubious competence parade and fight out their questionable views, prejudices, and theories and attempt to dispose of our fate.

The homosexual community is no longer content with this role and is insistent upon disposing of its own fate. This, of course, was the rationale behind the recent invasions by Gay Liberation Front groups of psychiatric conferences in San Francisco, Los Angeles, and Chicago, and of a similar invasion of a seminar on Theology and Homosexuality at Catholic University in Washington, D.C.

One irate doctor in Chicago is reported to have asked by what right the homosexuals were present. He missed the point. As subjects of the discussion, our moral right to be present was beyond question or valid challenge. By what right did he and his colleagues have the arrogance to discuss homosexuals and our condition, our problems and concerns (and propose solutions to them) in our absence? It can be predicted that in the future there will be few conferences dealing in whole or in part with homosexuality, in which homosexuals will not be present as active participants— with or without invitations—and psychiatrists and others had better prepare themselves for this.

We have not appointed psychiatrists—or theologians, moralists, legislators, lawyers, or others—as our spokesmen, our representatives, or our keepers. These people are presumptuous to attempt to formulate our problems and our concerns, or to imply that they speak with authentic knowledge of them. We saw what happened when, for years, whites spoke (in the best of good faith and with the best of good intentions) for blacks. Somehow things did not appear quite the same when blacks began to speak for themselves. The parallel is precise.

Where has psychiatry gone awry on this subject? On the Baltimore television program mentioned earlier, I asked the psychiatrist whether he and his colleagues were taking any steps to cure society's pathological phobia against homosexuality. He disavowed that this came within the proper area of operation of a psychiatrist. Thus I feel that he and psychiatry are demonstrating their profound irresponsibility and immorality.

The person who is sick and in need of therapy is not the homosexual fired from a job, but the employer firing him because of his homosexuality; not the government employee denied a civil service job, but the chairman of the Civil Service Commission who imposes a policy denying civil service jobs to homosexual citizens, and the Chief of the Investigations Bureau who tries to justify such policies; not the homosexual who gets beaten up, but the thugs who go out to "roll queers"; not the homosexual who is entrapped or enticed into a solicitation, but the policeman volunteering for such duty and making the arrest which he has created; not the homosexual teenager, but his parents who make his life miserable by imposing upon him their anxieties, hang-ups, hostilities, prejudices and negative attitudes toward homosexuality; not those homosexuals who seek their sex covertly in semipublic places, but the society which provides them with no other social resources and, by denying them a comfortable homosexual social life while in their younger, pattern-forming years, has forced them to accept the only outlets available to them and then blames them for the damage it has wrought.

Psychiatry has failed by omission and by commission to meet its responsibilities of changing society and society's attitudes. THAT is where the psychotherapy is needed!

To all of this, psychiatry, *as it presently defines its concerns with homosexuality,* not only is utterly irrelevant, but is deeply detrimental. This need not be so.

It is clear that most homosexuals have no desire to convert to heterosexuality and would not do so even if such changes were made easy and sure. Many psychiatrists piously claim that they attempt to convert to heterosexuality only those homosexuals who indicate that they wish such change. The situation is not at all as simple as that. The motivations for desiring such changes must be examined with some care—as most of those same psychiatrists would surely do if a *hetero*sexual came to them desiring change to homosexuality. Ordinarily, one would expect that the traffic of discontented people wishing to convert between two intrinsically and objectively equal states—black and white; Jewish and Christian; Protestant and Catholic; homosexual and heterosexual—would be proportional to the reservoir from which the traffic emanates. That is, that some ten times as many whites would choose to try to pass as black as vice versa, etc. However, in a situation of repression, discrimination and bigotry, where the traffic between the two states is totally one way, motives for desiring a change which represent submission to society's bigotry-based value judgments must be explored, not merely accepted.

A majority of those who wish to change to heterosexuality can well be considered to be in a class with blacks who try to "pass" as white because they have been brainwashed into a belief in the inferiority of their Negritude and the superiority of whites.

A far more reasonable—and acceptable—approach would be for the psychiatrist to get beyond his own "hang-ups" and value judgments, his own insistence that the goal of therapy must be adjustment to a maladjusted society, and to create in the homosexual pride in his homosexuality and the psychic resources to lead the life, rewarding and fulfilling to self and productive to society, of which he is fully capable as a homosexual.

One of the consequences of the "cure" obsession of many psychiatrists (rightly or wrongly attributed by the gay community to all psychiatrists) is that psychiatrists are shunned even by those homosexuals who could profit by psychotherapy. Some homosexuals are in need of psychotherapy, of course, just as many heterosexuals are. But they are not in need of conversion to heterosexuality. The standard request which I get from the occasional homosexual who comes to me for referral to a psychiatrist (there are not many such cases) is for "someone who isn't going to try to change me" (to heterosexuality). With good reason, homosexuals refuse psychotherapy or counseling which becomes a totally unwanted and totally unneeded assault upon their homosexuality.

Assistance is needed, therefore, not to change homosexuals to heterosexuality, but to reinforce the homosexual in his homosexuality, to restore or establish his self-esteem and self-confidence —in sum, to undo the damage done him by a hostile society.

This is an area where, by the default of psychiatry, many of the Gay Liberation groups are active. By setting up "consciousness raising" groups—effective, continuing group therapy sessions— efforts are being made through peer-reinforcement techniques to reinforce the homosexual in a sense of the rightness of his homosexuality. These activities also create the necessary sense of group solidarity and community so necessary for effective social action. Many of the slogans currently heard (*Gay is Good,* coined by this writer as a psychologically supportive and reparative device for the homosexual in precise parallel to the function served by *Black is Beautiful, Be Gay—Be Proud,* etc.) are intended to serve this function.

One might expect that a psychiatric profession genuinely interested in therapy would be offering professional assistance in these efforts. But since it is psychiatry which more than any other single force in modern society is responsible for the damage being repaired by these efforts, and which has a very real vested financial interest in creating such damage, it is not surprising that no assistance is forthcoming. After all, if all homosexuals stopped considering themselves sick, some psychiatrists would have to find someone else upon whom to prey in order to earn their keep!

The points made here need not be belabored further, but can be summarized simply. Psychiatry is totally irrelevant to the problems of homosexuals in a hostile society. At the very least, psychiatry and psychiatrists are ignored; more often they are attacked as "the enemy" incarnate—and with considerable justification. Psychiatrists have been discredited and dethroned as sources of wisdom, knowledge and authority. For many groups, psychiatrists represent the last major bastion of bigotry (along, perhaps, with the Federal government); some of the more militant groups feel it demeaning to descend even to debate with psychiatrists. Having defaulted in the areas in which they could assist us, and having shown themselves totally insensitive to the consequences of the theories which they irresponsibly promulgate, psychiatrists are felt to have nothing whatever of value to offer us and are thought to be doing us very real harm.

If, in order to remedy this unfortunate situation, psychiatrists wish to assist us and make themselves relevant to Gay Liberation, to the homophile movement, and to the homosexual community, they can work actively:

> to dispel in the popular mind the sickness-myth which they have created;

> to change society's attitudes toward homosexuals and homosexuality;

> to temper and ultimately to eliminate the prejudice felt and the discrimination, contempt, disdain, and dislike shown toward homosexuals;

> to create and implement new, effective methods, applicable to large numbers of people, of supporting and reinforcing the homosexual in his homosexuality, in order to repair the psychic damage done by society and by psychiatry.

I am sure that many psychiatrists reading this will both resent it and reject it. Nevertheless these *are* the feelings and views of a large and growing number of real homosexuals and these views are ignored at risk of exiling oneself to an ivory tower. A minority busy building up a sense of community, imbued with a feeling that *gay is good,* exhilarated by *gay pride,* actively entering the political arena, fighting discrimination, creating its own life style and remodeling society in the process, is not going to have much time, patience, or use for psychiatry and psychiatrists whose only theme is conformity to the anachronistic precepts and tenets of a sick society.

As much as anything else, Gay Liberation means liberation of homosexuals from psychiatry with its outmoded notions and its thralldom to questionable and outworn societal standards. One would hope that the next step, along with the other liberation movements springing up in our society today, will be Psychiatrists' Liberation. It is long overdue. In a spirit of forgiveness, charity, and humanity, we will be pleased to assist in the administration of therapy to a profession badly in need of it, in order to achieve its liberation.

Huey Newton

A Letter to the Revolutionary Brothers and Sisters about the Women's Liberation and Gay Liberation Movements

—*For many, Huey Newton is the archetype of the revolutionary figure. His association with the Black Panthers has been both intense and pervasive. With the conspicuous rise of militancy on the part of some homosexuals (both male and female), Newton sees the opportunity for still another oppressed group to join the revolutionary movement to correct the injustices perpetrated against minorities in this country. Homosexuals, Newton's reasoning goes, need not look far to understand the concepts of "minorities" and "oppression."*

During the past few years, strong movements have developed among women and among homosexuals seeking their liberation. There has been some uncertainty about how to relate to these movements.

Whatever your personal opinions and your insecurities about homosexuality and the various liberation movements among homosexuals and women (and I speak of the homosexuals and women as oppressed groups), we should try to unite with them in a revolutionary fashion. I say "whatever your insecurities are" because, as we very well know, sometimes our first instinct is to want to hit a homosexual in the mouth and want a woman to be quiet. We want to hit the homosexual in the mouth because we're afraid we might be homosexual; and we want to hit the woman or shut her

From *Berkeley Tribe* (September 5–12, 1970). Reprinted by permission of the publisher.

up because we're afraid that she might castrate us, or take the nuts that we might not have to start with.

We must gain security in ourselves and therefore have respect and feelings for all oppressed people. We must not use the racist type attitude like the White racists use against people because they are Black and poor. Many times the poorest White person is the most racist because he's afraid that he might lose something, or discover something that he doesn't have; you're some kind of threat to him. This kind of psychology is in operation when we view oppressed people and we're angry with them because of their particular kind of behavior, or their particular kind of deviation from established norm.

Remember, we haven't established a revolutionary value system; we're only in the process of establishing it. I don't remember us ever constituting any value that said that a revolutionary must say offensive things towards homosexuals, or that a revolutionary should make sure that women do not speak out about their own particular kind of oppression. Matter of fact it's just the opposite: we say that we recognize the women's right to be free. We haven't said much about the homosexual at all, and we must relate to the homosexual movement because it's a real thing. And I know through reading and through my life experience, my observations, that homosexuals are not given freedom and liberty by anyone in the society. Maybe they might be the most oppressed people in the society.

And what made them homosexual? Perhaps it's a whole phenomenon that I don't understand entirely. Some people say that it's the decadence of capitalism. I don't know whether this is the case; I rather doubt it. But whatever the case is, we know that homosexuality is a fact that exists, and we must understand it in its purest form: That is, a person should have freedom to use his body in whatever way he wants to. That's not endorsing things in homosexuality that we wouldn't view as revolutionary. But there's nothing to say that a homosexual cannot also be a revolutionary. And maybe I'm now injecting some of my prejudice by saying that "even a homosexual can be a revolutionary." Quite on the contrary, maybe a homosexual could be the most revolutionary.

When we have revolutionary conferences, rallies and demonstrations there should be full participation of the Gay Liberation movement and the Women's Liberation movement. Some groups might be more revolutionary than others. We shouldn't use the actions of a few to say that they're all reactionary or counterrevolutionary, because they're not.

We should deal with the factions just as we deal with any group or party that claims to be revolutionary. We should try to judge somehow, whether they're operating sincerely, in a revolutionary fashion from a really oppressed situation. (And we'll grant that if they're women, they're probably oppressed.) If they do things that are un-revolutionary or counterrevolutionary, then criticize that action. If we feel that the group in spirit means to be revolutionary in practice, but they make mistakes in interpretation of the revolutionary philosophy, or they don't understand the dialectics of the social forces in operation, we should criticize that and not criticize them because they're women trying to be free. And the same is true for homosexuals. We should never say a whole movement is dishonest, when in fact they're trying to be honest, they're just making honest mistakes. Friends are allowed to make mistakes. The enemy is not allowed to make mistakes because his whole existence is a mistake, and we suffer from it. But the Women's Liberation Front and Gay Liberation Front are our friends, they are potential allies, and we need as many allies as possible.

We should be willing to discuss the insecurities that many people have about homosexuality. When I say "insecurities," I mean the fear that they're some kind of threat to our manhood. I can understand this fear. Because of the long conditioning process which builds insecurity in the American male, homosexuality might produce certain hangups in us. I have hangups myself about male homosexuality. Where, on the other hand, I have no hangup about female homosexuality. And that's a phenomenon in itself. I think it's probably because male homosexuality is a threat to me, maybe, and the females are no threat.

We should be careful about using those terms that might turn our friends off. The terms "faggot" and "punk" should be deleted from our vocabulary, and especially we should not attach names normally designed for homosexuals to men who are enemies of the people, such as Nixon or Mitchell. Homosexuals are not enemies of the people.

We should try to form a working coalition with the Gay Liberation and Women's Liberation groups. We must always handle social forces in the most appropriate manner. And this is really a significant part of the population, both women and the growing number of homosexuals, that we have to deal with.

ALL POWER TO THE PEOPLE!

Daniel Curzon

Something You Do in the Dark

—In this selection from Daniel Curzon's novel, Something You Do in the Dark, *Cole Ruffner has just been released from prison and is trying to adapt himself to the "straight" world around him. He mulls over the past and as a consequence thinks of the events that led to his arrest, trial, and sentencing. Experiences such as his are not rare in the reportage of homosexual arrests—particularly in homosexual-oriented periodicals and newspapers.*

But I'm free now, by God! I earned the right to lie here, to think what I want to think. You'll never put me behind bars again. I swear it. He made himself remain quiet, directing the images into his mind. He had tried not to think clearly about the event for six months, for he had worn his brain out with reliving the scene, until he was weary, exhausted. But now he wanted to see if he could think about it again, even find some comfort in the details. *Three years ago? No, it couldn't be. Though sometimes it seemed longer than that—all those tedious, bland days of sitting in a cell. In August three years ago. Three years and three days ago:*

He drove through a public park, Rouge Park, to a "comfort station," even joking to himself about the name, thinking that all he wanted was a little comfort. The place was usually deserted after seven, but the attendants did not close it down until eight thirty. It was a well-known meeting place, for "quickies." The body built up its pressures, which had to be relieved. A fact of chemistry. There were always several men waiting inside, who leaned forward on the toilet stools to see who entered, not at all subtle. The officials of the park had removed the doors of the stalls to eliminate such sex acts, but the doorless stalls actually made cruising easier and prevented any sort of privacy, whereby the men would relieve their needs and depart, instead of lingering, startled by each opening of the outside door. Cole was on his way to a party given by Angie, a good friend, one of the girls who worked in his office. The irony was that he wanted to get sex off his mind, and he checked for police cars. None in sight.

He stood at a urinal, keeping his eyes down for a good five minutes, not especially interested in the older men sitting on the toilets. When he turned his head, one of them made slurping noises—disgusting, but they aroused him nevertheless. He started to face the man, when the door opened and a young man, very attractive, came in, right up to the next urinal. While glancing at Cole, he fumbled slowly with his zipper, and then began manipulating his penis, making the blood rush, beckoning with his head. Ordinarily, Cole would have waited, been much more cautious, but the man was so encouraging, and so attractive. Cole looked back over his shoulder at the other two men in the stalls, who obviously wanted him to take the offer. And so he did. He put out his hand, and when the man swung toward him, he cupped both hands around the sex.

The rest was blurred, somehow not completely formed in his mind. Mainly what he recalled was two men falling or jumping out of the ceiling, through a wire mesh. One of them must have injured his leg because he hopped around as he made the arrest. *It was really quite funny,* Cole told himself. *One detective hopping around like somebody playing hopscotch, shouting "cocksucker" over and over at him.* The handsome young man who was the decoy was washing his hands, saying nothing, wiping carefully, rolling the paper into wads as he tossed it casually into a wooden barrel.

They let the other two men in the booths go, hitting them a few times as a warning. But Cole they took to the unmarked Ford that was parked a few blocks away behind some willow trees. One of the men kept kicking him in the rear, at least seven or eight times, and Cole shouted for him to stop it, but all the man did was kick him harder. "There's some dirt on your clothes; I'm helping you, you cocksucker; I'm helping you!"

Inside the automobile the policemen shoved Cole to the far side, but they did not start the car right away, because the two in front were whispering to each other, while the biggest one, in the back seat with Cole, jabbed him gently in the ribs. "I'll let you go if you go down on me, kid," he said. "What do you say? All three of us—

and we'll let you go." Cole could not tell from the tone if the man was serious or merely trying to humiliate him further. "Come on, son, go to it; you like to do it anyway. God, my leg hurts!" He suddenly stuck it over to Cole's side of the car. "You're gonna pay for my injury, kid, don't you forget it." He grabbed Cole's head and pulled on the hair, forcing the head down into his lap. But Cole resisted, his throat blistered, sick. The cop rolled the head around, back and forth, across his crotch. A warmish, vague musty odor mixed with tobacco. "Get to it, boy. This here boy don't know how to do nothing."

The two men in the front seat looked back at the words. "What are you doing to that kid, Keel?"

"Just giving him a chance to earn his freedom, that's all."

"Aw, don't you ever get tired of this?"

Cole tried to see their faces clearly, to see what they meant. Were they serious? But he could detect nothing in the dimness. Then the man in the back grabbed Cole's cheek in a hard pinch. "Get going, son, and watch them teeth." He pulled down his zipper, arching his back to do it. As he did, the car started and backed up. "Come on, we'll let you go afterward."

Cole looked up at the silhouetted forms in the front. "Will you? Really?"

"What do you think? We're good to faggots, aren't we, Ralph?" The three of them snickered so that Cole did not know what he was expected to do; he sat still. "Give me a blow job, what do you say?" Tentatively, he leaned forward, then sat back. "Come on, kid." The policeman patted his own legs on either side of the fly. Cole leaned down again toward the man's stomach. "That's the way, son. Do your duty." Cole slowly put his face into the man's clothes, his own sweat plastering his hair over his brow, a few pubic hairs brushing against his nose. "That's the way, fairy, tickle my pickle." The cop put his hand on the back of Cole's neck and squeezed, then pressed down. "Lick it." Cole could hardly breathe; he hestitated. "I said lick it!" His tongue went out and touched the stub, which tasted like salt and moist talcum powder. "Lick harder; give it a go." Cole's heart swelled inside him, achingly, and he thought he would vomit. But he opened his mouth and surrendered. After a few seconds, the cop yanked him up by the collar. "You ain't nothing but a whore, are you?" He pushed Cole's face away and fastened the zipper. "Pig, slimy pig. Faggot. Queer faggot freak! Sister man, you make me puke. Let's get this thing moving faster." The man gestured at the two in front.

"Keel, you're brutal," the handsome man said quietly.

"You ought to know, Parris, with your cock hanging out all the time. I think you get a kick out of it."

The other did not respond, and Cole, his mouth gone totally dry, asked, "Where are we going?"

"We got a judge that wants to see you, sissy boy. You're going to pay for your crime against society, including this pain in my leg." He rubbed at his calf. "You've got three witnesses who saw you— three. Don't you know sucking's against the law."

"But I didn't—"

"Hey fellas, he doesn't know that cocksuckers go to jail. Just like drunk drivers, only longer. You know, we ought to put up a sign like they do along the streets."

"Come on, cut it out, lay off," the handsome, younger man said.

"You give in to these queers, Parris, and you see what happens!"

For a while after that no one spoke, until the florid-complexioned man in the back said, "You happened along at a bad time, boy." Cole said nothing, but the man continued, confidentially. "Not talking, eh? Well, there was a queer murder a few days ago; some young boys, two of them, found shot through the back. Since we haven't found the killer yet, all of you faggots are gonna pay." He spoke as if the natural order of reward and punishment was being announced. "Why don't you speak up, fairy. The last one we caught, a couple of days ago, bawled all over us."

"Let me go. I—"

"Shut up, freak!" the man pulled his leg back to his side, scraping Cole's ankle as he did, but Cole made no further attempts to speak.

The courtroom the next morning was filled with people, primarily grubby-looking, even the officials. Cole was brought in with the other men from the jail, mostly drunks, a few assault cases. His clothes were rumpled from his having tried to sleep in them all night. He had not been allowed to call a bondsman. That morning a lawyer was appointed to defend him, a man who did not even ask him what had happened or bother to give his own name. He asked only if Cole had a job and how much money he made a year. Cole accepted the lawyer, not knowing what else to do, never having needed one before, not at twenty-four.

"What do you plead?" the judge asked, a leathery-faced old man.

"Not guilty, Your Honor," the court lawyer pleaded for Cole.

Then one of the arresting policemen, the limping one, read his account of the arrest, adding details that were lies, saying that Cole had grabbed the decoy, who was minding his own business, that the defendant had even exposed himself in a public place. The man's voice seemed extremely loud, carrying throughout the whole court-room, but Cole was too embarrassed to look around to see. "The defendant also offered to bribe us by an obscene suggestion, Your Honor. But I won't go into the details since I won't press it," the heavy man said in conclusion.

"All right, what's your story?" the judge asked indifferently, scribbling some notes to himself as Cole talked.

Cole looked at his lawyer helplessly, wondering what he was supposed to say. Should he deny everything? "What can I say, Your Honor? I seem to be on the defensive, don't I?" He grinned, not knowing why. Did he think that charm would work a miracle? But the judge was not charmed; he wrinkled his nose when he looked up.

"What is your defense, if any?"

The lawyer answered for him. "The defendant, Your Honor, is employed."

For some reason that seemed to make a difference in his guilt. "Where?" the judge asked Cole.

"I work in the Federal Building."

"Do you work for the government?"

"Yes, I'm a cartographer, a map-maker."

"For the government?"

"Yes."

"I see. Why were you in a public lavatory?"

"Why does anybody go into one, sir?"

"Don't be smart," the lawyer whispered to him, before he looked up to the judge. "The defendant was driving around, Your Honor, and stopped to use the convenience."

"He knows that toilet is notorious. Since he has a government job, he ought to be more responsible. If they didn't hire you people in the first place," he said accusingly at Cole, "then they wouldn't have to worry about your carrying-on."

"I wasn't bothering anyone."

"On the contrary, sir, this man was acting in a very obvious lewd and lascivious manner," the heavy man broke in.

"And how were you acting in the car?" Cole shouted at him.

"What do you call that? Tell him what you made me do, tell him!"

"Stop shouting," the judge commanded. "We are not interested in what the officer did, but in what you did in that public lavatory."

"What do you mean you're not interested? He's guiltier than I am. Isn't he?" Cole turned to the other two policemen. "They know; they saw him."

"Well?" the judge asked them, but they shook their heads no.

"But you heard him last night! You do too know!"

When the two policemen again shook their heads, the judge said, "Enough of this. The case seems clear to me. Guilty as charged."

Then Cole went into a foolish rage. "You don't give a damn about justice. You leave my sex life alone, you hear me!"

His lawyer looked at him with contempt at his outburst.

"Have you said your piece?" the judge said sarcastically.

"I'm not guilty of any crime."

"Your conduct this morning here convinces me that you are a rather unstable person, and, according to your record, you were also picked up by the police at age nineteen for loitering. There's a pattern here. You need a bit of cooling off, it appears to me. It's persons like you who go stalking around these public parks, getting yourselves murdered, when you aren't committing the murders yourself. It's about time we put a stop to all of this. Six months in the Detroit House of Correction. Indecent Exposure and Lewd and Lascivious Behavior."

When a policeman came up behind Cole to escort him away, he shrugged off the man's hands. It couldn't be happening, it just couldn't be. He was dazed. Overhead a lazy blade-fan revolved, cooling nothing, just moving the oppressive heat around. "I won't go!" Cole yelled. Then he ran toward the railing that surrounded the judge's platform, toward the exit. Two other police officers came toward him from somewhere. To get away, he leaped over the railing but fell to the floor. He was up at once, grabbing papers from the court secretary's desk, throwing handfuls of paper at the advancing officers, more of them now. He lifted the shorthand typewriter the man had been using over his head with both hands. "Stay away, you bastards! Stay away!" The people in the courtroom were quiet, sitting staring at him from the blackish-brown rows that looked like pews. One man in the rear shouted encouragement to him: "Way to go, man. Give 'em hell." But before the words were finished, Cole was surrounded by men with pistols pointed at him, and he simply dropped the machine behind him; it merely bounced twice and settled back into an upright position, undamaged. His little demonstration cost him two more years in jail, for threatening a police officer and contempt of court.

Beside the pool, Cole laughed at himself, a small smirk that did not quite emerge from the mouth, a noise that could have been someone smothering. *King Kong Fights Airplanes on Empire State Building! King Cole Conquers Police! Why is it so funny now,* he wondered. *It was terrible then. Agonies and disasters become smart-aleck comments. Why can't my trial retain its form, remain the misery that it actually was? I have SUFFERED!* His self-smile dissolved, and he let his mind dwell on the faces of the three men in jail who had been the cause of yet six more months in prison:

One held his legs, another sat on his shoulders, and the third pulled down his trousers. It happened in the laundry room, amid all those soiled towels and briefs, little pieces of smut and hair dutifully soaped and bleached and rinsed away. He was tossed on a pile of laundry bags, his rear end lathered with a handful of detergent that the man had grabbed from a shelf. And then a sharp, slow pain as the man tried to penetrate him. All the man said was, "Hold still, buddy, and it won't hurt so much." *Cole wondered if he had really consented to the sodomy; he could have struggled harder. Nobody can be violated unless he wants to be, can he? But he had fought them.* The man clutched at his waist, panting, trying to work into rhythm, but he never quite succeeded; he came in less than a minute. It was while the second man was greasing himself with the semen that they were discovered by a supervisor. All of them were given another six months for "unnatural behavior," Cole included. No one believed him at the hearing when he protested, sometimes screaming, that he had been raped. They thought he was lying, for, after all, he was the pervert, as everyone knew. The men who had attacked him were just normal men—all had wives. As they said in the director's office, they were just horny.

Suzannah Lessard

Gay Is Good for Us All

—In this final selection, Suzannah Lessard, a highly respected reporter, gives the reader a glimpse into the burgeoning Gay Liberation Movement and also speaks to the question of the relation of radical lesbians to the Women's Liberation Movement. It is clear that the homosexual milieu, whether "Gay Lib" is successful or not, will never be the same again as a result of the quickening given to the dialectic between homosexuals and heterosexuals by the new homosexual radicalism.

"Oh no, not the fairies too!" said a woman watching the Gay Liberation Movement march up Sixth Avenue last June, with a quizzical, good-humored expression on her face, as though they were so many puppies. "I'm from Ohio. I think it's funny," said a tourist. "I'd like to kick the shit out of them," said a clean, tense young man turning on his heel. No one quite knew how to react. Few grasped the implications or viewed it as more than either a circus or an abomination. But the marchers were confident. They had taken the trick out of the trick mirror; the invisible homosexual was now massively visible. With what seemed hardly more than a flick of the wrist they had upturned a whole new complex of bigotry and exclusion into broad sunlight, and the astonished prejudices could do little more than blink.

And once again, with the emergence of the Gay Movement, the old image of society as a vertical structure with one group holding another in subjugation was transformed into something more like a many-leveled house of cards, suits straining against each other, Queens standing on Knaves, one-eyed Jacks trumping Queens, the ceiling of one set forming the floor of another, with only one

"Gay is Good for Us All" by Suzannah Lessard, from *Washington Monthly*, **II** (December, 1970), 39–49. Reprinted by permission of *The Washington Monthly*.

205

simple element in the complex of relationships—the position in the throne room of the white, male, heterosexual King.

The movement was born one night in August, 1969, when the New York police raided the Stonewall Inn, a gay bar on Christopher Street. It was by no means the first time—few of the many gay bars in the Village vicinity were immune to the arbitrary raids which usually ended in several arrests and many more bruises and broken heads. But this time, to the amazement of the Sixth Precinct, the homosexuals refused to take their punishment passively. The sissies fought back. Word of the brawl traveled, the gay community turned out in force, and the battle spread from the bar into what came to be known as the Christopher Street Riot, a free-for-all in which cars were overturned, fires lit, and police sent to the hospital. After that the image of the homosexual in the eyes of the world, and, more important, in his own eyes as well, was irrevocably altered.

Prior to Christopher Street, the two major homosexual organizations, the Mattachine Society and the Daughters of Bilitis, were small and necessarily timid. Though Mattachine did make statements to the effect that homosexuality was neither pathological nor depraved, its objectives were in fact limited to helping the homosexual adjust within the society, providing social activities and legal and medical help, and backing conservative campaigns to change the more flagrant anti-homosexual laws. They were limited because their members were limited: homosexuals tended to be isolated and inhibited, having taken the one course they could really afford, which was to pass for heterosexual in order to pursue careers and life within the society, both of which would likely be destroyed were their homosexuality exposed. So their endeavor was not to battle the dragon but to sneak around it, to "get by" with a minimum of pain.

Furthermore, most people view the homosexual as a criminal and a pervert, an attitude deeply embedded in the culture; and it would take rare assurance for a homosexual not to let this attitude pervade his own image of himself and further deter his drive to challenge it.

OUT OF THE CLOSET INTO THE STREET

Out of Christopher Street the Gay Liberation Front was formed. In New York and subsequently in every major city in the country, the Front recruited, held workshops, and started newspapers. Many of the members were also part of the New Left, and, like the women, they started by confronting prejudice among their peers, educating them to the oppressiveness of their attitudes and the problems of the homosexual. After 10 months they had grown big enough and become inwardly confident enough to organize a mass march up Sixth Avenue in New York. It was touch and go down to the wire, however. No one knew until the last minute whether more than a handful would actually show up, and few thought the march would reach its destination in Central Park without a violent confrontation with bystanders or the police.

But thousands and thousands turned out for the first big holiday from the closet. The festive mood was intoxicating. People in their Sunday best, their hippie best, lots of workshirt and jeans types, a few fantastic costumes—they looked more like a peace march to whom the President had just capitulated than *homosexuals*. They just didn't *look* queer, and that fact registered everything from horror to discomfort to plain surprise on the faces of people on the sidelines. As one marcher put it, "So much has been accomplished in terms of who we are. We are people." And not only were they people, but they were evidently quite happy. The happy homosexual was supposed to be an impossibility. These together struck a solid blow at the assumption that homosexuality is in itself distorting, sad, and sick. Rather, it becomes clear that the conditions under which society forces it to exist are the causes of all those traits—deviousness, self-deprecation, unstable relationships—that we have been accustomed to linking inextricably with the way of life.

This seemed to have been a discovery for the marchers as well. After lives of secrecy and guilt, coming out into the open with the assertion "Gay is Good" gave them a healthy sense of self many hadn't known for years. "Coming out has been a delight," a woman recently told me. "It's difficult to imagine what it was like before. We are conditioned not to remember pain."

The briefest glance uncovers the depth of prejudice which the movement hopes to vanquish. The psychoanalytic tradition describes homosexuality entirely in terms of sickness, arrested development, unhealthy parental relationships, etc. Upon learning that a friend is homosexual, most of us, however sympathetic, have a tendency to conjure up an image of his mother. We assume that something has gone wrong, that the person has become homosexual for negative reasons, because he was unable to deal with some problem, and hence his choice represents a failure of sorts. The masculinity cult in America colors all our attitudes. Qualities like courage, effectiveness, and leadership are considered superior and are associated with virility, and conversely, the "feminine virtues" of tenderness, docility, and patience are considered of lesser importance. Men are expected to embody virility, and women maternity. Deviates from these roles are thought to be "half a man" or "half a woman"—and inferior in areas which have nothing whatever to do with sexuality. To most straight people, it is simply self-evident that a heterosexual is "better" than a homosexual. The notion that it's not a misfortune to have a child become a homosexual is as strange as the suggestion of one member of the movement that when a child discovers he is homosexual, the parents, not the child, should go to a psychiatrist to try to overcome their hang-ups about homosexuality.

The legal tradition is even harsher. In all states but one (Illinois), sodomy is a crime with sentences running as high as 10 years' minimum and referred to in such phrases as "infamous crime against nature." Under this legal umbrella, discriminatory hiring practices exist unchallenged. For instance, the Civil Service Commission handbook on personnel states flatly that a homosexual is not suitable for service because his condition would automatically impair his efficiency as well as "inhibiting" those who were forced to work with him. This policy was recently overturned in a District of Columbia Court of Appeals, but the decision applies only to hiring within the D.C. Circuit. Further, because many homosexuals are reluctant to expose themselves to publicity, Civil Service has been able to pursue its old policy within the District with few challenges.

The armed forces also have policies to the effect that homosexuality is an incapacitating condition which undermines discipline and makes the individual incapable of leading a constructive life. These policies have led to the dishonorable discharge of many men as well as Wacs and Waves. The women's services are one of the few areas where intense job discrimination against lesbians exists. In most cases lesbians, who can in any event hide their homosexuality more easily than men, are discriminated against primarily as women.

Beyond these formalities, antihomosexuality permeates the popular culture. "Faggot" is a universal term of derision. Wherever homosexuals are portrayed in movies they are ridiculous or desperate or disgusting. The old man in "Midnight Cowboy" was revolting, and Joe Buck responded "naturally" when he hit him. The host in "Boys in the Band" was pathetic. Both lesbians in "Five Easy Pieces" looked ugly in a movie full of pretty people. These versions of the homosexual generally go unquestioned. They fulfill our preconceived notions and affirm heterosexual superiority.

It seems clear that this overall attitude is irrational, that there is no necessary connection between worthiness and sexuality, and that whether or not one considers homosexuality a sickness these policies and attitudes are a barbarous response. It would seem that attitudes towards homosexuality are far more unacceptable, far more degrading to those who hold them—as well as those who endure them—than homosexuality itself could ever be.

SISTERS

Bonds between Gay Lib and Women's Lib grew early. It was a natural affiliation; they both were rebelling against roles predetermined by sex and felt oppressed by the chauvinistic heterosexual male. Both worked to develop a sense of self-worth against the long-accepted condition of second-class citizenship. The women were also struggling with the influence of the psychoanalytic tradition which, as Kate Millett put it in speaking of Freud, "assumed that to be born female was to be born castrated" and therefore innately inferior to the potent male. It was not a smooth affiliation, however. Straight women found they had to struggle with sex chauvinism in dealing with the gay men and were, in turn, guilty of resisting the lesbian within their own ranks for fear the movement, which was already being ridiculed as "a bunch of dykes," would be discredited. However, despite the resistance they encountered in Women's Lib groups, the larger percentage of activist lesbians has chosen Women's Liberation as their primary point of identification and Gay Liberation second, thus bringing the gay struggle into the heart of the women's movement.

On the whole, society seems to be less outraged by lesbians than by male homosexuals. After all, within the context of sex roles, the male is rejecting kingship, thus blaspheming what society holds most holy—whereas the lesbian is rejecting servitude, a futile act for one born with the indelible marks of a servant. Secondly, it has long been the prejudice of Western tradition that women endure rather than enjoy sex (Freud insisted that their only pleasure came from a masochistic enjoyment of pain) and hence sex between women is nonsensical. Thirdly, because a woman's homosexuality is far less manifest, to the extent that she can apparently function perfectly within a marriage, lesbians seem to be a rarity rather than a social "problem." If anything, men find lesbians titillating, à la James Bond, Pussy Galore—a challenge, something to be conquered, coerced into the proper reverence for their irresistible powers. On the other side of the coin, lesbians are the gravest threat to the sex role power structure, for they are at the bottom of the pack, the ace if you will, and independent of men—so that in rebelling they have nothing to lose. This is what has brought them into a unique position within the women's movement. As a Radicalesbian statement put it, "Lesbian is the word that holds women in line."

The resistance to homosexuals within the Women's Lib movement has not been overcome in all factions. The more establishment oriented, such as the National Organization for Women, have adamantly insisted on their heterosexual purity (though even NOW is expected to come out with a statement on lesbians in the next month reversing its policy). But in the more radical groups, lesbians have evolved a very special role for themselves. As one woman said, "As lesbians we are truly independent of men, and it's very important for straight women to see that that's possible. We just aren't dependent on that candy bar"—the candy bar being the hope for some form of masculine approval. Some women have even gone so far as to become "political lesbians"—that is, to become lesbians on purpose so as to utterly sever their dependence on men, presumably in order to eventually reenter relationships with men from a position of equal inner strength. That is certainly an extreme; a more moderate measure is for a woman to reply to the question of whether she is or is not a lesbian in the affirmative regardless of fact, thus reducing the word to meaninglessness and eliminating the fear of being called a "dyke" for stepping out of the homebody, "real woman" role which society has cut out for her.

So, though the relationship has been trouble-fraught (in some places they're not speaking to each other), Gay Lib and Women's Lib have played crucial roles in each other's development. Together they expose the underbelly of society in a more extensive, penetrating way than either could alone, uncovering the depth and extent to which predetermined masculine/feminine roles have governed social dynamics, not only allowing but often forcing one group of people to exploit another.

HO-HO-HOMOSEXUAL

A sector of Gay Lib has extended its horizons beyond Women's Lib. A strong element in the Gay Liberation Front of New York brought radical politics explicitly into the Gay platform, ultimately causing a split within the New York group. A break-off group, the Gay Activists Alliance (GAA) was then formed. The GAA limits its activities to gay liberation per se and works, though militantly, within the system, while the GLF men consider themselves revolutionaries first. Though groups in other cities haven't split, the same elements exist in all, the more militant factions resolving their position within the whole by forming radical caucuses. GLF women in general identify primarily with the Women's Lib movement; the more revolutionary lesbians having formed their own group, Radicalesbians, which like the GLF/New York men identifies primarily with political revolution. These groups are by no means mutually exclusive.

The revolution-oriented gay men and women explain their fusion of the two causes thus (their arguments being greatly reduced here): the basic unit of the sex role structure is the family in which the woman performs menial chores for the man, who is thus freed to pursue more lofty ambitions. The family is also the basic consumer unit of the capitalist system, which stresses the connection between worthiness (you can read power here) and the acquisition of objects. This is directly related to the sex role nature of the family, in that among the objects a man accumulates is his wife (this is a version of the thesis that men treat women primarily as sex objects), hopefully beautiful, efficient, and at the service of his pleasure. This relationship between the acquisition of goods and power over women is emphasized unequivocally in advertising, the lubricant of capitalism in its function of engendering greed. Capitalism, then, is based on the assumption that people are greedy for goods—and the power that goods bring. It assumes that these basic facts cannot be changed, that social planning can only be corrective within the system, not redirective. The result of this power-acquisitive urge has been racism, imperialism, and sexism. Revolution says these "facts of nature" can be changed, but to do so you have to raze the system which nourishes them. In other words, to achieve true gay liberation you have to do away with capitalism which, in its present form, is deeply intertwined with sexism—just as in order to achieve black liberation you must dissolve the system, because in the same power-oriented manner it induces people of one race to beat up on another. And this is why the causes of the nigger, the dyke, the bitch, and the faggot are one and the same and why these Causes Incorporated must be geared to the overthrow of capitalism.

It is easy to punch holes in this argument, to call it simplistic, metaphorical, in parts fanciful, but that would be, I think, a dodge to avoid recognizing a certain genius at work in it. The genius is in great need of refinement, granted, but it is there. My reaction to the argument at this point is that somehow it doesn't manage to produce its own kernel. And while I'm no great defender of capitalism it seems clear that sexism, racism, and imperialism have occurred under every system, Marxism included, and that by doing away with capitalism you will by no means insure yourself against these evils. The revolutionary gays will agree with me there, but counter that while oppression can certainly exist without capitalism, the particular form of capitalism which has actually evolved is so deeply rooted in oppression that it would be impossible to purge the system without in effect destroying it.

The merging of Gay Lib and Women's Lib directly with revolution raises another issue: how do you describe these groups—are they a class, a caste, or what? This is more than a semantic issue, because the confusion in definition represents, I think, a real confusion within these groups in terms of who they are. The terms class and caste are really relevant only in a metaphorical sense; the social structure one combats as a gay person or a woman is far more kaleidoscopic, more mercurial than what one combats as an economically oppressed person. "People use the economic thing to negate the gay movement," said a black member of GLF. "They don't stop to consider how many gay people belong to economically oppressed groups." NOW is currently waging a battle with the FCC over the equal priority of sex and race discrimination in hiring practices: "Without equal enforcement against sex discrimination, employers are encouraged to discriminate on every other one

of the prohibited bases—race, color, creed, and national origin—
as long as they do so against women." But because women and
homosexuals have numbers among the oppressed class does not
make them as a group an oppressed class, though the dynamics of
discrimination described above are very real and suggest the nature
of the bond, of the common denominator which they share. Women
and homosexuals, respectively, belong to groups, or kinds, with
certain common traits which society has arbitrarily invested with
symbolic meaning—i.e., that your value as a lawyer, doctor, thinker,
is discernible through those traits—female, homosexual—which
actually tell nothing whatever about your value in those capacities.

But whatever the exact role and definition of any group within
the structure, all discriminations, as suggested by the NOW statement, aid and nourish each other—witness the KKK slogan
"Don't be half a man, join the Klan"—and, conversely, there is a
kinship between all oppressed groups. When one group relates its
condition to another, however metaphorically, there is a sudden
subjective realization of kinship which transcends all antagonisms.
When a black man leers and clucks at me in the street I feel angry,
helpless, and misused, but if I connect these feelings to what he
must endure at the hands of whites, then despite my antagonism,
nonetheless real, I feel a spontaneous sense of kinship. Just so, a
homosexual's sympathy for the black cause is clinched into something far more compelling than sympathy when he realizes that
to be black in a small town would be very much like being gay in
a small town. This is why the GLF was so persistent in courting
the black militants. They weathered ridicule and then abuse—
black militants have tended to be a super-macho cult—but persisted and won the Panthers over to a recognition of the common
elements in their plight. In August, Huey P. Newton wrote in a
public letter:

> Whatever your personal opinions and your insecurities about
> homosexuals and women (and I speak of the homosexuals and
> women as oppressed groups), we should try to relate to them in a
> revolutionary fashion. . . . We must gain security in ourselves and
> therefore have respect for all oppressed people. . . . When we have
> revolutionary conferences, rallies, and demonstrations, there should
> be full participation of the Gay Liberation Movement and the
> Women's Liberation Movement . . . (they) are our friends . . . the
> terms "faggot" and "punk" should be deleted from our vocabulary,

and especially we should not attach names normally designed for homosexuals to men who are enemies of the people, such as Nixon and Agnew. Homosexuals are not enemies of the people.

When recently the homosexuals marched down to the New York House of Detention, the prisoners leaned out the window and cheered. When they marched up Sixth Avenue one of the most sympathetic comments was from a drunken bum: "It's wonderful," he said, "they have a place in this world, too" and hitched up his ragged overalls. This is not to say all prejudices have been overcome within these groups; many Women's Lib advocates refuse to deal with gay men's groups—"they're male dominated, aren't they?" —and a heterosexual virility bias is undoubtedly still deeply entrenched in the Black Panther Party. But the contrary tendency is there and growing while the macho mood is fading.

When people realize they're all up Queer Street together, the bonds of kinship can grow denser and stronger than any of the divisive factors of class, or caste, or suit, or kind. Whatever your politics, the cross-hatching of supportive relationships which have sprung up in the far left, not out of expediency but out of a discovery of a real human bond and an energetic effort to overcome the most deeply ingrained prejudices, go far to controvert the notion of the "incorrigibility of human nature" which, whether or not it is the outgrowth of capitalism as the revolutionaries charge, seems indeed to have permeated social attitudes in this country.

THE SPOILS OF KINGSHIP

And the culprit, the white male heterosexual king who sits in the throne room guarding his birthright, the recipient of all this wrath, what of him? Isn't the throne room as vicious a dungeon of his humanity as those in which he keeps his underlings?

The faces of men commuting on trains between affluent suburbs and their high-level work in the big-time world of the city are blank and worn beyond their years. They don't seem like people in the flush of fulfillment, the inheritors of the earth, or for that matter like cruel, arrogant nobles gripped with the excitement of power. They sit on the train between battlefields wrapped in their newspapers, for a spell excused from guarding their titles, and they seem in this rare unself-conscious moment a tired, dreary lot. It would seem that rather than the possessors they themselves are the spoils of kingship. Their wives, however bored and discontented with their role, have observed intimately the price their husbands have had to pay, and with the thought of that cost can turn to their laundry with a fleeting, perhaps, but distinct, sense of reprieve.

Just as the black militants for a long time seemed to be aspiring to the bourgeois ideals of the white society they challenged, Women's Lib groups for a time emphasized their desire to live like those men who they felt oppressed them. Those early days, again like those of the first black militants, were marked by simplistic rhetoric, humorlessness, and inflexibility. But as the movement developed, confidence was gained, and discussions began to probe more deeply, the realization evolved that the roles assigned to men were not enviable, but in ways as pernicious to the men themselves as to women. Men have been the most rigorously programmed of all. From childhood it is impressed on them that they must be dominant, the strong authoritative guardians of weaker human beings —and to the extent that they are, they are "real men." To the extent they fail in this role, to the extent they betray "feminine" traits of docility, repugnance to violence, and tenderness and also unsureness, a need for comfort, and timidity—to that extent they are "womanly." And in the eyes of society, the womanly man is a pathetic thing indeed. Since a major tenet of both Women's Lib and Gay Lib is that the division of "traits" between the sexes is for the most part arbitrary and without foundation in reality, it follows that men are as arbitrarily conditioned as women. A less vituperative look at that sex—and not just those stodgy commuters—reveals that the same behavior which women find oppressive is in many instances evidence of the strain their predetermined role has put on their humanity. Why do so many men compulsively talk louder than women, interrupt them, and make it difficult for them to contribute their side of a conversation? Why do they constantly have to make it clear that they are "important" and that they speak with authority, the more so in instances where they don't have any particular authority? Why do they find it so painful to be found wrong, especially by a woman, sometimes insisting that they are right despite overwhelming evidence to the contrary? These very common ways, rather than suggesting that men are naturally overbearing, suggest more that they are insecure, fearful of insignificance, not strong and right, unable to dominate.

A most telling quality along these lines is the American heterosexual male's inability, in varying but widespread degrees, to laugh
at himself. Even worse than being found wrong by a woman is to
be joshed by her, no matter how friendly the manner. If she does
so she is likely to be called a ball-breaker, a bitch, a dyke. Women,
homosexuals, and blacks have in general been quite ready to laugh
at themselves, admittedly sometimes to a pathological degree—the
clown-like minstrel, the charming, absent-minded idiot, the mincing drag queen. But there is a wide territory between in which an
ease with oneself and one's human failings provides a leaven without which self-seriousness, ambition, assertiveness—all good things
in themselves—become strident, intractable, and dissociated from
reality, more a liability to self-realization, not to mention peace
and happiness, than an asset. It is significant that in the early days
of black militancy and Women's Lib, members of those movements
were, like the white heterosexual king they rebelled against, noteworthy for their lack of humor about themselves—as well as for
other white male traits such as intractable insistence that they were
"right" and refusal to let anyone else be heard.

These qualities have by no means been purged from those movements, but they have diminished considerably for many reasons,
among them greater confidence, and a redirection of energies from
a drive to parallel the white male oppressor into an effort to
evolve a whole new image of man and society which will change
things for the better for everybody, including Massah King. As
time goes on and the movement develops, it also becomes apparent that those who retain the qualities of stridency and humorlessness are those newest to the movements, who have rejected the
security of their designated roles but have not yet been able to
overcome the sense of their own racial or sexual unworthiness.
And so this behavior appears to be a kind of therapy, a necessary
stage, like a neurotic in psychoanalysis acting out his neurosis in
the extreme before he is cured. This only reconfirms the notion
that men act that way because they are insecure.

And why shouldn't they be insecure? No human being is om-
nipotent, all-knowing, and self-sufficient. Men as well as women
feel sorrow and tenderness, fear and need of comfort. The accepted
solution has been that when a man wavers and is afraid, his good
wife should "build up his ego," to make him feel courageous and
unwavering and important, all those things a man is supposed to
be. The endeavor is to quell his real emotions rather than deal

with them: repress, repress. It's little wonder that men shout, insist on constant service as evidence of their manliness, and have a hard time laughing at themselves. Not enviable.

Gay Liberation has played a crucial role in dissipating the deeply rooted reverence for the image of the king-male. Many gay women had long rejected that image; and so, utterly indifferent to it, they provided straight women with living examples of independence from that candy bar. Gay men were in an equally unique position, for not only had they been victimized by those who play the male role, but they had also suffered because they had been *made* to play it themselves. It took women a long time to begin accepting lesbians, and it took the blacks a long time to begin accepting both the women and the gay people, because both movements have been trapped within the norms of the throne room. The tendency towards fusion of these groups with each other augurs a motion away from stridency and inflexibility and towards the ideal of a world built according to human needs rather than according to power. The redefinition of those needs is a far greater revolution than any straight political rearrangement could in itself accomplish.

The king will be liberated when the whole pack of role cards falls—when he is not restricted by the king-male role. Much of the physical violence that wracks the country is committed by males between 15 and 25—the period in which traditionally a boy proves his manhood. The masculinity curse also drives the less gory but more common psychological violence, which pervades business meetings, dinner parties, and the home—as people pierce, jab, and scrape to wrest some form of triumph and have it saluted. It's the crying of uncle that's at stake in the worst cases, psychological submission, and the king-male must abhor that most of all. He strains to make sure someone is below and knows it.

The masculinity complex lives in our national throne room. The last three Presidents have been nearly obsessed with proving their toughness; Presidents have bled the nation white to keep from backing down in Vietnam—to keep from looking chicken in backbone warfare.

But when more men feel that they no longer *need* to be the king-male—or share his compulsive desire to be crowned, to reign virile and proud and appreciated—maybe there will be fewer bloodied people, fewer good things ravaged, and maybe even fewer wars.

Utopias have an air of death about them. Fortunately, they never come true. They are deathly because they omit the basic mystery of life and reduce existence to a smooth-running machine. Utopias are humorless. But Life, Death, Beauty, Ugliness, Good, and Evil are here to stay and will insure us against all utopias, so one can look at the vision projected by all these new developments without fear for the future.

The vision of these sexual freedoms is not a very full one, a kind of comprehensive liberation in which all oppressed groups unbind each other for a hazy new purpose. Reasonable as the idea is, it seems to exist in a thin, improbable future.

It also seems to include the seeds of disasters, such as large numbers of people, having no role assigned to them, going out of their minds for lack of identity—like a lot of bureaucrats without their bureaucracy. But as things change, the vision firms up and even becomes a little part of reality—like the Panthers' trying to accept the Gay Liberation people. A large part of it all lies in just getting used to separate ideas, such as that homosexuals are just as good as heterosexuals. America seems to be on the brink of a Dark Age which will tolerate none of these new ways. But on the other hand, as a man marching up Sixth Avenue on that bright euphoric Sunday said to me, "There's a lot of people in this."